Iḥyā’ ‘Ulūm al-Dīn
Vol. II

IMAM AL-GHAZĀLĪ

ESSENTIAL

Iḥyā' 'Ulūm al-Dīn

THE REVIVAL OF THE RELIGIOUS SCIENCES

Completely revised edition of Fazlul Karim's translation

Volume II

The Norms of Daily Conduct

IBT

Islamic Book Trust

Kuala Lumpur

First published 2015
Reprint 2017
Islamic Book Trust
607 Mutiara Majestic
Jalan Othman
46000 Petaling Jaya
Selangor, Malaysia
www.ibtbooks.com

Islamic Book Trust is affiliated with The Other Press.

Perpustakaan Negara Malaysia Cataloguing-in-Publication Data

Ghazzali, 1058-1111
Essential Ihya' 'Ulum al-Din : The Revival of the Religious Sciences: Revised edition of Fazlul Karim's translation.
Volume II / Imam al-Ghazali.
ISBN 978-967-0526-16-4
1. Islam--Doctrines. 2. Religious life--Islam.
I. Fazlul Karim. II. Title.
297.2

Front calligraphy
Prayer from the Qur'an 20:114 written in Arabic calligraphy.
Translation: "Say, 'My Lord, increase me in knowledge.'"

Printed by
SS Graphic Printers (M) Sdn. Bhd.
Lot 7 & 8, Jalan TIB 3
Taman Industri Bolton
68100 Batu Caves, Selangor

Contents

Translator's preface ix

Book 1: The rules of eating and drinking

Introduction 3

1 The rules of eating alone 4

2 The rules of eating with others 8

3 Hospitality 9

4 The rules of entertaining guests 13

Book 2: The secrets of marriage

1 The merits and demerits of marriage 25

2 The rules of marriage 36

3 Rules observed after marriage 40

Book 3: Earning a livelihood

Introduction 57

1 The excellence of earning a livelihood 58

2 Sources of livelihood 62

3 Justice 67

4 To do good in mutual transactions 72

5 Not to be forgetful of religion and the hereafter when doing business 76

Book 4: The lawful and unlawful

Introduction 83

1 The merits of lawful earnings and the demerits of unlawful earnings 84

2 The different degrees of doubtful things 95

3 Arguments and questions 100

4 Knowledge of the lawful and unlawful 103

5 Allowances and gifts from rulers and kings 105

6 Frequenting rulers 110

7 Miscellaneous issues 116

Book 5: Love and brotherhood

Introduction 121

1 The merits of friendship and brotherhood 122

2 The duties of friendship and brotherhood 139

3 Duties to a Muslim 156

4 Duties to neighbours 174

5 Duties to relatives 178

6 Duties to slaves and servants 183

Book 6: The rules of living in seclusion

Introduction 187

1 Merits and demerits of secluded living 191

2 Benefits of society 198

3 Rules and regulations of secluded living 202

Book 7: Rules and regulations of travelling

Introduction 207

1 Rules of travelling, from beginning to end 208

2 Rules of travelling 214

Book 8: Music and ecstasy

Introduction 223

1 Different opinions about listening to songs 224

2 Effects and rules of listening to songs 236

Book 9: Enjoining good and forbidding evil

Introduction 249

1 Merits of enjoining good and forbidding evil 250

2 The integrals and conditions of enjoining good and forbidding evil 258

3 Corrupt practices prevalent in society 268

4 Enjoining rulers to do good, and forbidding them from evil 270

Book 10: The character and conduct of the Prophet (ṣ)

Introduction 287

1 The Prophet's learning through the Qur'an 288

2 The Prophet's character and conduct 292

3 The Prophet's good manners 294

4 The Prophet's words and laughter 296

5 The Prophet's eating 298

6 The Prophet's clothing 300

7 The Prophet's pardoning 302

8 The Prophet's dislikes 305

9 The Prophet's generosity 307

10 The Prophet's bravery and heroism 309

11 The Prophet's modesty 310

12 The Prophet's figure and constitution 311

13 The Prophet's miracles 313

Index of Qur'anic verses 317

Index 321

Translator's preface

"The Norms of Daily Conduct" is the second volume of Imam al-Ghazālī's world-renowned masterpiece *The Revival of the Religious Sciences.* The present work is an attempt to translate it from the original Arabic not too literally but in substance. The volume deals with the norms of conduct in daily life including eating and drinking, marriage, earnings and trade, lawful and unlawful earnings, duties towards Muslims, neighbours, servants and slaves, the harms and benefits of seclusion and society, journey, music, enjoining good and forbidding evil and the character and conduct of the Holy Prophet (ṣ).

A literal translation is avoided in order to omit the unnecessary arguments of sects and things prevailing in the world and to omit the sayings of less important sages. But no verse of the Qur'an or saying of the Prophet (ṣ) has been omitted.

I pray that Allah Almighty guide everyone in accordance with the teachings of the Holy Qur'an, the Sunnah and the spirit in which *Ḥujjah al-Islām* (the Proof of Islam), the title given to Imam al-Ghazālī, wrote the *Revival,* about which it has been said, "If all the books of Islam were destroyed except for al-Ghazālī's *Revival,* it would be but a slight loss."

Book 1
The rules of eating and drinking

Introduction

All praise is due to Allah, who conducts the whole of creation in an orderly manner, who gives sustenance according to a measure, who increases the strength of animals by food and drink and who nourishes religion and good deeds by good foods and drinks.

The object of the wise is the vision of the Lord in the next world, which can only be gained by knowledge and action, which one cannot devote oneself to without a healthy body, which is also not possible without food and drink which are absolutely necessary and which are consumed according to prescribed rules. For this reason, some learned sages said that food and drink appertain to religion. Allah says, "Eat of the good things and do good" (Qur'an, 23:51). If a man consumes food and drink for helping his knowledge, actions and God-fearingness, his food and drink are considered worship. But he should not spend his time on them uselessly and remain busy like a lower being which roams from field to field eating and drinking. For that which is a means of access to religion must show him the lights of religion, which are its manners and uses. A religious man must stick to these and control his passion and greed for food and drink by weighing them in the balance of Sharīʿah. The Holy Prophet (ṣ) said, "A man can acquire virtues in all his actions, even in a morsel of food he lifts to his mouth and to the mouth of his wife."

1

The rules of eating alone

The rules of eating alone are of three kinds: those before eating, those while eating and those after eating.

Rules before eating

There are seven rules before eating. The first is that the food be lawful. Allah ordered the eating of good and lawful food and prohibited bad and unlawful food, as there is benefit in the former and harm in the latter. Allah says, "Do not swallow up your property among yourselves by false means" (Qur'an, 2:188). The root of religion is lawful food because it is the basis of all religious acts.

The second is to wash the hands before eating. The Prophet (ṣ) said, "Washing before eating prevents poverty, and washing after eating prevents frivolous thoughts." Dirt and germs which stick to hands as a result of manual labour can be removed by washing. So washing before eating is necessary as ablution before prayer is necessary.

The third is to place the food on the ground, as it is the way of the Prophet (ṣ). Whenever any food was taken to him, he kept it on the ground because it is the sign of humility. Moreover, he would not eat food from anything except a big dish with others. It is said that four things were innovated after the Prophet (ṣ): to eat on tables, to sift food with a sieve, to use soap and to eat to one's heart's content. These things, though not unlawful, do not befit a humble man.

The fourth is to eat sitting straight. The Prophet (ṣ) said, "I do not eat while reclining, for I am a mere slave, and I eat as a slave eats and sit as a slave sits." To eat reclining is also bad for the stomach.

The fifth is to intend to gain strength for worship. And one should promise to eat little, as a full stomach prevents one from worship. The purer the intention is for religion, the less is the greed for food. The Prophet (ṣ) said, "The son of Adam needs no more than some morsels to keep up his strength. Doing so, he should consider that a third of his stomach is for food, a third for drink and a third for breathing." If the intention is true, one should not extend one's hand towards food if one is not hungry.

The sixth is to be satisfied with the food served and not be greedy for varieties of curries. Food is honoured only when one does not wait for curry. The Prophet (ṣ) said, "When the time for supper and the time for the nightfall prayer coincide, first have supper."

The seventh is to have many people partake of the food. The Prophet (ṣ) said, "Eat all together, as there are blessings in it." He also said, "The food of which many hands partake is best."

Rules while eating

One should:

- begin the meal with the words "in the name of Allah" and end it with "All praise is due to Allah."
- eat with the right hand.
- begin and end the meal with salt.
- take little morsels and chew each morsel well.
- not extend the hand to a morsel until swallowing the previous one.
- not speak of the defects of the food, for the Prophet (ṣ) never did it. When he liked a food, he ate, and when he did not like it, he did not eat it.

- eat what is closest, except in the case of fruits, as this was the practice of the Prophet (ṣ).
- eat from the rim or centre of a bowl.
- not cut bread or meat with a knife because the Prophet (ṣ) said, "Cut meat with your teeth" and "Honour the principal foods, as Allah sent them from the blessings of heaven."
- eat food which has fallen on the ground. The Prophet (ṣ) said, "If any morsel of food falls down, pick it up and remove the dust attached to it and do not leave it for the Devil."
- lick the fingers, for the Prophet (ṣ) said, "Do not wipe your hands with a cloth until you lick your fingers because you do not know in which part of the food there is blessing."
- not blow on hot food, which is prohibited, but be patient until it is easy to eat.
- eat odd numbers of dates, grapes and other fruits which can be counted.

The rules of drinking water

One should:

- not, unless thirsty, drink water when eating because it is better and keeps the stomach sound.
- say, "In the name of Allah," and drink slowly. The Prophet (ṣ) said, "Drink water in sips rather than in gulps."
- not drink water standing or lying, as the Prophet (ṣ) prohibited it unless one has an excuse.
- not breath or yawn into a pot.
- say the following invocation of the Prophet (ṣ) after drinking: "All praise is due to Allah, who has made it delicious and sweet by His grace and has not made it salty or distasteful for our sins."
- drink water with three breaths, saying afterwards, "All praise is due to Allah," and hand it back with the words "in the name of Allah."

Rules after eating

One should:

1. stop eating before becoming full.
2. lick the fingers, wipe them with a towel and wash them.
3. pick up the fallen crumbs of food, as the Prophet (ṣ) said, "Whoever eats what lies on the dining cloth will remain safe and pass his life in comfort, and his children will remain safe."
4. use a toothstick, not swallowing what comes out of the teeth as a result.
5. lick the dish and drink any liquid in it. It has been said that whoever licks his dish and drinks the liquid in it will get the reward of manumitting a slave.
6. express sincere gratitude to Allah for what He has given one to eat, regarding food as a gift from Him. Allah says, "Eat of the good things which We have provided you with, and give thanks to Allah" (Qur'an, 2:172). Thus, whenever one eats lawful food, one should say, "All praise is due to Allah, by whose mercy good deeds are completed and blessings descend. O Allah, give us good food and engage us in good deeds." If one eats doubtful food, one should say, "All praise is due to Allah under all circumstances. O Allah, do not let it lead us to transgress You." In addition, after the meal, one should say, "All praise is due to Allah who provided us with sufficient food and drink and gave shelter to our leader and chief," and recite Sūrah al-lkhlāṣ (Qur'an, 112) and Sūrah Quraysh (Qur'an, 106). If one eats food prepared by someone, one should say, "O Allah, give him abundant good and bless him in what You have provided him." After drinking milk, one should say, "Bless what You have provided us, and increase it for us."
7. remain seated until the dining cloth is lifted.
8. wash the hands with soap.

2

The rules of eating with others

There are seven. One should:

1. not begin eating when there is an elderly or honourable man present, but rather let him begin.
2. not remain silent at the time of eating, but rather talk.
3. not wish to eat more than your friend. It is not lawful to eat more when food is equally distributed unless one's friend gives you consent.
4. eat in such a way that there remains no need of saying to your companion, "Eat, eat!" Rather, one should eat according to one's habit.
5. find nothing wrong in washing one's hands in a basin. If the same basin is used by all for washing hands, the following rules should be observed: None should spit in it, the chief guest should be honoured, the basin should be moved to the right, a servant should pour water on the hands and when rinsing the mouth, let the water fall from the mouth gently.
6. not watch his companions eat, nor stop eating before he does.
7. not do anything others deem unclean or talk about things which bring to mind things which are deemed unclean.

3
Hospitality

Its excellence

There is great merit in showing hospitality to guests and entertaining them. Ja'far al-Ṣādiq said, "When you sit with guests on a dining cloth, sit for a long time, as no account of that time will be taken."

Al-Ḥasan al-Baṣrī said, "Accounts will be taken of what one spends on oneself, one's parents and others, but no account will be taken of what one spends on food for one's Muslim brethren, as Allah would be embarrassed to ask him about that."

There are many *ḥadīths* to this effect. The Prophet (ṣ) said, "Angels like a person as long there is food before him"; "When your Muslim brethren lift up their hands after they finish eating, no account will be taken of someone who eats the remaining food"; "No account will be taken of the food which someone gives to his Muslim brother"; and "No account will be taken of three things: the predawn meal of a faster, what a faster breaks his fast with and what a person eats with his Muslim brother."

Ibn 'Umar said, "To take good food on one's journey and give it to one's companions is an indication of one's generosity." Some Companions said, "To eat together is a sign of good conduct." A *ḥadīth* says, "Allah will say to a man, 'O son of Adam, I was hungry and you did not give Me food.' He will reply, 'How could I have given You food when You are the Lord of the universe?' Allah will say, 'A Muslim brother of yours was hungry, but you did not give him food. If you had given him food, it would have reached Me.'"

The Prophet (ṣ) also said, "Honour someone who comes to see you"; "There are high places in paradise whose outer sides are visible from the inner sides. These are for those who are modest in treatment, give food and pray at night when people are asleep"; "The best of you is the one who gives food"; and "If a man feeds his Muslim brother until he is full and gives him drink until his thirst is quenched, Allah will distance him from hell by seven ditches, the distance between every two of which is what could be walked in five hundred years."

The rules of entering people's houses and the presentation of food

When a person enters the house of his friend to have a meal, he should not enter it suddenly, as it is prohibited. Allah says, "Do not enter the houses of the Prophet (ṣ) unless permission is given to you for a meal, not waiting for its cooking being finished" (Qur'an, 33:53). The Prophet (ṣ) said, "Whoever joins a feast without invitation is a transgressor."

If a man goes to the house of another for some need and the time of meal comes, he should not have the meal without being requested to do so. If the host invites him to have the meal, he should see whether it has been said willingly or out of shame. If it was the latter, he should decline.

To go to the house of a close friend for food was the practice of the Prophet (ṣ), who, with Abū Bakr and 'Umar, used to go to the house of Abū al-Haytham and Abū Ayyūb al-Anṣārī to have meals. In the beginning, they used to have meals in the houses of the Madīnan Helpers (*Anṣār*). Allah says, "Or your friends' (houses). It is no sin in you that you eat together or separately" (Qur'an, 24:61). The Prophet (ṣ) also once had a meal in Barīrah's house without her permission. When al-Ḥasan al-Baṣrī was asked about friends, he said, "A friend is someone with whom the soul is at ease and the heart at rest."

Regarding the rules of presenting food, a person should not go to too much trouble to prepare food. Instead, he should place before the guest whatever is available. If he has neither food nor money, he should not go into debt or make difficulties for himself. If he has available what is necessary for his own consumption and his nature does not allow him to present it, it is not necessary for him to do so.

A person should present to his guest food which is better than what he eats. A sage said, "If any of my friends comes to me, I do not care what I feed him, as I do not want to trouble myself for his sake. Rather, I present to him whatever I have. And if I put myself out for him, I would not welcome him." It is said that once, when 'Alī was invited, he said, "I can accept your invitation on three conditions: do not buy anything from the market for me, do not hoard up what is in your house and do not trouble your family members." Salmān said, "The Prophet (ṣ) ordered us not to put ourselves out for a guest with something we do not have, but to present him with what is ready." It has been reported that whenever the prophet Yūnus's friends came to see him, he used to place before them pieces of bread and vegetables from his garden and say, "Eat. If Allah did not curse those who put themselves out, I would have put myself out for you." Anas said that they used to present a guest with dried bread and dried dates and say, "We do not know who carries a greater sin: someone who dislikes the food presented to him or someone who dislikes to present what he possesses."

A guest should not suggest or demand anything in particular, as this may be troublesome for the host. According to a *ḥadīth*, the Prophet (ṣ) would prefer the easier of two things. A sage said, "Eating is of three kinds: eating with poor people, where each one gives precedence to the other, eating with cheerful brethren and eating with worldly men with good manners."

The host should ask his guest what kind of food he likes, as there are merits in giving the guest what he wants. The Prophet (ṣ) said, "Whoever takes care to fulfil the desires of his Muslim brother, his sins are forgiven, for Allah will please one who pleases his Muslim brothers." He also said, "Whoever gratifies his brother in what he craves, Allah writes for him a million merits, forgives a million of his sins, raises him a million degrees and will feed him from three gardens: Firdaws, 'Adn and al-Khuld."

A person should never ask a guest, "What food shall I bring for you?" Rather, he should present to him whatever food is available. Sufyān al-Thawrī said, "When your Muslim brother meets you, do not say to him, 'What food will you eat? What food shall I bring you?'" A Sufi said, "If poor people come to you, give them food. If theologians come to you, ask them about theological problems. If reciters of the Qur'an come to you, show them the *miḥrāb*."

4

The rules of entertaining guests

There are six manners of entertaining guests: inviting, accepting the invitation, attending, presenting food, eating and departing.

Inviting

The Prophet (ṣ) said about the entertainment of guests, "Do not trouble yourself for a guest, lest you think bad of him. For whoever thinks bad of a guest thinks bad of Allah, and Allah also thinks bad of him." He also said, "There is no good in someone who does not entertain guests." The Prophet (ṣ) once passed by an owner of many camels and cattle who did not entertain him. A woman who had some goats only entertained him by sacrificing a goat. With that, the Prophet (ṣ) said, "Look at these two people—these traits are solely in the hand of Allah, and He gives them to whomever He wishes." Once, a guest came to the Prophet (ṣ) and said, "As I have a guest, tell that Jew to give me a loan. I shall repay it in the month of Rajab." The Jew said, "By God, if you do not give me something as a pledge, I will not give you the loan." Upon being informed of this, the Prophet (ṣ) said, "By Allah, I am trustworthy in the heaven and trustworthy in the earth. If he gives me a loan, I shall repay it. Take my shield and give it to him as a pledge."

Whenever the prophet Ibrāhīm wished to have a meal, he would walk a mile or two, searching for a guest to eat with him. For this he was named Abū al-Ḍayfān (Father of Guests). The custom of entertaining guests is still prevalent by the side of his grave in commemoration of that attribute of his. Not a single night passes there without one to three hundred guests being entertained. The manager of this place says that up to this day, no night has passed without a guest there.

The Prophet (ṣ) was once asked, "What is faith?" to which he replied, "The giving of food and the exchange of greetings." He also said, "Giving food and praying at night when people are asleep expiate sins and raise one's rank." When asked what an accepted pilgrimage is, the Prophet (ṣ) said, "Giving food and speaking good words."

Anas said, "Angels do not enter a house which a guest does not enter." There are many other traditions regarding the merits of entertainment.

The rules

A person should not invite irreligious men or transgressors, as the Prophet (ṣ) said, "May your food be eaten by religious men," praying for a person who had invited him; "Eat only the food of religious men, let only religious men eat your food and invite the poor"; and "The worst feast is a marriage feast to the rich are invited and not the poor."

He should not neglect relatives in his hospitality, as it creates loneliness and the severing of kinships.

He should be careful when inviting friends and acquaintances because singling out individuals creates loneliness in the hearts of the rest. He should follow the Prophet's practice of giving food and bringing joy to the hearts of the believers.

He should not invite a person who will not join a feast, or a person who will offend the guests. Instead, he should only invite someone who will willingly accept the invitation. Sufyān al-Thawrī said, "Whoever invites a person who is averse to accepting his invitation commits a sin. And if the guest accepts his invitation, the host commits two sins, as the guest comes to him in spite of his unwillingness."

Finally, he should feed a religious man, as it helps his religion. Conversely, he should not feed a sinner, as it encourages sin.

Accepting the invitation

To accept an invitation is recommended, though some say it is obligatory, as the Prophet (ṣ) said, "If I am asked to eat goat's thigh, I shall accept it." There are five rules for accepting an invitation.

The first is not to distinguish between the poor and the rich, since this is pride, which is prohibited. Similarly, those who accept the invitation of the rich but not that of the poor are also considered proud and opposed to the ways of the Prophet (ṣ). The Prophet (ṣ) used to accept the invitation of slaves and the poor. Once, while riding a camel, al-Ḥasan ibn 'Alī, was passing by a group of poor people who were begging by the side of a pathway and eating food in a dusty place. They said, "O grandson of the Prophet (ṣ), join us and eat." He at once got down, sat with them on the ground, ate with them, then mounted his camel and said, "I accepted your invitation. Now accept my invitation. They accepted it, and he entertained them on a fixed date."

The second is not to refuse an invitation on account of distance. The Torah says, "Visit a sick man even if he is a mile away, join a funeral prayer even if it is three miles away and meet with a friend for the sake of Allah even if it is four miles away." The Prophet (ṣ) said, "If I were invited to Kurā' al-Ghamīm (several miles from Madīnah), I would accept it." He once broke his fast there in Ramaḍān and shortened his prayer.

The third is not to refuse an invitation owing to fasting, but rather to attend a feast and break the fast so as to incur the pleasure of the host, as it brings greater rewards than that of optional fasting. The Prophet (ṣ) said, "Your brother has gone out of his way, and you say, 'I am fasting.'" Ibn 'Abbās said, "The best virtue is to eat with friends after breaking an (optional) fast." Entertaining guests include giving antimony, scents or scented oils.

The fourth is not to accept an invitation when you know that unlawfully earned food will be served or there will be irreligious practices, such as the serving of unlawful food and wine, the use of gold or silver cups or plates or the singing of immoral songs. And acceptance of the invitation is not lawful if the host is a tyrant, transgressor or innovator.

The fifth is to accept an invitation not for the satisfaction of your stomach, but intending to gain strength for acquiring merits in the next world. Also, a person should intend to be careful of disobeying Allah, since the Prophet (ṣ) said, "He who does not accept an invitation disobeys Allah and His Messenger"; intend to honour his believing brother, as the Prophet (ṣ) said, "He who incurs the pleasure of a believer incurs the pleasure of Allah"; intend to meet a believer in order that he may love him, as the Prophet (ṣ) imposed this condition; and intend to be free from defamation, so that it will not be said that he did not attend owing to pride, bad disposition or disdain for a Muslim brother. If a person has one of the above intentions, he will draw near to Allah.

A sage said, "I wish to have an intention in all my actions, even in food and drink." The Prophet (ṣ) said, "All actions are judged by the intention, and every man gets what he intends. So the emigration of one who emigrates for the sake of Allah and His Messenger is for Allah and His Messenger. And whoever emigrates for worldly gain or for marrying a woman will get what he emigrates for." Intending to do something unlawful has no effect, so a person should not intend anything unlawful.

Attending

One should:

- not sit in the middle to occupy the best space.
- neither delay in attending, as the guests may be waiting, nor attend before the fixed time, as the host may not have prepared food beforehand.

- not sit in such a manner as to inconvenience others. If there is a fixed place for one, one should not sit elsewhere. The Prophet (ṣ) said, "Satisfaction with a little sitting space for the sake of Allah is an aspect of humility."
- not look towards the place from which the food comes, as it is contrary to good manners.
- entertain the person sitting by one's side and talk with him.
- show guests the direction of prayer, the lavatories and where they can perform ablution.
- if one is a host, be the last to wash one's hands.
- upon seeing anything opposed to Sharī'ah, remove it if able, or else go away expressing dislike for it.

Presenting food

There are five rules. The first is to serve food to a guest without delay, as this honours the guest. The Prophet (ṣ) said, "Let whoever believes in Allah and the last day honour his guest." The "honoured guests of Ibrāhīm" (Qur'an, 51:24) were those he honoured by placing food before them without delay, as indicated by Allah's words "He made no delay in bringing them a roasted calf" (Qur'an, 11:69). Ḥātim al-Aṣamm said, "Hastiness comes from the Devil except in five cases of the *sunnah* of the Prophet (ṣ): to give food to a guest, to bury a dead man, to give a grownup a daughter in marriage, to clear a debt and to repent for a sin."

The second is to serve fruits or fruit juice first, if available, as they help digestion. The Qur'an also enjoins the serving of fruits first. Allah first says, "Fruits such as they choose" (Qur'an, 56:20), and then, "The flesh of fowl such as they desire" (Qur'an, 56:21). Thus, the best thing to serve after fruit is meat and *tharīd* (flat bread torn into small pieces and soaked in broth along with pieces of meat). The Prophet (ṣ) said, "The superiority of 'Ā'ishah over women is like the superiority of *tharīd* over other foods." After that, sweets should be served.

To honour a guest with meat is indicated by Allah's words about Ibrāhīm, who brought a fatted calf to his guest. This is one of the two things meant by honouring. Regarding good foods, Allah says, "We sent to you manna and quails" (Qur'an, 2:57). The Prophet (ṣ) said, "The best curry is meat." After mentioning manna and quails, Allah says, "Eat of the good things that We have given you" (Qur'an, 2:57), meat and sweet things being among them. In this regard, a sage said, "Sweet things after food are better than many curries."

The third is to serve the best foods first, so that guests may eat to satisfaction and not eat much after. A habit of those who indulge in luxurious living is to first serve inferior foods and then better foods, which contradicts the practice of the Prophet (ṣ). It was the custom of early sages to serve all the foods to their guests at the same time. Also, a menu of food should be given to each guest, so that he may know what foods are available.

The fourth is not to remove the remnants of food until the guests have had their fill. The fifth is to serve a sufficient quantity of food, since to serve less indicates lack of good manners. One day, varieties of dishes were served to Ibrāhīm ibn Adham. Thereupon, Sufyān al-Thawrī said to him, "O father of Isḥāq, do you not fear that this is extravagance?" Ibrāhīm said, "There is no extravagance in food." Ibn Mas'ūd said, "We have been prohibited from accepting the invitation of someone who boasts about his food."

Departing

When leaving a feast, a one must observe three rules. The first is to accompany the guest to the door. This is recommended because the Prophet (ṣ) said, "Whoever believes in Allah and the hereafter should honour his guest" and "Etiquette towards a guest requires that he should be accompanied to the front door." Abū Qatādah reported that when a delegation from the Negus came to the Prophet (ṣ), he himself began to serve them. His Companions said to him, "O Messenger of Allah, we are sufficient for you." He said, "Never. They honoured my Companions, and I wish to repay them."

The second is to welcome guests with a smiling face and good words and to bid them farewell. When al-Awzāʿī was asked, "What is hospitality?" he said, "A smiling face and pleasant words. Bid farewell to the guest in good spirits, even though he may not be perfect." The Prophet (ṣ) said that in this way a person can earn the rank of someone who fasts and prays.

The third is that a guest should not leave without the permission of the host and without satisfying him. If a person is a guest, he should not reside with the host for more than three days, as many a time a host is vexed with a guest because of his long stay. The Prophet (ṣ) said, "Hospitality is for three days, and whatever exceeds that is considered an act of charity." If, however, the host sincerely requests that the guest stay longer, it is lawful for him to stay. The Prophet (ṣ) said, "One bed is for the host, one is for his wife, one is for the guest and a fourth is for the Devil."

Miscellaneous rules and prohibitions of eating

- One should avoid eating in markets as far as possible.
- ʿAlī said, "Allah averts seventy kinds of disasters from someone who begins eating with salt. Whoever eats seven dried dates daily, every worm in his stomach is destroyed. Whoever eats twenty-one reddish raisins daily will not feel any pain in his body."
- Meat begets meat.
- *Tharīd* is the food of the Arabs.
- If sweet things are eaten, the stomach grows large and the buttocks becomes slack.
- Beef creates diseases, milk has a cure, its clarified butter has a medicinal effect and fat removes its like of disease.
- There is nothing better than fresh grapes for a woman in childbed.

- Fish saps the body.
- Reciting the Qur’an and using a toothstick removes sputum.
- Whoever wishes to live long should eat in the morning, eat very little at night, wear shoes, not entertain a man with clarified butter, have little sexual intercourse and wear simple clothes. These are also the injunctions of religion.
- Once, the governor al-Ḥajjāj said to a physician, “Tell me what medicine to use.” The physician said, “Do not marry anyone except a grown-up girl; do not eat meat except the meat of a stout and strong animal; do not eat food unless it is well cooked; do not use medicine unless you are ill; do not eat fruits unless they are ripe; do not eat food unless it is chewed well; eat what you like, but do not drink water after it; do not eat anything after drinking water; do not withhold stool or urine; sleep a little after breakfast; and walk a little after dinner before going to bed, but not less than a hundred steps.” It is said that if urine is withheld, it is harmful to the body, just as everything around a stream is destroyed when its watercourse is blocked.
- The rupture of a vein causes disease, and skipping dinner causes old age.
- A physician said to his son, “Do not go out of the house without eating food in the morning, as there is patience in it, and it removes thirst and greed for food.”
- Just as a diseased man who gives up a patient’s diet suffers, so a healthy man suffers if he goes on a patient’s diet.
- Someone said, “Whoever takes care of his diet can be certain that he will have no disease, has no doubts about his well being and is in a sound state of health.”
- It is better to carry food to a house wherein a man has died. When Ja‘far ibn Abī Ṭālib died, the Prophet (ṣ) said, “The family members of Ja‘far are busy owing to his death and cannot prepare food, so take them something to eat.” This is recommended.

- Do not eat the food of a tyrant or an oppressor. If there is no alternative, eat a little, but do not eat their best foods. It is reported that when Dhū al-Nūn al-Miṣrī was sent to prison, he did not eat for three days. He had a foster sister who sent food to him through the guard of the prison, but he did not eat it. He sent news to her, saying, "Your food is lawful, but it has reached me through the hand of an oppressor." This is the height of God-fearingness.
- Imam al-Shāfiʿī said, "Four things make the body strong: to eat meat, to use perfume, to bathe frequently and to wear linen. Four things make the body idle: excessive sexual intercourse, excessive thinking, excessive drinking of water in times of hunger and excessive pepper. Four things strengthen eyesight: to sit facing the direction of the prayer, to use antimony before sleeping, to look at green things and to keep clothes clean. Four things weaken eyesight: to look at unclean and impure things, to watch someone be hanged, to look at female genitals and to sit with your back to the direction of the prayer. Four things increase sexual prowess: to eat the meat of sparrows, truffles, pistachios and watercress. Sleep is of four kinds: to lie with belly upwards, which is the sleep of the prophets; to sleep on one's right side, which is the sleep of worshippers; to sleep on one's left side, which is the sleep of rulers; and to sleep on one's front, which is the sleep of the Devil. Four things increase wisdom: to give up useless talk, to clean the teeth, to keep the company of the learned and to keep the company of the pious. Four things are considered worship: to not take a step without having made ablution, to prolong prostration, to keep attached to the mosque and to recite the Qur'an much."
- Imam al-Shāfiʿī said, "If a man enters a bathroom after becoming hungry and delays eating after exiting it, it is a wonder that he is alive. If a man eats soon after cupping, it is also a wonder that he is alive."

- Imam al-Shāfi'ī said, "I do not see any better medicine than the water of violets for epidemic diseases. The body should be anointed therewith, and it should be taken as a drink. And Allah knows best."

Book 2
The secrets of marriage

1

The merits and demerits of marriage

Know, dear readers, that there are differences of opinion among scholars about the merits of marriage. Some say that it is better for worship, while others say that to remain unmarried is a means of increasing acts of worship. The following are the proofs that marriage is better.

The Qur'an

Allah says:

> *Marry those among you.* (Qur'an, 24:32)
>
> *Do not prevent them from marrying their husbands.* (Qur'an, 2:232)
>
> *Certainly We sent messengers before you and gave them wives and children.* (Qur'an, 13:38)
>
> *They who say, "O our Lord, grant us in our wives and our offspring the joy of our eyes."* (Qur'an, 25:74)

Among the prophets who did not marry is 'Īsā, who will marry after his second advent.

Ḥadīth

The Prophet (ṣ) said:

> Marriage is one of my practices, and whoever diverts from my practices is not from me.

Marriage is my way, and whosoever loves my conduct should follow my way.

Marry and multiply, for on Resurrection Day I will boast upon seeing your numbers in comparison with other nations.

Whoever does not marry fearing poverty is not of me.

Let those who have the means get married.

Let whoever has strength get married, as marriage averts eyes and protects private parts. And whoever has no means to marry should fast, as fasting to him is like castration.

"Castration" is used metaphorically to mean sexual impotence during the fast.

When there comes to you a man whose religion and trust please you, get him married. If you do not, there will be disasters and quarrels in the world.

This is encouragement to marry out of fear of disturbance and disorder.

He who marries and gives in marriage becomes entitled to Allah's care.

He who marries fulfils half of his religion, so let him fear Allah regarding the second half.

Generally, the private parts and stomach create disorder in a person's religion, and marriage removes that disorder.

The actions of a man come to an end except three: a religious son who prays for him, recurring charity and a religious book.

A religious son is impossible without marriage.

Traditions from Companions and early Muslims

'Umar said, "Two things prevent marriage: inability and being a sinner," implying that religion does not prohibit marriage.

Ibn 'Abbās said, "No act of worship is complete without marriage."

'Umar had many wives and would say, "I marry for children."

A Companion renounced the world, stayed with the Prophet (ṣ) and spent many nights with him. The Prophet (ṣ) asked him, "Will you not marry?" He said, "O Messenger of Allah, I am a poor man and have no means. Shall I be deprived of serving you?" The Prophet (ṣ) remained silent. The Prophet (ṣ) again put this question to the Companion, but he replied as before. The Companion then thought, "The Messenger of Allah knows well what will bring us near Allah and what is good for us in this world and the next. I shall certainly marry." The Prophet (ṣ) asked him a third time, 'Will you not marry?" He said, "O Messenger of Allah, get me married."

A hermit surpassed all the people of his time in worship. When his case was mentioned to the prophet of his age, he said, "How good he is! But he is lacking one thing." Grieved, he asked that prophet about it, and he said, "You have not married." The hermit said, "I am a poor man. I have no means to bear its expense." The prophet said, "I will give my daughter in marriage to you." And he did.

A man said to Ibrāhīm ibn Adham, "Glad tidings to you. You can engage yourself in worship because you are alone." Ibrāhīm said, "Your prayer amid your family is better than all my spiritual works." The man asked, "Then why do you not marry?" He said, "I have no need for women and do not wish to have any connection with any woman."

Someone said, "The rank of a married man in comparison with that of an unmarried man is like the rank of someone engaged in jihad in comparison with a devotee. And one *rak'ah* of prayer by a married man is better than seventy by an unmarried man."

Reasons for not marrying

The Prophet (ṣ) said, "After two hundred years, a man without a wife and children will be better." He also said, "A time will come when a man will be destroyed by his wife, parents and children:

they will demand of him beyond his means, and he will enter paths in which he will lose his religion and perish."

A tradition says, "One of the two sources of comfortable living is having less children, while one of the two sources of poverty is having many of them." Abū Sulaymān al-Dārānī was once asked about marriage, and he replied, "Abstaining is better than enduring women, and enduring them is better than suffering hellfire." He also said, "He who seeks three things becomes attached to the world: livelihood, marriage and writing stories."

Al-Ḥasan said, "When Allah wishes good for a man, He does not keep him engaged in family and wealth."

The benefits of marriage

There are five benefits of marriage. The first is to have children and is the main reason why marriage is contracted. The object is to preserve lineage so that the world will not lack humans.

There are four objects of having children: an increase in human population, the love of the Prophet (ṣ), the prayers of religious children after one's death and, if the children die first, their intercession.

The first object is very subtle and not easy to grasp. It is an inherent truth, and the following is its proof. Suppose the owner of a piece of land hands over the seeds of the crops and the instruments of cultivation to a servant, and gives him the land for cultivation as well, But the servant does not cultivate it, does not use the instruments and destroys the seeds. It is clear that the master will be angry with the servant. Similarly, Allah created man and woman, and created the life germ for the production of children in the back of a man and in the breast of a woman. The uterus is the fertile field and the male organ and the female organ are the instruments of cultivation. He also created in the male and female a desire to procreate by using the instruments of their organs. The Prophet (ṣ) also clearly proved this by saying, "Marry and multiply." Whoever does not marry destroys the seeds, does not use the instruments and goes against the object of Allah. For this reason, to kill a child or bury him alive is prohibited.

A person might ask, "If the object of Allah is to preserve lineage, then why has He prescribed its destruction by death?" Life and death, though opposed to each other, are the will of Allah, just as love and hatred, though opposed to each other, are His will. Allah says, "He does not like ungratefulness in His servants" (Qur'an, 39:7); "I have never hesitated over anything as I hesitate over taking the soul of my Muslim servant. He dislikes death, and I do not like to trouble him, but there is no escape from death"; "We have ordained death among you" (Qur'an, 56:60); and "Who created death and life" (Qur'an, 67:2). So the words of Allah "We have ordained death among you" and "I do not like to trouble him" do not contradict each other.

The second object is an expression of love for the Prophet (ṣ) and an effort to increase the number of his followers, which he will boast about on Resurrection Day. The Prophet (ṣ) said, "A straw mat in the corner of a house is preferable to a barren woman"; "The best among your women is a lovely woman who produces many children"; and "An ugly woman with children is better than a beautiful woman without children." It appears from the above traditions that the object of marriage is to have children and not only to satisfy sexual passion.

The third object is that if anybody leaves a religious son or daughter, he or she may pray for his or her deceased parents. A *ḥadīth* says that at death, the actions of a man end except three, a religious child being one of them. Another says, "Supplications are offered to the dead on platters of light." If a child is religious, his parents get the rewards of his pious actions and invocations, as they have earned them, but they are not punished for his sins as nobody bears the burden of another. Allah says, "We will unite with them their offspring and We will not diminish to them aught of their work" (Qur'an, 52:21), but their good deeds will increase owing to the good deeds of their children.

The fourth object is that if a child dies before his parents, he can intercede for them. The Prophet (ṣ) said, "A child will carry his parents to paradise," and in another tradition, "He will draw his parents as I draw your clothes." He also said, "It will be said to the child, 'Enter paradise.' He will go to the door of paradise and say in an angry tone, 'I will not enter paradise without my parents.' It will then be said to him, 'Admit his parents along with him into paradise.'"

Another *ḥadīth* says, "Children along with others will be brought to the place of judgement. It will be said to the angels, 'Take their children to paradise.' While they are waiting at the door of paradise, it will be said to them, 'Welcome, Muslim children. Enter. There is no reckoning for you.' They will ask, 'Where are our parents?' The guard will reply, 'Your parents are not like you. They have sins and faults for which they will be summoned and taken to account.' With that, they will make tremendous noise before paradise, and Allah will say, 'What is this cry for?' They will say, 'Lord, the children of the Muslims say, 'We will not enter paradise except in the company of our parents.'' Allah will say, 'Leave them all, so that they can take their parents to paradise.'"

The Prophet (ṣ) said, "Someone whose two children predeceased him will be safe from hell." He also said, "Allah, by His mercy, will admit into paradise someone whose three prepubescent children predeceased him." He was asked, "O Messenger of Allah, what if two of them predeceased him?" He said, "Even if two predeceased him."

The second benefit of marriage is to be safe from the Devil, to satisfy lust and to safeguard the private parts. The Prophet (ṣ) said, "If a man marries, half of his religion is saved. So he should fear Allah concerning the remaining half" and "Let whoever is unable to marry, fast, as fasting for him is a means of controlling passion." The pleasure which lies in sexual intercourse is only a sample of happiness in the next world. For to encourage pleasure which someone cannot enjoy is pointless. Thus, if an impotent male were encouraged to seek the enjoyment of sexual intercourse, or were a young boy encouraged to seek rule and power, encouragement would be useless. So Allah created pleasure in this world with the object that if people experience pleasure, they will be eager to have lasting pleasure in the next world and will perform acts of worship.

Ibn 'Abbās said, "The worship of a man does not become perfect without marriage." Commenting on the words of Allah "Man is created weak" (Qur'an, 4:28), 'Ikrimah and Mujāhid said that man cannot refrain from women. Fayyāḍ ibn Najīḥ said, "When the male organ of a man becomes erect, two thirds of his intellect go away." Explaining the words of Allah "(Seek refuge) from the evil of the utterly dark night when it comes" (Qur'an, 113:3), Ibn 'Abbās said they mean "Seek refuge from the Devil when the male organ becomes erect." The Prophet (ṣ) said, "O Allah, I seek refuge in You from the evils of my ears, my heart and my semen." He also said, "I ask You to purify my heart and safeguard my private parts."

Al-Junayd said, "Sexual intercourse is as necessary for me as food." The Prophet (ṣ) said that if the look of a man falls on a woman, he should cohabit with his wife, for that would ward off temptation from his soul. Jābir reported that the Prophet (ṣ) once looked at a woman and soon after went to his wife Zaynab and fulfilled his desire. Then he came out and said, "If a woman approaches, she does so in the image of the Devil. So if one of you sees a woman who pleases him, let him go to his wife, as that woman has what his wife has." He also said, "Do not go to a woman in the absence of her husband, for the Devil runs through your veins like the circulation of blood." He was asked, "In your case also?" He said, "In my case also, but Allah has helped me against him, and he has submitted to me," meaning "I have been saved from the machinations of the Devil."

Once, a young man said to Ibn 'Abbās, "I am a young man and have no wife. I fear sin in most cases, and many a time I seek relief by masturbation. Is there any sin in it?" Ibn 'Abbās turned his face from him and said, "How disgusting! It is better to marry a slave girl than that. Nevertheless, it is better than fornication."

Sexual passion is so strong in some men that one wife cannot satisfy them, and so they are permitted to marry four wives. 'Alī married seven days after the death of Fāṭimah. It is said that al-Ḥasan took many wives, but not more than four at a time. The Prophet (ṣ) said to al-Ḥasan, "You have my character and appearance." He also said, "Al-Ḥasan is from me, and al-Ḥusayn is from 'Alī." Some of the Companions had three or four wives, and those who had two wives were many.

The third benefit of marriage is that it brings peace of mind, which is necessary for worship. Allah says, "He it is who created you from a single being, and of the same (kind) did He make his mate, that he might incline to her" (Qur'an, 7:89). 'Alī said, "Give peace to the mind, as it becomes blind when it becomes disturbed."A *ḥadīth* says that the there are three special times for a wise man. He speaks secretly with his Lord at one time, takes account of his actions at another time and remains busy with his food and drink at another time. Another version says that a wise man is not desirous of anything except three things: to earn the livelihood of the next world, to earn the livelihood of this world and to taste lawful things.

The Prophet (ṣ) said, "For every desire there is eagerness, and for every eagerness, there is a natural disposition. He whose natural disposition leads to my way is guided"; "After complaining to Jibrīl about the lessening of my sexual passion, he advised me to eat *harīsah*"; and "From your world, three things have been made dear to me: scent, women and prayer, my delight." This comfort is necessary for peace of mind.

The fourth benefit of marriage is leisure for worship. The wife lessens the duties of the man in terms of cooking, making the bed, washing dishes and other chores. A chaste and religious wife helps here husband with these. Sulaymān al-Dārānī said, "A religious wife is not of this world, for she liberates you for the hereafter. She frees her husband by performing household duties and satisfying his sexual passion." The Prophet (ṣ) said, "Let one of you have a grateful heart, a remembering tongue and a chaste wife helping him for the next world." 'Umar said, "After faith man has been given nothing better than a virtuous wife. And no wealth is as valuable to a man as a chaste wife." The Prophet (ṣ) said, "I have been preferred to Adam by two gifts: Adam's wife was his helper in a sinful act, while my wives are my helpers in my religious affairs; and the Devil was disobedient to Adam, but he submitted to me and commands me only to what is right."

The fifth benefit of marriage is that there are some duties arising out of marriage which are considered acts of worship: to maintain a family, to have patience with the character and conduct of the wife, to bear the hardships of the family members, to try to do good to them, to show them the path of religion, to earn for them lawful things and to educate the children. The Prophet (ṣ) said, "One day of a just ruler is better than seventy years of worship. And the task of ruling a family is no less than that of a king"; "Be careful. Every one of you is a ruler, and every one of you will be asked about his subjects"; and "What man spends on his family is considered an act of charity. Even if he lifts a morsel of food to the mouth of his wife, he will get rewards."

A scholar mentioned his actions during his pilgrimage, jihad and other good works to another scholar, who said, "Your religious acts are nothing compared to those of the *Abdāl*." The first asked him, "What acts are those?" He said, "They are a lawful income and spending on one's family." The Prophet (ṣ) said, "He whose prayer is good, who has a big family, whose wealth is little and who abstains from defaming Muslims will be in paradise with me like these two fingers." He also said, "Allah loves a poor man who has a big family but refrains from begging." A *ḥadīth* says that if the sins of a man become many, Allah preoccupies him with the burden of children to expiate his sins. A wise man said, "There are offences which cannot be expiated by anything except family burdens." The Prophet (ṣ) said, "If a man has three daughters and spends on their maintenance, Allah makes paradise his reward, unless he commits an unpardonable sin."

The harms of marriage

There are three harms of marriage. The first is that earning a lawful income becomes difficult as a result of marriage. A *ḥadīth* says that a man with a mountain of good deeds will be made to stand before the Balance and will be questioned concerning his wealth, his expenditure, his maintenance and other matters. Also, it is said that on Resurrection Day, children will say to Allah, "O our Lord, take him to account for his duties towards us. He did not teach us what we did not know and gave us unlawful food to eat without our knowledge." The Prophet (ṣ) said, "Nobody will meet Allah with a greeter sin than that of keeping his family members uneducated." Very few people are safe from this danger.

The second harm is failure to fulfil one's duties towards family members, to tolerate their character and conduct and to endure harm from them. The Prophet (ṣ) said, "It is sin enough for a man not to fulfil his duties of maintenance for which he is responsible." He also said, "The fleeing of a man from his family is like that of a slave from his master: his prayer and fast are not accepted until he returns." Whoever neglects his duty of maintenance is like a fleeing man even though he remains present. Ibrāhīm ibn Adham refused to get married, saying, "I do not wish to let any woman sin, and I have no need for woman."

The third harm of marriage is that the wife and children may distract one from the remembrance of Allah, encourage one to hoard up wealth and seek objects of pride and boast. Whatever diverts attention from Allah is a cause of misfortune. Ibrāhīm ibn Adham said, "He who sticks to the thighs of his wife gets no benefit."

These are the benefits and harms of marriage. Whether marriage is better or not depends on the personal character of the person. Thus, marriage is good for someone who is not diverted from the remembrance of Allah and from the path of honesty and virtue. Conversely, marriage is bad for someone who is diverted from the remembrance of Allah. And if one needs to control his sexual passion, marriage is necessary. ʻĪsā did not marry in spite of his high and lofty position as a prophet. The Holy Prophet (ṣ), who has been given the highest rank among men, had several wives, and yet he did not forget Allah for a moment. He would even receive revelation when he was in the same bed with his wife ʻĀ'ishah.

2
The rules of marriage

The marriage contract

The marriage contract has four conditions: (1) the consent of the guardian or, if there is no guardian, the ruler or his representative; (2) the consent of a grownup girl, whether unmarried or a widow; (3) two adult witnesses who will inform the audience of the girl's consent; and (4) the proposals and acceptances of the bride and bridegroom.

Some rules of marriage

- The proposal is to be submitted to the guardian of the girl.
- The engagement must be read before the marriage along with proposal and acceptance. The guardian of the girl will say, "All praise is due to Allah, and blessings be on Allah's Messenger. I give my daughter in marriage to you." The bridegroom will say, "All praise is due to Allah, and blessings be on Allah's Messenger. I accept her in marriage with this dowry."
- The bride should be informed of the condition of the bridegroom. It is better that they see each other before marriage.
- Two witnesses are necessary.
- One should have the intention to follow the way of the Prophet (ṣ) by marriage and to seek children.

- It is good to perform the marriage ceremony in the month of Shawwāl, as the Prophet (ṣ) married ʿĀ'ishah in Shawwāl and consummated the marriage in Shawwāl.
- The bride should not be the wife of another man, in her waiting period (*ʿiddah*), an infidel, a slave, related to the bridegroom, a woman who has cursed her husband or in *iḥrām*.

The qualifications of the bride

There are eight qualifications. The first is religion. The bride should be religious and possess good conduct. This is the main quality of the bride. Once, a man came to the Prophet (ṣ) and said, "O Messenger of Allah, my wife does not repulse any foreign touch." The Prophet (ṣ) said, "Divorce her." He said, "I love her." The Prophet (ṣ) said, "Then keep her." The Prophet (ṣ) said, "A woman may be married for her wealth, beauty, reputation or religion. If you marry a religious woman, may your hands be covered with dust." Another *ḥadīth* says, "Whoever marries a woman for beauty and wealth is deprived of her beauty and wealth. If a man marries for the protection of his religion, Allah gives him the means of beauty and wealth." The Prophet (ṣ) said, "Do not marry a woman only for her beauty, as it may be a cause of her ruin. Nor marry a woman only for her wealth, as her wealth may make her disobedient. Marry her only for her religion." He laid great stress on her religious habits because a religious wife helps her husband with his religion.

The second is good conduct. If the wife is harsh and rough and ungrateful, her harms outweigh her benefits. It is related that an Azdī traveller met the prophet Ilyās, who ordered him to marry and prohibited him from monkery. Then he said to him, "Do not marry four kinds of women: a woman who always seeks dresses without any reason, a woman who boasts about her wealth before other women, a woman who is a sinner and unchaste and who have friends (Allah says about such women, 'Nor receiving paramours' (Qur'an, 4:25)) and a woman who takes pride before her husband with haughty words." 'Alī said, "There are some characteristics which are bad for a male but good for a female: miserliness, pride and cowardice. When a woman is a miser, she protects her wealth and her husband's wealth and possessions. When she is proud, she becomes soft and rejects doubtful talks. When she is a coward, she keeps her distance from her friends and is afraid to go to any place of defamation for fear of her husband."

The third is beauty. Beauty is sought from a girl as it saves one from fornication. For this reason, it is recommended to see a bride before marriage. The Prophet (ṣ) said, "When any of you wishes in his heart to marry a woman, let him look at her, as it generates mutual love." He also said, "If any of you wishes to marry a woman of the Madīnan Helpers (*Anṣār*), let him look at her, as there is something in their eyes." It is said that they had yellow in their eyes. Al-A'mash said, "The result of a marriage which is performed without looking is sorrow and anxiety." Mālik ibn Dīnār said, "A man does not marry an orphan girl, who remains pleased simply with food and clothes and whose expenses are low. People marry girls of good fortune and wealth, who demand fine foods and clothes." Imam Aḥmad married a deaf woman, although he had a beautiful cousin. He did not desire comforts and pleasures. The Prophet (ṣ) said, "Of all your women, the best one is she who gives her husband pleasure when he looks at her, obeys him when he orders her and protects her body and his possessions when her husband is absent."

The fourth is dowry. The Prophet (ṣ) said, "The best woman is she who is beautiful and whose dowry is little." He prohibited dowry beyond one's capacity. To some of his wives he gave a dowry of only ten dirhams and some household articles, and to others he gave two measures of wheat or dates or two measures of maize. Some of the Companions of the Prophet (ṣ) fixed the dowry at a piece of gold which, it is said, equalled only five dirhams. A *ḥadīth* says that there is good in a woman who is given in marriage without delay, who gives birth to a child without delay and for whom a small amount of dowry is fixed. One should not marry coveting many goods from the bride, though mutual presents are recommended and signs of one's love. The Prophet (ṣ) said, "Give presents and it will beget mutual love, but do not seek too many presents from each other." Allah says, "Bestow not favours that you may receive again with increase" (Qur'an, 74:6).

The fifth is that the bride is able to bear children. The Prophet (ṣ) said, "Marry lovely and childbearing women."

The sixth is virginity. The Prophet (ṣ) said to Jābir, who married a woman who had previously married, "Why have you not married a virgin girl, whom you could play with and who could play with you?" There are three benefits of marrying a virgin. One is that she loves her husband. Women who have had a husband before are generally addicted to them. Another benefit is that the love of the husband for his wife becomes complete. Finally, a virgin girl will not yearn for a previous husband.

The seventh is that the bride comes from a respectable family. This is because if she comes from a good family, she can teach her children good manners and good conduct. The Prophet (ṣ) said, "Exercise care in choosing a woman for your semen, for a hereditary quality is wont to return."

The eighth is that the bride is not a near relative, as this would lessen desire. The Prophet (ṣ) said, "Do not marry a near relative, for the child is born weak." He also said, "Whoever marries his daughter to a transgressor cuts off his blood tie."

3

Rules observed after marriage

After marriage, twelve rules should be observed. The first rule is that there is a marriage feast, which is recommended. Anas reported that the Prophet (ṣ) once saw paleness in the face of ‘Abd al-Raḥmān ibn ‘Awf and said, “What is it?” He said, “I have married a woman for a piece of gold.” The Prophet (ṣ) said, “May Allah bless you both. Give a feast with a goat.” When the Prophet (ṣ) married Ṣafiyyah, he gave a feast with grapes and wheat. He said, “To give a feast on the first day is a duty, on the second day recommended and the third day for show, and Allah will disgrace whoever does an act for show.”

It is recommended to bless the bridegroom, saying, “May Allah unite you both in good.” It is also recommended to proclaim the marriage. The Prophet (ṣ) said, “What distinguishes between the lawful and unlawful in marriage is the tambourine and the voice.” He also said, “Proclaim this marriage, perform it in the mosque and beat the tambourine for it.”

The second rule is that the husband treats his wife well. Allah says, “Treat them kindly” (Qur’an, 4:19) and, in upholding their rights, “They have made with you a firm covenant” (Qur’an, 4:21). The Prophet (ṣ) gave three instructions at the time of his death. Soon after, he was unable to speak. He said, “Prayer, prayer! Do not impose on your slaves what you cannot support. As for your women, they are prisoners in your hands. You have taken them as trusts from Allah and have made their private parts lawful with the words of Allah.” He also said, “If a man endures his wife’s ill-treatment of him, Allah will give him the rewards He gave Ayyūb for his patience amid disasters. If a wife tolerates her husband's ill-treatment of her, Allah will give her the rewards He gave to Āsiyah, the wife of Pharaoh." To have patience when the wife gets angry and when she makes trouble is following the Prophet's good treatment of his wives. It is not enough merely to restrain oneself from troubling the wife.

At times the wives of the Prophet (ṣ) argued with him. Once, the wife of the Prophet (ṣ) placed her hand on the chest of the Prophet (ṣ) and gave him a push, and her mother rebuked her. The Prophet (ṣ) then said, "Leave her, as she does more than this." Once, there was an altercation between the Prophet (ṣ) and 'Ā'ishah, and Abū Bakr was asked to arbitrate. 'Ā'ishah said to the Prophet (ṣ), "Speak, but speak only the truth. At once, Abū Bakr gave her such a slap that her mouth began to bleed. Then he said, "O enemy, will he speak anything but the truth?" Then she took refuge with the Prophet (ṣ).

The third rule is to play around with the wife after bearing her hardships, which gives pleasure to her. The Prophet (ṣ) used to joke with his wives and come down to the level of their intelligence in deeds and manners. And he ran races with 'Ā'ishah. One day 'Ā'ishah won the race, but on another day the Prophet (ṣ) won it and said, "This is revenge for that day." The Prophet (ṣ) said, "The most perfect believer in faith is someone who is the best in good conduct." He also said, "The best of you is someone who treats his wife the best."

In spite of his sternness, 'Umar said, "Stay in the house with your wife like a boy. When the wife demands things from her husband, he should treat her like a man." Luqmān said, "A wise man should live in his house like a boy, and when he is among others, he should be found a man." A *ḥadīth* says, "Allah dislikes a man who is harsh to his family and self-conceited." The Prophet (ṣ) said to Jābir, "Have you not found a virgin to marry? You could play with her, and she with you." A desert woman described her husband after his death, saying "By Allah, he was fond of sports, and when it was dark, he remained silent."

The fourth rule is not to play with one's wife so much that her manners are ruined and fear leaves her heart. Rather, one should be moderate, not giving up one's duties, and strike fear in her heart when she does evil. 'Umar said, "Disagree with women, as there is blessing in disagreeing with them." Someone said, "Take advice from them, but disagree with them." The Prophet (ṣ) said, "Whoever becomes the slave of women is ruined." He said this because if a husband acts according to the wishes of his wife, he becomes her slave and is thus ruined, since Allah has made him her master. The right of a husband is that the wife should obey him, and the husband should not obey her. Allah says, "They met her master at the door" (Qur'an, 12:25), "her master" being her husband.

Imam al-Shāfi'ī said, "If you honour three kinds of men, they will disgrace you, and if you disgrace them, they will honour you: a wife, a servant and a Nabataean," as evil and lack of intelligence predominate in them. The Prophet (ṣ) said, "A religious woman among ordinary women is like a crow with a white belly among a hundred crows."

Luqmān advised his son, "O dear son, fear an unchaste wife, as she will make you grow old before you grow old. Fear the harms of women, as they do encourage good. Beware of unchaste women." The Prophet (ṣ) said, "Seek refuge in Allah from three calamities," and among them he mentioned "an unchaste wife" because she will make you old before you get old. In another version, "If you go to her, she will rebuke you. If you do not go to her, she will be treacherous to you."

When the Prophet (ṣ) fell seriously ill and could not come out to the mosque for prayer, he told Abū Bakr to lead the prayer. 'Ā'ishah said, "My father's heart is soft. When he finds your place vacant, he will be perturbed." The Prophet (ṣ) replied, "When you prevent Abū Bakr from leading the prayer, you have been swayed by your low desires and have strayed from the right path."

When the wives of the Prophet (ṣ) disclosed their secret talks with the Prophet (ṣ), Allah revealed, "If you both turn to Allah, then indeed your hearts are already inclined (to this)" (Qur'an, 66:4). He said this regarding his good wives. The Prophet (ṣ) said, "No nation ruled by a woman ruler will prosper."

The fifth rule is to be moderate in jealousy. This means one should not go to extremes in misjudging, in acting adversely or in spying on hidden matters. The Prophet (ṣ) prohibited seeking out the faults of women. According to another version, he prohibited going suddenly to them. Once, the Prophet (ṣ) returned with his Companions from a journey to Madīnah and said to them, "Do not go suddenly to your wives tonight." Two of them went to their wives without paying heed to his words and found disagreeable things in their houses.

A famous *ḥadīth* says, "A wife is like a rib. If you try to make it straight, it will break. If you leave it as it is, it will become more crooked." This refers to rectifying her character. The Prophet (ṣ) said, "There is a type of jealousy which Allah hates: to become jealous of the wife without justification, as this is the type of suspicion which has been prohibited." Some types of suspicion are sinful. 'Alī said, "Do not become jealous of your wife lest evils come out." To disclose a sin in its proper place is necessary, as it is praiseworthy. The Prophet (ṣ) said, "Allah has jealousy, and a believer also has jealousy. Allah has jealousy when a servant commits a sin." He also said, "Do you wonder at the jealousy of Sa'd? By Allah, I am more jealous than him, and Allah is more jealous than I. Because of His jealousy, He made unlawful both open and secret indecencies."

The Prophet (ṣ) said, "I was taken to paradise in the night of my ascent and found a palace there. I asked, "For whom is this palace?" It was said that it is for 'Umar. I wished to see 'Umar therein, but remembered his jealousy. 'Umar wept and said,

"O Messenger of Allah, shall I be jealous because of you?" The Prophet (ṣ) said, "There is jealousy which Allah loves and jealousy which He hates. There is also pride which He loves and pride which He hates. The jealousy which He loves is jealousy which results from suspicion, and the jealousy which he hates is jealousy which results from unfounded suspicion. The pride which He loves is pride during jihad and the pride of a man at the onset of danger. The pride which He hates is pride about a useless thing."

The Prophet (ṣ) once asked Fāṭimah what is good for a woman. She said that she should not look at another man, nor should another man look at her. The Prophet (ṣ) drew her close to him and said, "This daughter is a worthy child of a worthy father," deeming her reply good. 'Umar ordered the females to stay in their houses if they dressed well. He said, "Accustom your women to staying in their houses." During his life, the Prophet (ṣ) ordered the women to be present in the mosques. 'Ā'ishah said, "If the Prophet (ṣ) saw the condition of women after his death, he would prohibit them from going outside." The Prophet (ṣ) permitted women to go outside for the 'Īd celebrations.

The sixth rule is to spend moderately and be neither stingy nor extravagant. Allah says, "Eat and drink and be not extravagant"and "Do not make your hand to be shackled to your neck nor stretch it forth to the utmost (limit) of its stretching forth" (Qur'an, 17:24). The Prophet (ṣ) said, "The best of you is the best of you to his wife" and "A dinar spent for the sake of Allah, a dinar spent on ransoming a slave, a dinar given in charity to a poor man and a dinar spent on your wife—the one which earns you the greatest reward is the one spent on your wife." Someone said, "'Alī had four wives. Every four days, he would buy meat for a dirham for each of his wives." Ibn Sīrīn said, "It is commendable to give a weekly feast for family members."

The seventh rule is that a husband teaches his wife religious matters, as all men have been given orders to save the members of their families from the fire. Allah says, "Save yourselves and your families from a fire' (Qur'an, 66:6). So to teach religious knowledge, articles of faith and all the questions of religion is necessary.

The eight is that, if there is more than one wife, the husband should treat them equally. For example, if the husband wishes to take a wife with him on a journey, he should let his wives cast lots, as the Prophet (ṣ) used to do this. The Prophet (ṣ) said, "If a man has two wives and prefers one to the other, he will appear on Resurrection Day with a crooked limb." The husband should be equitable in spending nights with them and giving them presents. Loving them equally, however, is not necessary, as the heart cannot be divided equally. Allah says, "You have it not in your power to do justice between wives, even though you may wish (it)" (Qur'an, 4:129). The Prophet (ṣ) used to divide the nights equally among his wives and said, "O Allah, this is my effort. Do not make me responsible for what is not in my power and capacity, but in Your power." The Prophet (ṣ) loved 'Ā'ishah more than any other wife, and his wives knew this.

The ninth rule is to appoint two people, one from the husband's side and one from the wife's, to arbitrate between them when there is a dispute. If they seek reconciliation, Allah will reconcile them. The wife should be separated gradually and not all at once. At first she should be given advice. If this is fruitless, the husband should sleep in another bed. This should be done for one to three nights. If this is fruitless, he should beat her mildly, not breaking a bone, causing her to bleed or slapping her on the face. The Prophet (ṣ) was once asked about the rights of wife over her husband. He replied, "If the husband eats, he should give her food. If the husband puts on clothes, he should give her clothes. He should not be insolent or beat her excessively. And he should avoid her only in cohabitation." He can get angry with her and avoid her for not observing her religious duties for up to thirty days. The Prophet (ṣ) once remained absent from his wives for one month.

The tenth rule is to observe the etiquette of sexual intercourse. A person should commence with the name of Allah, then read Sūrah al-Ikhlāṣ (Qur'an, 112) and say, "Allah is greatest. There is no deity but Allah. O Allah, if You take out semen from my back, make it a good child." The Prophet (ṣ) said, "When any of you goes to his wife, let him say, 'O Allah, protect me from the Devil, and protect what you have given us from the Devil.' The result is that the Devil will not be able to harm a child born from such intercourse."

He should not face the direction of the prayer at the time of intercourse, and he should cover his and his wife's body. The Prophet (ṣ) used to cover his head, close his mouth and say to his wife, "Remain quiet."

A *ḥadīth* says, "When any of you goes to his wife, he should not fall suddenly on her but rather speak words of love and kiss her." The Prophet (ṣ) said, "Let none of you fall suddenly on his wife like a lower animal. Let him send a messenger before cohabitation." Someone asked, "What is the messenger, O Prophet." He said, "Kisses and words of love." The Prophet (ṣ) also said, "Three qualities are considered deficiencies in a male: that he meets someone whose acquaintance he wishes to make, but parts with him before learning his name and lineage; that he is treated kindly, rejects the kindness shown to him and cohabits with his wife or concubine without talking with her or kissing her; and that he is unable to hold back his ejaculation before his wife's."

It is not recommended to cohabit with one's wife on the first, middle and last days of the lunar month. It is recommended to cohabit on the night before Friday.

After he ejaculates, let him keep his body on her breasts until she ejaculates, as she does so late. It is painful for her to be separated from her husband when her sexual passion rises high.

A young husband should cohabit with his wife once every four days. Depending on the nature of the wife, this may be increased or decreased. To cohabit with the wife during her period is unlawful.

It is, however, lawful to enjoy her without sexual intercourse. Allah says, "So go into your tilth when you like" (Qur'an, 2:223). It is also allowed to sleep beside her during this time.

The eleventh rule is to ejaculate only in the place of tilling—the womb—for whatever Allah has decreed will come to pass. The Prophet (ṣ) said similarly. There are differences of opinion among scholars regarding coitus interruptus. One party says that it is lawful under all circumstances, another that it is unlawful under all circumstances, another that it is lawful with the consent of the wife and another party that it is lawful with female slaves, but unlawful with free women.

To us coitus interruptus is lawful. But it is offensive because virtue, producing a child, is abandoned. The Prophet (ṣ) said, "If a man cohabits with his wife, written for him the reward of producing a child who is martyred fighting in the way of Allah." He said this in consideration of rewards because, if a child is born to him, he would receive a reward of being the cause of his existence and strengthening him for jihad. And this is only possible if he ejaculates into the uterus.

That coitus interruptus is lawful is supported by analogy with the Qur'an. Though there is no clear verse regarding it, it can be inferred thus: it is not unlawful to abstain from marriage or to abstain from sexual intercourse after marriage or abstain from ejaculation after sexual intercourse. It is true that rewards of these actions are forgone, but abstaining from them is not unlawful. For a child is born after semen is deposited into the uterus, which has four stages: marriage, cohabitation, patience until ejaculation and waiting until the sperm is implanted into the uterus.

The life of a child coming into existence has several stages as well. First, the semen in the uterus is mixed with female ova. When both mix, it is a crime to destroy it. It is not a crime, however, to destroy it before they mix. Second, if it forms into a clot of blood and a lump of flesh, it is more detestable to destroy it. Third, if life is infused into that lump of flesh, it is even more detestable to destroy it. Fourth, when the child is born, destroying it is the most detestable.

If semen is mixed with the menses of a woman, it is condensed, as when something is mixed with milk, milk is condensed. This is just like a proposal and acceptance, which constitute an agreement or contract. Both things are necessary for a contract. If there is a proposal but no acceptance, there is no sin in breaking it. The ejaculation of semen is like a proposal and its entering uterus is like its acceptance. If it is ejaculated outside, the proposal is lost, and there is no sin in it. Therefore, to ejaculate outside the uterus, before it is mixed with female ova, is not a sin.

Should you say, "If there is no sin in coitus interruptus, it is still bad, as the purpose of semen is to produce a child, and if it is not done, it is secret polytheism," I would answer that the motives for coitus interruptus are five. The first is to preserve the beauty and health of the wife and thus to enjoy her always. If semen is destroyed with this motive, it is not unlawful. The second is to prevent the birth of too many children, in which case it is not unlawful. To maintain too many children is very difficult. Doubtless, perfection and virtue arise from dependence on and faith in Allah's guarantee to give sustenance to all creatures, but abandoning what is preferable is not a crime. The third is for fear of having a daughter, in which case it is unlawful. The Arabs before Islam used to bury their daughters alive and they feared the birth of daughters, but this was prohibited in the Qur'an. If marriage or sexual intercourse is abandoned with this motive, it will be a sin. Without this motive, however, these are not sinful. Thus, if semen is ejaculated outside the uterus with the above motive, it will be a sin. The fourth is to protect the honour of the woman, to keep her neat and clean and to save her from maintaining children, in which case coitus interruptus is unlawful.

Should you say, "The Prophet (ṣ) said, 'He who abstains from marriage for fear of child birth is not of us,'" I would answer that coitus interruptus is like abstaining from marriage. His words "he is not of us" mean "he is not of our way." And should you say, "The Prophet (ṣ) also said, 'Coitus interruptus is secret murder' and then recited the verse 'And when the female infant buried alive is asked for what sin she was killed'" (Qur'an, 81:9), we would answer that there is an authentic *ḥadīth* about the legality of coitus interruptus, and that "secret murder" in the above *ḥadīth* means "secret polytheism." Thus, it is offensive and not unlawful.

'Alī said, "Life, comes into being after seven stages." Then he read these verses "Certainly We created man of an extract of clay. Then We made him a small seed in a firm resting-place. Then We made the seed a clot. Then We made the clot a lump of flesh. Then We made (in) the lump of flesh bones. Then We clothed the bones with flesh. Then We caused it to grow into another creation. So blessed be Allah, the best of the creators" (Qur'an, 23:12-14) and "And when the female infant buried alive is asked for what sin she was killed" (Qur'an, 81:9).

A *ḥadīth* in *Ṣaḥīḥ al-Bukhārī* and *Ṣaḥīḥ Muslim* says that Jābir said, "We used to practice coitus interruptus in the lifetime of the Prophet (ṣ), when the Qur'an was being revealed. When this news reached the Prophet (ṣ), he did not prohibit us from it." Another *ḥadīth* reported by Jābir says, "A man came to the Prophet (ṣ) and said, "I have a slave girl who serves us and gives water to the palm trees. I cohabit with her, but I do not want her to conceive." The Prophet (ṣ) said, "Practice coitus interruptus with her if you wish, but what has been decreed will come to pass." After some time, the man came to the Prophet (ṣ) and said, "The slave girl has conceived." The Prophet (ṣ) said, "What has been decreed will come to pass."' This is in the *ṣaḥīḥs* of al-Bukhārī and Muslim.

The twelfth rule is to observe five rules if a child is born. The first is not to be pleased with the birth of a son and displeased with the birth of a daughter. The Prophet (ṣ) said:

> If a man has a daughter, teaches her good manners, gives her good food and gives to her charity out of what Allah has given

him, she becomes a cause of his fortune and makes the path to paradise easy for him after saving him from hellfire.

If a man has two daughters or sisters and teaches them good manners until they are married, he and I will be in paradise like these two fingers.

If a Muslim goes to the market, purchases something and, after returning home, gives it first to his daughters and not to his sons, Allah will look at him, and Allah will not punish someone at whom He looks.

If a man brings a good thing to his family from the market, its rewards are like those of charity. He should first give it to his daughter and then to his son. He who incurs the pleasure of his daughter will get the rewards of weeping out of fear of Allah. And if a man weeps out of fear of Allah, Allah makes his body unlawful for hell.

If a man has three daughters or sisters and tolerates their hardships and ordeals, Allah will admit him into paradise. (A man asked him, "O Messenger of Allah, if a man has two?" He said, "Even if he has two." The man again asked him, "If he has one?" He said, "Even if he has one.")

The second is to give the call to prayer (*adhān*) in the ears of the child. Rāfi' related that his father said, "I saw the Prophet (ṣ) proclaiming the call to prayer in the ears of al-Ḥasan when he was born." The Prophet (ṣ) said, "Give the call to prayer in the right ear of the newly born child and the call to commence (*iqāmah*) in his left ear." When the child begins to talk, he should be taught "There is no deity but Allah"; these should be his first words. On the seventh day, he should be circumcised.

The third is to give a good name to the child. The Prophet (ṣ) said, "When you give a name, give a name of servitude"; "The best names are 'Abdullāh and 'Abd al-Raḥmān"; "Name with the names of Allah, and do not give my surname as a surname"; "Do not give both my name and my surname"; and "On Resurrection Day, you will be called by your names or the names of your fathers."

The fourth is to sacrifice two goats for a son and one for a daughter, which is called *'aqīqah*. There is no harm if only one goat is sacrificed for a son. Also, it is recommended to give in charity the weight of the child's hair in gold or silver. The Prophet (ṣ) ordered Fāṭimah to shave the head of al-Ḥusayn on the seventh day and to give silver after weighing his hair.

The fifth is to besmear the vertex of the child's head with dates or sweet things. Asmā' said 'Abdullāh ibn Zubayr was born in Qubā'. When he was brought before the Prophet (ṣ), he prayed for him, rubbed dates on his body and put some of his saliva into his mouth. Then he rubbed dates on his scalp and prayed for him. He was the first child born in Islam.

Divorce

Divorce is lawful, but of all lawful things, it is the most detestable to Allah, as Allah says, "If they obey you, do not seek a way against them" (Qur'an, 4:34).

If a person's father dislikes his wife, he should divorce her. Ibn 'Umar said, "I loved my wife very much, but my father, 'Umar, did not like her. When he ordered me to divorce her, I informed the Prophet (ṣ) of it, and he said, 'O son of 'Umar, divorce her.'" This shows that his duty towards his father is greater.

The Prophet (ṣ) said, "If a woman seeks divorce from her husband without any reason, she will not breathe the fragrance of paradise." In other words, paradise is unlawful for her. In another version, the Prophet (ṣ) said, "Women who seek divorce are hypocrites."

With respect to divorce, the husband should observe four matters. First, he should not divorce the wife during her period. When 'Umar divorced his wife during her period, the Prophet (ṣ) said, "Tell him to take her back and keep her until her menstrual discharge stops. Thereafter, she will have monthly menses and will be pure. Then he may divorce her or take her back. This is the period of waiting which Allah enjoins." Second, he should not divorce her three times at once because if he has regrets within the period of waiting, he can take her back. Third, after the divorce, he should give maintenance and presents to the ex-wife. This is obligatory for the husband. Fourth, he should not disclose the secrets of his ex-wife after the divorce. This has been prohibited in sound *ḥadīths*.

The husband's rights

There are many traditions that magnify the rights of the husband. The Prophet (ṣ) said:

> If the wife of a man dies while he is pleased with her, she will enter paradise.
>
> When a woman prays five times a day, fasts the month of Ramaḍān, protects her private parts and obeys her husband, she will enter the paradise of her Lord.
>
> Childbearers, mothers, wet nurses who are compassionate towards their children, and those who pray will enter paradise provided that they do not wrong their husbands.
>
> I peeped into hell and found that the majority of its inmates are women. (He was asked, "Why, O Messenger of Allah?" He said, "They curse a lot and enrage their mates.")
>
> I peeped into paradise and found that there are few women there. I asked, "Where are the women?" I was told, "Two things of reddish colour preoccupied them: gold and saffron."
>
> (Upon being asked about the husband's rights) When he wants her, she should not refuse, even if she is on a camel's back. She should not give anything from his house in charity without his permission. If she does, she commits a sin and her husband gets rewards. She should not observe optional fasts without his permission. If she does, and becomes hungry and thirsty, it will not be accepted from her. And if she goes out of his house without his permission, the angels curse her until she returns to his house or until she repents.

> If I ordered anybody to prostrate before another, I would order a woman to prostrate before her husband, as the duties towards him are many.

> When a woman stays in her house, she draws nearer to Allah. Her prayer in the courtyard of her house is more meritorious than her prayer in a mosque, and her prayer in her room is better than her prayer in her courtyard.

The husband's rights are many, but two of them are essential. One is safeguarding and sheltering. The other is to be spared unnecessary demands and the need for having to provide them if they are unlawful.

Also among the obligations of the wife is that she not spend extravagantly the wealth of her husband, but protect it. The Prophet (ṣ) said, "It is unlawful to give in charity the food in his house without his permission, unless the food would be spoilt." Asmā' said to her daughter when she was getting married, "You are now going to spend a life in which you will have to live long, you are going to the bed with a person who is not of your acquaintance and you are going to love someone whom you did not love before. Make for him a world which will be heaven for you and prepare for him a bed which will be a pillar for you. Be his slave so that he might become your slave. Do not go willingly to him, lest you become to him an object of hatred. Do not remain far from him, lest he forget you. When he is near you, be near him. When he is distant from you, protect your nose, ears and eyes. Do not let him get from you anything except a sweet smile. Do not let him hear from you anything except pleasant words. And do not let him see in you anything except beauty."

She should safeguard her husband in his absence and seek his pleasure in his presence. The Prophet (ṣ) said, "If a woman troubles her husband, the black-eyed houri says, 'Do not trouble him. May Allah destroy you. Now he is with you, but perchance he will leave you soon and come to us.'"

When the husband dies, she should not express sorrow for more than four months and ten days. The Prophet (ṣ) said, "It is unlawful for a woman who believes in Allah and the next world to grieve for more than three days except in the case of the death of her husband, for whom she should grieve for four months and ten days, during which she should stay in his house."

Finally, she should do all the household chores to her utmost capacity.

Book 3
Earning a livelihood

Introduction

Allah has made the next world the place of reward and punishments and this world the place of efforts, troubles and earning a livelihood. Earning a livelihood is not the aim of human life but a means to the hereafter. Thus, the world is a seed ground for men, who are of three kinds. One kind forgets the hereafter and makes earning a livelihood the sole object of life; this kind will be destroyed. Another kind makes the hereafter the sole object of life and remains busy earning a livelihood. And another kind adopts a middle course, keeping its goal of returning to the next world fixed while earning a livelihood.

He who does not adopt the middle path in earning a livelihood will not get the pleasure of the straight path. And he who makes the world a means of earning the next world adopts the rules and regulations of Sharī'ah in seeking it and gets the pleasure of the middle path.

1
The excellence of earning a livelihood

The Qur'an

Allah says:

> *We made the day for seeking livelihood.* (Qur'an, 78:11)
>
> *We made in it means of livelihood for you; little it is that you give thanks.* (Qur'an, 7:10)
>
> *There is no blame on you in seeking bounty from your Lord.* (Qur'an, 2:198)
>
> *Others who travel in the land seeking of the bounty of Allah.* (Qur'an, 73:20)
>
> *Disperse abroad in the land and seek of Allah's grace.* (Qur'an, 62:10)

Ḥadīth

The Prophet (ṣ) said:

> There are sins which are not expiated by anything except the anxieties of earning a livelihood.
>
> The truthful tradesman will be resurrected on Resurrection Day with those of great faith and martyrs.

> He who seeks a lawful livelihood, refrains from begging, puts in effort for family members and is kind to neighbours will meet Allah with a face which will be bright like a full moon.
>
> Allah loves a person who adopts the path of labour to save himself from depending on others, and He hates a person who gains knowledge thinking it is a means of livelihood.
>
> Allah loves the believing trader.
>
> The best lawful income is that which a person earns himself.
>
> Take to trade, for in it is nine-tenths of sustenance.
>
> I have left no command which, if obeyed, will not bring you near paradise and keep you distant from hell. And I have left no prohibition which, if obeyed, will not keep you distant from paradise and bring you near hell. The trusted Spirit inspired my soul that no man will die until he receives his full measure of sustenance, although it may come to him late. So fear Allah and seek livelihood in a lawful manner. I enjoin you to earn a livelihood in a just manner. Let nobody say, "Abandon the seeking of livelihood." Let not a delay in earning a livelihood encourage you to earn it illegally, for disobedience to Allah cannot bring what is His.
>
> The markets are the repositories of the food of Allah. He who comes to them gets something therefrom.
>
> If anyone of you gathers firewood with a rope and seeks livelihood by bearing it on his back, it is better than to beg men, whether they give or not.
>
> If a man opens for himself one door of begging, Allah will open for him seventy doors of begging.

One day, the Prophet (ṣ) was seated in the mosque of Madīnah with his Companions when a stout and strong young man ran past the mosque on his way to his shop. The Companions said, "Woe to this young man! If only his body and health ran in the way of Allah!" The Prophet (ṣ) then said, "Do not say this. If this young man runs with the object of not depending on others and refraining from begging, he is in the way of Allah. And if he strives to support his weak parents or weak children, he is in the way of Allah. But if he tries to show his health out of pride, he is in the way of the Devil."

Once, the prophet 'Īsā asked a man, "What do you do?" He said. "I worship." 'Īsā asked, "Who gives you food?" He said, "My brother." 'Īsā said, "Your brother worships better than you.'"

Traditions from Companions and early Muslims

Luqmān advised his son, "O dear son, avoid poverty by lawful earnings, because he who is poor is afflicted with three qualities: laxity in religious actions, weakness in intellect and loss of manliness. A greater fault than these three is to keep it secret from people."

'Umar said, "Let none of you refrain from earning a livelihood. Instead, say, 'O Allah, give me sustenance.' And know for certain that the heaven will not rain gold and silver." Once, while Jābir was sowing seeds in his field, 'Umar said to him, "If you do good, you will not depend on people. It will save your religion, and you will be honoured by them."

Ibrāhīm ibn Adham was asked, "Which is better: a truthful merchant or a devotee?" He said, "A truthful merchant is dearer to me, as he is in jihad. The Devil comes to him by way of weight and measure and buying and selling, and he engages in jihad against him.' 'Umar said, "No place is dearer to me than where I seek livelihood for my family members and where I buy and sell."

When a strong tempest arose at sea, the passengers of a boat asked Ibrāhīm ibn Adham, "Do you not see this calamity?" He answered, "I do not consider this a calamity; depending on men for a need is a calamity."

Once, the Prophet (ṣ) was asked about the livelihood of beasts and birds. He said, "They go out hungry in the morning and return full in the evening." In other words, they go out in search of their livelihood.

Once, al-Awzāʿī saw Ibrāhīm ibn Adham bearing a load of firewood on his back and said, "O Abū Isḥāq, why are you taking such trouble? Our brethren are enough for you." He said, "O Abū ʿAmr, leave me alone in this matter, as I have come to know that if a man waits in a place of disgrace seeking a lawful livelihood, paradise is sure for him."

The object of trade and commerce is to gain either necessary livelihood or to gain enormous wealth. The latter is the root of attachment to the world, which is the basis of all sins. It is better for four people not to beg: one busy with physical acts of worship; a friend of Allah busy exercising the soul and the spiritual sciences; a mufti, a scholar of Ḥadīth or a person who is learned and teaches; and a person who busy with the administration of the affairs of Muslims, such as rulers and kings. These four kinds of people remain busy with the affairs of the public or with their religious affairs. The Prophet (ṣ) was not commissioned to be a trader, but directed to glorify Allah. For this reason, when Abū Bakr became the caliph, other Companions advised him to give up his business and fixed for him a monthly allowance from the state treasury. After his death, he advised his sons to return the money to the treasury.

2

Sources of livelihood

Four things are necessary when earning a livelihood: lawful earnings, justice, kindness and fear for one's religion. We shall discuss each separately.

Lawful earnings

Earnings can be sought in six ways: trade, usurious gain, buying in advance, renting things and hiring people's services, partnerships and loans. Knowing the rules of Sharīʿah about each of these is obligatory, just as seeking knowledge is obligatory for every Muslim. It was reported that ʿUmar used to visit the markets, instruct some inexperienced traders, whip them and say, "Nobody who lacks knowledge of trade will carry on doing business in our markets."

Trade

Trade has three integrals: the buyer and the seller, the commodities and the contract.

The buyer and the seller

No transaction is valid with a minor, insane person, slave or blind man. Minors and insane people are not legally responsible. No transaction is valid with a slave unless it is permitted by his master. Similarly, a transaction with a blind man is unlawful unless his representative consents to it. It is lawful to transact with an unbeliever, but it is unlawful to sell arms to him.

The commodities

Six conditions apply to commodities. First, they should not be impure, such as dogs, pigs, dung, stool, wine, the teeth of elephants and the fat of impure animals. Second, they should be beneficial and necessary. Scorpions, rats, snakes, worms and insects under the earth are unlawful in trade. Also unlawful are musical instruments, toy idols of animals and clothes on which there are animal pictures. Third, they should be in possession of the seller. Fourth, they should be fit for transfer according to Sharīʿah. Thus, runaway slaves, fish in the water, birds in the air, foetuses in the wombs of animals and milk in udders cannot lawfully be sold. Fifth, they should be known, fixed and certain. Lastly, they should be in the possession of the owner. If the buyer sells it before possessing it, it will be unlawful.

Contract

The contract for buying and selling should be expressed in clear and unambiguous terms. Intention plays an important part in it. No condition can lawfully be imposed by one party after the agreement is final. Sales in an auction are lawful if the terms are proclaimed beforehand. Imam al-Shāfiʿī, however, held that auctions are unlawful.

Usurious gain

Allah made usury unlawful, and there is a strict prohibition against it. The question of usury arises in only two cases: in transactions with cash, gold and silver and transactions with foodstuffs. Usury occurs in these two cases only under two conditions: if something is bought on credit and not in cash and if something is exchanged for a smaller quantity of the same thing. It is unlawful to sell a fixed quantity of gold or silver for a fixed quantity of more gold or silver on credit. It is also unlawful to receive in cash the value of a thing which will be delivered in the future.

Three rules should be observed regarding gold and silver. First, a large quantity of counterfeit coins cannot be exchanged for a smaller quantity of authentic coins, as this kind of transaction is unlawful. A small quantity of a thing cannot be exchanged for a greater quantity of the same thing. Second, there is no fault in selling a large amount of silver for a lesser amount of gold, because they are different things. Third, if gold and silver are mixed, and the quantity of each is not known, the transaction is unlawful.

The foodstuffs of the seller and buyer may be the same or different. When they are the same, it is lawful to exchange them, and the rules concerning things of the same type are applicable. Thus, it is unlawful to exchange a goat for mutton, wheat for bread and milk for clarified butter, butter or cheese.

Buying in advance

Eight conditions apply to buying in advance. First, the quantity and kind of a thing for which an advance payment is made should be fixed. Second, the principal thing or money should be paid in advance where the agreement was made, otherwise, the transaction will be unlawful. Likewise, the thing or money should be delivered where the agreement was made. Third, the thing that is given in advance must be an exchangeable commodity. such as food stuffs, animals, minerals, cotton, milk, meat. Fourth, the weight and quantity of the thing given in advance must be fixed. Fifth, the time of the delivery of the thing should also be fixed. Sixth, the place where the commodity is to be delivered should be clearly stated, as there might be a difference in price where it is to be delivered. Seventh, the thing to be advanced should have no connection with another thing, such as "the crops of this land" or "the fruits of that garden." Eighth, it is unlawful to buy in advance rare and precious such a rare jewel, a beautiful slave or a slave girl.

Renting things and hiring people's services

It has two integrals: the fee and the utility or service. If wages are in cash, it must be fixed like the price of a thing sold. If the remuneration is a salary or rental fee, its kind and quantity should be fixed. It is unlawful to let a house on condition that the tenant must construct the building or house, as the cost of the house is unknown. It is also unlawful to exchange skin for skin from the body, skin for carrying an animal and an outer cover for crushing wheat.

The service is what is sought for the fee. It should be fixed, and should not be given to a broker. It is unlawful to maintain an animal in exchange for milk, to maintain a garden of grapes in exchange for grapes or to lease a garden in exchange for its fruits. The person performing the service should possess the strength required to do the job. Thus, it is unlawful to hire a weak man to carry out a task which is beyond his strength and capacity. It is also unlawful to appoint a representative to carry out one's personal obligation, such as hiring someone to fight in jihad or do acts of worship. But it is lawful to make pilgrimage on behalf of another person who is incapable, to bury or carry a dead man, to be an imam in prayer for a fixed term, to proclaim the call to prayer, to teach the Qur'an and the like for a fee.

Partnerships

There are three integrals: capital, profit and the type of partnership. With regard to the capital, it will be fixed, paid in cash and handed over to the managing agent. It is unlawful for the capital to be anything other than money.

As for the profit, what shares the capitalists and traders should get should be settled beforehand. If the profit is fixed for the trade, it is unlawful. No condition should be imposed concerning fixed commodities and times. A trader who can utilise the capital according to his wish in the business becomes the representative or agent of business.

A partnership of four types, three of which are unlawful. It is unlawful to divide the work in a joint business. If a partner puts up capital and another partner possessing honour only uses his influence in the business, it will be unlawful. If, however, they each put up an equal amount of capital, and the profit is divided equally among them, it is lawful.

3
Justice

It is unlawful to trouble the public by unjust dealings, oppression and deceit and fraud. There are two kinds of loss by deceit and fraud. One kind is for the general public and the other is for special people. Public loss is of many kinds. One kind arises from hoarding foodstuffs, waiting for their prices to rise. This is a form of oppression, and the Sharīʿah curses such people.

The Prophet (ṣ) said, "If a man hoards up foodstuffs when they are dear for forty days to sell them for higher prices, he is displeased with Allah, and Allah also is displeased with him." Someone has said that he commits the sin of murdering all people. ʿAlī said, "If a man hoards up foodstuffs even for a day to sell them for higher prices, his heart becomes hard." The Prophet (ṣ) said, "He who takes foodstuffs from one place to another and sells them on that day according to the market rate will get the rewards of charity." According to another version, "he will get the rewards of setting a slave free."

The Qur'an says, "Whoever inclines therein to wrong unjustly, We will make him taste of a painful chastisement" (Qur'an, 22:25). This applies to hoarding up to get more profit.

A pious merchant sent foodstuffs by sea to his agent in Baṣrah with the instruction that he should sell it as soon as they reached him. When the commodities reached Baṣrah, the merchants there told the agent to hoard them for a week and then sell, as this would bring greater profit. His agent did accordingly and sold them after a week for a higher price and informed his master. His master wrote to him, "You have acted contrary to my wish. It was not my wish to incur a loss in religion and profit from commodities. I have committed a sin for hoarding, so distribute all the proceeds to the poor and the destitute. Perhaps, I may expiate my sin of hoarding."

It is therefore prohibited to hoard up foodstuffs for getting greater profit depending on the kinds of food and the time. It is not prohibited to hoard up foodstuffs which are for livelihood, such as medicine and saffron. There are differences of opinion with regard to hoarding things which resemble principal foodstuffs, such as meat, fruits and the like, which appease hunger and which are taken as alternatives to principal crops.

With regard to time, there are things whose hoarding becomes unlawful during times when there is a high demand for foodstuffs which are not readily available. To delay selling foodstuffs in such times is harmful to the public. But when there are no such circumstances, it is lawful to delay, as the public do not suffer by it. When there is famine, it is harmful to hoard up even such things as honey, clarified butter and meat. So the lawfulness and unlawfulness of hoarding foodstuffs depend on whether the public suffers harm or not.

To use counterfeit coins is a form of oppressing the public. The first man who uses such coins will get the sins of every person who subsequently uses them. This is similar to introducing a bad custom. A sage said, "To transfer a counterfeit coin to another is worse than the theft of a hundred coins, as theft is confined to one sin, while the circulation of a counterfeit coin is endless, continuing year after year until it is destroyed." Allah says, "We write down what they have sent before and their footprints" (Qur'an, 36:12) and "Man shall on that day be informed of what he sent before and (what he) put off" (Qur'an, 75:13).

There are five rules regarding counterfeit coins. First, if a man has counterfeit coins, he should throw them in wells, rivers and tanks. Second, every merchant should have knowledge of counterfeit coins to save himself and protect Muslims from them.

Third, if he tells others that they are counterfeit, he will not be absolved from its sin if he knew they were counterfeit when he received them. Fourth, he who receives counterfeit coins to destroy them is absolved from its sin and receives the blessings of the Prophet (ṣ), who said, "May Allah show kindness to someone whose buying is easy, whose selling is easy, whose clearance of debt is easy and whose demand is easy." Fifth, a counterfeit coin is one which has no gold or silver. A coin which has gold or silver cannot be called counterfeit. But in a place where a kind of coin is prevalent, another kind of coin is unlawful there.

It is injustice for a merchant to cause loss, and it is justice not to cause a Muslim loss. The general rule is to love for others what one loves for oneself. This should be observed in four ways. The first way is not to praise one's goods. To say that a thing possesses a quality which it does not is falsehood. If a buyer purchases a thing on the basis of such a description, it will be an act of deceit. A person will be taken to account for every word he utters. Allah says, "He utters not a word but there is by him a watcher at hand" (Qur'an, 50:18). The Prophet (ṣ) said, "In false oaths, there is much loss for commodities and less profit." He also said, "Allah will not look at three people on Resurrection Day: a proud, disobedient person, a person who behaves harshly after giving charity and a person who sells things by making oaths."

The second way is not to conceal the defects of the commodities. Someone who does this is an oppressor, a deceiver and a fraud. Deceit is unlawful. Once, the Prophet (ṣ) saw a man selling foodstuffs, and it pleased him. The Prophet (ṣ) then entered his hand into the the foodstuffs and found moisture in them. He asked him, "Why are there wet things in them?" He said, "Rain melted them." The Prophet (ṣ) said, "Has not the rain fallen on top of the crops? He who defrauds us is not one of us."

Once, the Prophet (ṣ) took a pledge of allegiance to Islam from Jarīr. When he was about to go, the Prophet (ṣ) extracted a promise from him that he would do Muslims good. Thereafter, whenever

Jarīr was making a transaction, he would disclose the defects of his goods and give the customer the option of purchasing them. Someone said to him, "You will not make a profit like this." He said, 'I promised the Prophet (ṣ) that I would do every Muslim good."

The Prophet (ṣ) said, "It is unlawful to sell a thing without disclosing its defects, and whoever knows of the defects but does not warn others commits a sin."

A man had a cow, and he milked it everyday and sold the milk after mixing it with water. One day, there was a flood which drowned the cow. One of his sons said to him, "The waters which you mixed with the milk accumulated and washed away the cow with a strong current."

The Prophet (ṣ) said, "When the buyer and seller tell the truth and wish well, their transaction is blessed. When they conceal and tell lies, blessing is withdrawn from them." Another *ḥadīth* says, "Allah's hand remains on two partners as long as they do not betray each other. When they do, He withdraws His hand from both."

It becomes easy to be good to people if a person knows that profit in the next world is better than the wealth and treasures of this world, and that these will end with the end of life, whereas his sins and virtues will remain. So how can a man prefer evil to good? The Prophet (ṣ) said, "The words 'There is no deity but Allah' will appease the wrath of Allah from creatures as they do not prefer worldly affairs to otherworldly affairs." Another *ḥadīth* says, "Whoever utters 'There is no deity but Allah' with sincere faith will enter paradise." He was asked, "What is sincere faith?" He said, "To be careful about what Allah has prohibited." The Prophet (ṣ) also said, "He who regards unlawful things as lawful does not believe in the Qur'an." So deceit in buying and selling and in mutual transactions is unlawful.

The third way is not to conceal the weights and measures of the commodities, but rather to use a balance and weights. Allah says, "Woe to the defrauders who, when they take the measure (of their dues) from men, take it fully, but when they measure out to others or weigh out for them, they are deficient" (Qur'an, 83:1-3).

The way to be saved from this is to give more when you measure out to others and take less from them when you take by measure. When the Prophet (ṣ) purchased something, he used to tell the seller, "Weigh according to the price and give a little more." Sulaymān said to his son, "O dear son, sin enters between two transactions just as seeds enter mills." Allah says, "That you may not be inordinate in respect of the measure. And keep up the balance with equity and do not make the measure deficient' (Qur'an, 55:8-9). And he who takes more and gives less is included in the verse "Woe to the defrauders who, when they take the measure (of their dues) from men, take it fully" (Qur'an, 83:1).

The fourth way is to be honest. The Prophet (ṣ) said, "Do not meet the riders who bring commodities, for the owner of the commodities has, after they are brought into the market, the option of breaking an agreement with those who met them in advance."

4

To do good in mutual transactions

Allah has ordered us to adopt good and just dealings and to do good to people. He says, "Do good (to others) as Allah has done good to you" (Qur'an, 28:77), "Surely Allah enjoins the doing of justice and the doing of good" (Qur'an, 16:90) and "Surely the mercy of Allah is nigh to those who do good" (Qur'an, 7:56). Doing good means to do something which benefits another.

Though doing good is not obligatory, it brings rewards and ranks. The rank of doing good can be attained by one of six actions. The first is not to make much profit. Sale is for profit, and there is no profit unless a thing is sold at a price higher than what it was bought at. To make less profit is doing good, but to make a greater profit is not unlawful. Once, a man paid the salesman of Yūnus ibn 'Ubayd four hundred dirhams for a bundle of clothes which was to be sold for two hundred dirhams. Yūnus said to his salesman, "Why did you not love for another what you love for yourself? Return half." 'Alī used to roam in the bazaar of Kūfah with a stick and say, "O merchants, take your dues and give others theirs. Do not refuse little profit or else you will be deprived of greater profit."

'Abd al-Raḥmān ibn 'Awf was asked, "What was the cause of your success?" He said, "Three things: I never refused a profit, I sold everything in cash and not on credit and I did not delay selling anything."

The second is to suffer loss. If a buyer buys from a poor man, there is no harm in paying a higher price in order to do good to him and enter the prayer of the Prophet (ṣ) "May Allah like whoever makes his buying and selling easy." When he purchases something from a rich man, he may seek greater profit.

The third is to be generous when seeking payments and debts. One can do this in three ways: to accept less at times, to give an extension on the payment and to ask for the money in a cordial manner. The Prophet (ṣ) said, "May Allah show mercy to an easy purchase, easy sale, easy payment of a price and easy payment of a debt"; "Forgive and you will be forgiven"; and "If a man grants a needy man time to repay a debt or remits it, Allah will make his account easy" (according to another version, "Allah will give him shade on the day when there will be no shade except that of the Throne").

The Prophet (ṣ) once spoke of a person who oppressed his soul very much and was engaged in sins. When he is presented on Judgement Day, it will be found that he has no good deeds. He will be asked, "Did you not do any good deed?" He will say, "No, but I gave loans to people and would say to my children, 'Grant time to the wealthy and remit the poor.'" Allah then will say, "I am more fit in this matter than you." Then Allah will forgive him.

The Prophet (ṣ) said, "I saw written on the door of paradise, 'One act of charity brings ten rewards, and one loan brings eighteen rewards.'" It is said that charity may not always reach those who are truly poor, but none except the needy bears the disgrace of a loan. If a man sells something to another, neither realising its price nor demanding it, it is considered a loan.

When al-Ḥasan al-Baṣrī was selling his donkey for four hundred dirhams, the purchaser said to him, "Reduce it by a hundred dirhams," and he did so. The purchaser then said, "Do good to me." Al-Ḥasan said, "I will reduce it by another hundred dirhams." Then he accepted two hundred dirhams and said, "This is how good is done to a person." A *ḥadīth* says, "Accept your dues with pardon, whether it is paid in full or not, and Allah will make your reckoning easy."

The fourth is to do good when repaying a debt. A person does this by clearing the debt before the creditor demands it. The Prophet (ṣ) said, "The best among you is he who repays his debt in a good manner." Also, he should clear the debt before its due date, and pay more than what he borrowed. The Prophet (ṣ) said, "If a man has the intention of paying back a loan when he takes it, Allah entrusts His angles with keeping him safe, and they pray for him until he clears his debt."

Once, a creditor came to the Prophet (ṣ) demanding the repayment of a debt which due date had expired, but he was unable to do so. The man used harsh words with the Prophet (ṣ), and the Companions were about to attack him when he said, "Leave him, as a creditor has the right to speak." The Prophet (ṣ) also said, "Help your brother, be he oppressed or an oppressor." He was asked, "How can we help an oppressor?" He said, "By prohibiting him from oppression."

The fifth is to accept the return of an item one sold if the buyer thinks he has suffered loss, as nobody except a repentant or suffering man intends to return an item he purchased. None should remain satisfied with causing loss to his Muslim brother. The Prophet (ṣ) said, "If a man forgives the sin of a repentant man, Allah will forgive his sins on Resurrection Day."

The sixth is to sell things to the needy on credit and not to demand from them when they are in want and are not well-off. The religious men of yore kept account books in which they wrote the names of unknown poor customers. And if they could not pay, they forgave them.

Trade and commerce are places of trial for the religious. For this reason, it has been said that when the neighbours of a person praise him, when the companions of a man on a journey praise him and when fellow traders in the market praise him, he should complain about his good character. Once, a witness went to depose before 'Umar, who said to him, "Bring to me someone who knows you." When he brought a person to him, the man began to praise his character. 'Umar asked him, "Is he your closest neighbour?" He said, "No." He asked him, "Were you his companion on a journey?" He said, "No." He asked him, "Did you do business with him?" He said, "No." He said, "So you do not know him." He then said to the man, "Go and bring someone who knows you."

5

Not to be forgetful of religion and the hereafter when doing business

Know, dear readers, that nobody should forget his religion and the next world during the course of his trade and earning a livelihood. If he forgets them, he will be ruined and be one of those who exchange their next world for this world. A wise man is he who protects his capital, which, in reality, is his religion and matters relating to the next world. A sage said, "To a wise man, the best commodity in this world is what is absolutely necessary for him in this world, for what is necessary in this world is praiseworthy in the next." Mu'ādh ibn Jabal said in his will, "What has been decreed for you from the fortunes of this world will surely come to you. But it is more necessary for you to seek the fortunes of the next world, so begin your actions for the fortunes of the next world." Allah says, "Do not neglect your portion of this world" (Qur'an, 28:77). In other words, "Do not let your portion of fate in this world make you forget your portion of your fate in the next, as this world is a seed ground for the next."

What completes a trader's religion

There are seven things. The first is to keep his faith firm and complete and have good intent at the start of his trade. He should trade to save himself from depending on others, abstain from greed for what others have, be satisfied with lawful earnings, earn to keep on the paths of religion and to maintain his family. He, moreover, should intend to do Muslims good and love for them what he loves for himself. Finally, he should follow the path of equity, justice and excellence and enjoin good and forbid the evils he finds in the market.

The second is to intend to fulfil a communal obligation such as trade, commerce or industry, believing that, if the various kinds of trade and industry are abandoned, it will be difficult for people to manage their livelihood, and the majority of people would be destroyed. One people are responsible for one kind of job. If everyone remains busy with only one kind of job, other jobs would not get done and, as such, people would be destroyed. In this regard, the Prophet (ṣ) said, "Difference among my people is a blessing." A *ḥadīth* says, "Trading in cloth is the best of all your trades, and sewing is the best of all industries." Another *ḥadīth* says, "If the inhabitants of paradise could trade, they would trade in cloth. And if the inhabitants of hell could trade, they would trade in the exchange of coins."

There are four trades which are said to weaken the intellect: weaving cloth, selling cotton, weaving thread and teaching. This is because most of the people in these trades are women, boys and men of weak intellect. And just as the intellect strengthens by association with intellectuals, so also it weakens by association with non-intellectuals.

The third is to not let worldly markets obstacles in the way of otherworldly markets, which are mosques. Allah says, "Men whom neither merchandise nor selling diverts from the remembrance of Allah and the keeping up of prayer and the giving of poor-rate" (Qur'an, 24:47) and "In houses which Allah has permitted to be exalted and that His name may be remembered in them" (Qur'an, 24:36). So you should work for the next world in the early part of the day until market time, remain attached to the mosque and remain busy with regular devotions.

The early Muslims made the early and last part of the day for the next world and the middle part for this world. A *ḥadīth* says, "If the angels who write records of deeds write, 'The remembrance of Allah and good deeds in the early and last part of the day,' Allah forgives one's sins between those two times." Another *ḥadīth* says, "The angels of day and night meet with one another at the dawn and midafternoon prayers. Allah then says, 'In what condition have you found My servants?' They will say, 'We saw them praying and left them while they were praying.' Allah says, 'I bear witness before you that I have forgiven them.'"

The fourth is to continue remembering Allah in addition to carrying out the above duties in the markets. Remembering Allah in the markets is meritorious. The Prophet (ṣ) said, "Among the heedless, a person remembering Allah is like a warrior behind a fleeing enemy or like a living man among the dead," or, according to another version, "like a living tree amid dried trees." He also said, "If a man says the following after entering the market, Allah will reward him thousands of merits: 'There is no deity but Allah, alone, without partner. His is the kingdom, and His is all praise. He gives life and takes it. He is eternal and will not die. In His hands is good, and He has power over all things.'"

'Umar said, "O Allah, I seek refuge in You from infidelity and all the sins committed in the markets. O Allah, I seek refuge in You from the oaths of sinners and the wailings of losers."

The Prophet (ṣ) said, "Fear Allah wherever you are,' as markets, mosques and houses are all the same to those who fear Allah, who live for Him, who die for Him and of whose life Allah is the cornerstone.

A sage said, "He who loves the next world loves a true life, and he who loves this world remains thirsty."

The fifth is not to be too greedy in the markets and in trade. A *ḥadīth* says, "Do not travel by sea except for the greater pilgrimage, the lesser pilgrimage and jihad." The Prophet (ṣ) said, "The worst of places is the market." Ḥammād would trade in wool rugs, and when he made a certain profit, he would close his business. Once, Ibrāhīm ibn Adham said to a person who was going to his pottery business, "You are seeking livelihood, but death seeks you."

The sixth is to keep away from doubtful things, even after giving up unlawful things. A person should leave places of doubtful earnings and restrain himself from eating doubtful things. Once, a man brought milk to the Prophet (ṣ), who asked him, "Where did you get this milk?" The man said, "We got it from goats." He asked, "Where did you get the goats?" He said, "From such-and-such a place." Then the Prophet (ṣ) drank it and said, "We are prophets and have been forbidden to eat anything except good things and to do anything except good deeds." The Prophet (ṣ) said, "Allah has commanded believers to do what He has ordered the prophets to do, saying, 'O you who believe, eat of the good things that We have provided you with' (Qur'an, 2:172)." The Prophet (ṣ) inquired about the source of a thing and the source of its source, and not beyond that.

A person should not do business with someone who is associated with oppression, treachery, theft and usury. The Prophet (ṣ) said, "He who prays for an oppressor to live a long life loves to be disobedient to Allah in His world"; "When any transgressor is praised, Allah becomes displeased"; and "He who honours a transgressor helps destroy Islam."

The seventh is to review the accounts with a co-worker, as you will be taken to account for your transactions with everyone on Resurrection Day. A wise man said, "I saw a merchant in a dream and asked him, 'What has Allah done to you?' He said, 'Fifty thousand account books have been opened before me.' I asked, 'Are all these records of sin?' He said, 'You will find a record for each person you have dealt with in the world. All have been recorded in these account books.'"

Book 4
The lawful and unlawful

Introduction

The Prophet (ṣ) said, "It is obligatory for every Muslim to seek lawful earnings." The lawful are clear, and the unlawful are also clear. But between these two are doubtful things which are unclear and difficult to know. All things fall into one of these three categories, which will be discussed in seven chapters.

1

The merits of lawful earnings and the demerits of unlawful earnings

The Qur'an

Allah says:

> *O men, eat the lawful and good things out of what is in the earth, and do not follow the footsteps of Satan.* (Qur'an, 2:168)

Allah ordered for eating good things before doing good deeds. The object of this order is eating of lawful things.

> *Do not swallow up your property among yourselves by false means.* (Qur'an, 2:188)

> *O you who believe, be careful of (your duty to) Allah and relinquish what remains (due) from usury, if you are believers. But if you do (it) not, then be apprised of war from Allah and His Messenger; and if you repent, then you shall have your capital.* (Qur'an, 2:278-279)

> *Whoever returns (to usury), these are the inmates of the fire; they shall abide in it.* (Qur'an, 2:275)

There are innumerable verses regarding the lawful and unlawful.

Ḥadīth

The Prophet (ṣ) said:

> It is obligatory for every Muslim to seek lawful earnings.

> He who strives to maintain his family with lawful earnings is like a fighter in the way of Allah, and he who seeks lawful earnings after restraining himself attains the rank of a martyr.

> If a man eats lawful food for forty days, Allah illumines his heart and lets wisdom flow from his heart through his tongue.

According to another version, "Allah grants him renunciation of the world."

> Eat lawful food and your supplication will be heard.

> There are many men who have dishevelled hair and dust-laden dresses, are tired from travelling, whose food is unlawful, whose dress is unlawful and who have been maintained by unlawful food. If they raise their hands and say, "O Lord! O Lord!" how can their supplication be heard?

> An angel residing in Jerusalem proclaims every night, "Neither optional nor obligatory acts of worship will be accepted from a person who eats unlawful food."

> If a man purchases a cloth with ten dirhams, and if one of the dirhams is unlawful, his prayer will not be accepted as long as a portion of that cloth remains on his body.

> The fire of hell is fit for flesh which has been grown by unlawful food.

> If a man does not care where he earns his wealth from, Allah will not care by which path he will enter hell.

> There are ten shares of worship, nine of which are in lawful earnings.

> He who seeks lawful earnings until the evening spends the night forgiven and rises at dawn with Allah pleased with him.

> If a man earns a livelihood by sinful acts and gives it in charity, as an act of kindness or spends it in the way of Allah, Allah will throw him into hell after collecting everything.

> The best of your religion is to keep away from unlawful things.

> If a man meets Allah after refraining from unlawful things, Allah will give him the reward of all of Islam.

In an earlier scripture, Allah says with regard to those who refrain from unlawful food, "I am embarrassed to take them to account."

> One dirham of usury is more serious to Allah than thirty acts of fornication.

> The stomach is the fountain of the body, and the veins come out of it. When the stomach is sound, the veins come out with health, and when it is unsound, they come out with disease.

Food in religion is like the foundation of a building. When the foundation is strong and firm, the building stands straight and remains erect, and if the foundation is weak and crooked, the building inclines to one side. Allah says, "Is he, therefore, better who lays his foundation on fear of Allah and (His) good pleasure, or he who lays his foundation on the edge of a cracking hollowed bank, so it broke down with him into the fire of hell?" (Qur'an, 9:109).

> The wealth a man earns from unlawful things will not be accepted from him, even if it is given in charity. If he leaves it after his death, he will increase the fire of hell therewith.

Many traditions have been mentioned in the book "Earning a Livelihood," so I do not wish to repeat them here.

Traditions from Companions and early Muslims

It has been reported that Abū Bakr once drank a little milk given to him by his female slave and asked her about it. She said, "I got it for prophesying for some people." Thereupon, he thrust his fingertips into his throat and vomited in such a way that he nearly died. Then he said, "O Allah, I seek Your forgiveness for what remains in my throat and to my stool." In another version, it is said that when the Prophet (ṣ) was informed of it, he said, "Do you not know that Abū Bakr does not allow anything into his stomach except lawful food?" Similarly, when 'Umar mistakenly drank the milk of a camel which was *zakāh*, he thrust his fingers into his throat and vomited it.

'Ā'ishah said, "You are heedless of the best act of worship, which is scrupulousness."

Al-Fuḍayl said, "He who takes care of what he admits into his belly, Allah records him as someone with great faith (*siddīq*). So, O needy man, consider what you break your fast with."

Sufyān al-Thawrī said, "Whoever gives unlawful wealth in charity is like someone who washes impure clothes with wine. Impure things can only be purified by water, and there sins cannot be expiated without lawful things."

Yaḥyā ibn Mu'ādh said, "To perform religious duties is Allah's secret treasure; supplication is its key and lawful food is its teeth."

Ibn 'Abbās said, "The prayer of a man in whose stomach is unlawful food is not accepted by Allah."

Sahl al-Tustarī said, "The truth of faith does not reach a man who does not possess four qualities: performing obligations along with recommended acts (*sunnah*), being careful about eating, abstaining from prohibited things openly and secretly and observing these rules with patience until death." He also said, "Whoever wants the signs of a person with great faith to be opened up for him should only eat lawful things and only follow the ways of the Prophet (ṣ)."

It is said that the heart of a man who eats doubtful things for forty days becomes enveloped with darkness. That is the meaning of the verse "Nay! Rather, what they used to do has become like rust upon their hearts" (Qur'an, 83:14).

Ibn al-Mubārak said, "To return a coin of doubt to its owner is better than giving a hundred thousand dirhams in charity."

Sahl said, "The limbs of a man who eats unlawful food become disobedient, whether he does so willingly or unwillingly, knowingly or unknowingly. And the limbs of man who eats lawful food become obedient to him and help him in doing good deeds."

A well-known *ḥadīth* says, "There is reckoning for lawful things in the world and punishment for unlawful things." The narrator added, "There is rebuke for doubtful things."

A religious man served food to a *badal.* Without eating it, the latter asked him about it and said, "We only eat lawful food. In so doing, our hearts remain firm, our states last, the affairs of heaven are disclosed to us and we see the next world. If we ate what you eat for three days, our sure knowledge would disappear and fear and spiritual vision would leave our hearts." The man said to him, "I fast throughout the year and recite the Qur'an thirty times a month." The *badal* said to him, "The drink you saw me drink at night is dearer to me than your reciting the Qur'an thirty times in three hundred units of prayer." Deer milk was his drink.

The Torah says, "If a man does not care where he gets his food from, Allah also will not care through which door of hell He will throw him into hell."

Classes of lawful and unlawful things

There are two classes of unlawful things: the inherently unlawful and unlawful earnings.

The inherently unlawful

The inherently unlawful include wine, blood, pork and dead animals.

Things fit for eating in the world are of three kinds: minerals such as salt, vegetables and animals. Minerals are of different kinds. What grows from the earth is lawful to eat unless it is harmful.

Vegetables are lawful to eat unless they take away the intellect, take life or ruin health. The things which take away the intellect are wine and intoxicants; the things which destroy life are poisons and the things which ruin health are medicines taken outside its time.

Animals are of two kinds: what is edible and what is inedible. Birds, beasts and land and aquatic creatures fit for eating and sacrificed according to the rules of Sharīʿah are lawful to eat. What is not sacrificed according to the rules of Sharīʿah or is dead is unlawful, except for fish, locusts and worms in foodstuffs and fruits. If a person does not like a particular food, it is offensive for him to eat it.

The Prophet (ṣ) said, "Immerse a fly if it falls into a food." If an ant falls into a food, it does not become impure. But if a portion of flesh from a dead man falls into a food, all of it becomes unlawful to eat, not on account of impurity, as a man does not become impure after death, but out of horror.

Animals, if sacrificed according to Sharīʿah, are lawful, except for their blood and what is attached to its impurities. One drop of an impure substance renders food unlawful.

Unlawful earnings

There are two kinds of earnings: those gained willingly or unwillingly and those which are gained unexpectedly. The former is of two kinds: those gained without the owner's knowledge, such as minerals underneath the ground, and those gained from the owner himself. Further, the latter is of two kinds: those gained from him by force and those gained with his permission. Those gained by force is again of two kinds: those gained due to the owner's fall, such as the booties of war, and those gained from him by virtue of the power of ruling authorities, such as *zakāh* and other economic liabilities. Similarly, those gained with his permission are of two kinds: those gained from him through exchange, such as trade, dowry and wages, and those not gained through exchange, such as gifts. Thus, earnings are of six kinds.

1. Those gained without owners: These include acquiring minerals, making barren land fertile, gathering firewood from

jungles, taking water from rivers and taking grass. All of these things are lawful provided there is no owner.

2. Those which are lawfully gained by force: These include the booties of war, which are lawful for all Muslims when a fifth is taken from them and divided justly among those entitled to them. It is unlawful to take booty from those unbelievers with whom there is treaty.
3. Those which are lawfully gained by force in spite of the owner's prohibition: These include *zakāh*, which can only be taken by the ruling authorities.
4. Those gained through exchange with the owner's consent: These are lawful and include commercial transactions.
5. Those which are gained with the owner's consent, but not through exchange: These include gifts and wills, which are lawful.
6. Those gained unexpectedly: These are lawful and include possessions gained by inheritance after the execution of the will and the deduction of necessary expenses, such as funeral expenses, expiations for religious obligations and pilgrimage expenses.

Different degrees of lawfulness and unlawfulness

Know, dear readers, that every unlawful thing is bad, but there are different degrees of unlawfulness. Likewise, all lawful things are good, but there are different degrees of lawfulness.

There are four degrees of lawfulness:

1. The forbearance of just and ordinary Muslims: This is the lowest degree. It is to save oneself from the unlawful.
2. The forbearance of pious men who refrain from lawful things verging on the unlawful: A jurist will rule such things lawful, as their unlawfulness is debatable, but the pious keep away from even the doubtful.

3. The forbearance of God-fearing men who keep aloof from even those things which are undoubtedly lawful: This is because if a person falls into the habit if doing the lawful, there is a chance that he may do something doubtful. The Prophet (ṣ) said, "A man cannot reach the degree of the God-fearing until he gives up things free from doubt for fear of doing doubtful things."
4. The forbearance of God-fearing men who give up the undoubtedly lawful, even if there is no fear of doing doubtful things: This is because they fear that those things may not be for Allah. Such people are called "those with great faith" (*ṣiddīqūn*).

Examples

No example is necessary in the case of the first degree, as the unlawful are clear, and a religious man must keep himself distant from them.

As for the second degree, it is not obligatory to abstain from lawful things bordering on the unlawful, but it is recommended. The Prophet (ṣ) said, "Give up what raises doubt in your mind and take what does not raise doubt in you." He also said, "Eat the hunted game on which there are marks of shooting and which die in your presence. And do not eat what you do not see shot but later find dead." Though it is not unlawful, it is the forbearance of the pious.

As for the third degree, a *ḥadīth* says, "A man cannot reach the degree of a God-fearing man until he gives up things free from doubt for fear of things of doubt." 'Umar said, "We have given up ninety percent of the lawful for fear of falling into the unlawful." Abū al-Dardā' said, "Piety reaches perfection when a servant fears a very small thing. And even when he sees a lawful thing, he abstains from it for fear of falling into the unlawful." Some examples are given below.

A religious man took out a loan of a hundred dirhams. When he came to pay back the loan, the creditor took only ninety-nine dirhams. 'Alī ibn Ma'bad said, "I rented a house, and wanted to write a letter and therefore took a little earth from its wall to soak the ink of the letter. While I was sleeping, I dreamt that a man was saying, 'O 'Alī ibn Ma'bad, know that tomorrow, on Resurrection Day, the owner of the house will demand the little earth you used.'" Because of what he did, he fell from the rank of the God-fearing.

During the caliphate of 'Umar, the musk of Bahrain gained as result of battle reached him. His wife began to measure it when he said, "I do not want you to touch it and say afterwards that something of it remained on your hands because of it. This belongs to Muslims in general, and you cannot get more than what you are entitled to."

Once, musk was measured before the caliph 'Umar ibn 'Abd al-'Azīz. He kept his nose shut lest its smell enter it. He said, "What benefit does it have besides its scent? It is the only benefit sought from it."

One time, the Prophet's grandson al-Ḥasan ibn 'Alī put into his mouth a dried grape which was *zakāh*. The Prophet (ṣ) said, "Throw it away! Throw it away!"

A man once went to see his friend at night. Soon after his death, he put out the light and said, "This oil has become inheritance."

'Umar gave his wife some musk to sell, and she sold it to another seller. At the time of the sale, she broke off a piece with her teeth, and some of it remained on her fingers. 'Umar smelt the scent on her and said, "You have taken the scent of the Muslims." He said this only to be a truly God-fearing man, and what she did was not unlawful.

Aḥmad ibn Ḥanbal said, "To smell the scent of a tyrannical ruler destroys the piety of a man."

When 'Umar became the caliph, he had only one wife, whom he loved very much. He, however, divorced her, fearing she might ask him to commit a sin and he might listen. For this reason, things which were undoubtedly lawful were even given up for fear of falling into doubtful things. Being habituated to many lawful things, one is led to unlawful things, such as too much eating and excessive use of scent. If too much food is eaten, sexual passion rises high and leads to unlawful cohabitation. Similarly, to look at beautiful buildings and the pomp and grandeur of the rich may tempt one to follow them.

There is no benefit in whitewash the walls of a building. Aḥmad ibn Ḥanbal held that it was offensive. When the Prophet (ṣ) was once asked about painting in the mosque, he said, "There is no *'arīsh* like the *'arīsh* of Mūsā." *'Arīsh* is a pearl-like antimony used as paint. The Prophet (ṣ) did not deem it lawful.

The ancient sages said, "The religion of a man whose cloth is thin is also thin."

As for the fourth degree, to those with great faith, those things which entail no transgression and which do not help in the commission of sin are lawful. The object of their every action is to please Allah, and piety is in all their deeds. They live for Allah and believe that what is done for other than Allah is unlawful. They follow the verse "Say 'Allah' and then leave them to plunge in their vain discourses" (Qur'an, 6:91). This is the rank of those who believe in Allah's oneness. Following are some examples of their piety.

Once, Yaḥyā ibn Kathīr used a medicine, and his wife said to him, "Walk for a while in the house, so that the medicine may work." He said, "I do not know of such a walk. I have been counting my breaths for the last thirty years." He did not consider walking connected with religion.

Al-Sarī said, "Once I got on a hill and saw a fountain and vegetables. I wished to eat something of the vegetables and drink the water. I thought that I would eat a lawful thing today. Then an unseen voice said, 'Wherefrom has the strength which has brought you to this stage come?' Then I became repentant and begged forgiveness."

Dhū al-Nūn al-Miṣrī was once imprisoned and had to go without food. When he became hungry, a woman sent some food to him through one of the men of the prison. But he did not eat it on the grounds that the hand of an oppressor gave it to him.

Bishr al-Ḥāfī did not drink the water of a canal dug by a tyrannical ruler, although this was lawful. Similarly, Abū Bakr vomited the milk he drank for fear that he would gain strength to commit sins.

Once, a servant of a sage took some of the firewood of a transgressor. He later put its fire out on the grounds that it was unlawfully earned.

These are some examples of the piety of early sages and pious men. Piety reaches its climax in the fourth degree, which is the degree of those with great faith.

2
The different degrees of doubtful things

The Prophet (ṣ) said, "The lawful are clear, and the unlawful are also clear. But between them are doubtful things which most people do not know. He who saves himself from doubtful things purifies his honour and religion. He who falls into doubtful things may fall into unlawful things, just as a shepherd who grazes his flock of sheep round a reserved grazing ground may fall into it." What is troublesome and unknown to the majority of people is doubtful things, so they should be discussed.

A lawful thing is what is naturally free from unlawfulness, such as the water of the sky. An unlawful thing is that which is naturally unlawful, such as an intoxicant, wine, stool or what is earned by unlawful methods such as oppression and usury. These are fixed and clear. Between the lawful and unlawful are doubtful things which change the state of the lawful and unlawful. A lawful thing becomes unlawful when it goes into the possession of another and doubt arises. If a man gets a fish and thinks that it has come from someone else, there arises doubt in his mind, whether it is lawful or unlawful for him. This doubt should have justification and not be mere conjecture. Doubt arises from of two conflicting beliefs.

Places where doubt arises

There are four places where doubt arises:

1. The lawful and unlawful. Doubt can arise from the lawful and unlawful in four ways.

The first is that a man knows a thing to be unlawful beforehand, but later there arises doubt as to its lawfulness. It is compulsory to give up this doubt and consider it unlawful. For instance, a hunted animal falls into the water and is later taken out dead. To eat its meat is unlawful—there is no doubt about it. The Prophet (ṣ) said to 'Adī ibn Ḥātim, "Do not eat it. Perhaps, your dog has not killed it." Whenever anything was brought to the Prophet (ṣ), he used to enquire about it if doubt arose in his mind until he knew whether it was a present or *zakāh*.

The second is that a person doubts that a lawful thing is lawful owing to peculiar circumstances. For instance, two men were quarrelling with each other, and one said to the other, "You are a hater." A God-fearing man should leave them while having doubt about them.

The third is that a thing is basically unlawful, but a reason to doubt its unlawfulness is so strong that it becomes lawful. In other words, it becomes subject to doubt and its lawfulness predominates. For instance, an animal, after being shot, disappeared. Afterwards, it was found with only one wound on its body. So it might have died for other reasons, raising doubts about the lawfulness of its meat. A God-fearing man refrains from eating such meat. The Prophet (ṣ) said, "As long as you find the mark of your arrow on its body, eat it, even if it disappeared from you."

The fourth is that a thing is lawful, but becomes unlawful owing to a ruling of Sharī'ah. For instance, a pot is lawful, but there arises doubt whether there is any impurity in it. So to drink water from it becomes unlawful.

2. A mixture of lawfulness and unlawfulness. When something lawful and something unlawful become mixed, doubt about its lawfulness arises. This mixture is of three kinds.

The first is a mixture of an unlawful thing and a definite number of lawful things, such as a mixture of the meat of a dead goat and the meat of sacrificed goats. Doubt about these things should not be entertained, as there is no evidence that the meat of a dead goat has been mixed. If there is reasonable doubt that the meat of a dead goat has been mixed, it will be unlawful.

The second is a mixture of a definite number of unlawful things and an indefinite number of lawful things, such as a mixture of one foster sister or even ten foster sisters with the women of a town. One can marry any woman of the town if the foster sisters cannot be identified. Or if interest in a certain town is prevalent, it is not unlawful to accept the coins of that town. The third is a mixture of an indefinite number of lawful things and an unlimited number of unlawful things. In such a case, if the unlawful things can be identified, it will be unlawful to enjoy them, otherwise it will not. But to abstain from a doubtful thing is a sign of piety. The soldiers of Yazīd looted Madīnah for three days, yet the Companions did not prohibit the people from buying and selling the goods of the Madīnan market, which consisted of the stolen goods. Moreover, if there is impurity on the pathways, prayer can be said on them, as the earths of pathways are pure. The Companions sometimes prayed with their sandals and shoes.

3. Any sin found in any cause which makes a thing lawful relates to either the thing itself, its end, its beginning or another thing in exchange of it. But it is not a sin which nullifies an agreement or any cause which makes a thing lawful.

Sins relating to a thing itself includes buying and selling after the call to the Friday prayer, cutting wood with a stolen axe and selling something which was sold to another, none of which are unlawful things.

Sins relating to the end of a thing include all extravagant expenses which lead to sin, such as selling grapes to those who prepare wine and selling instruments to dacoits. There is a difference of opinion among jurists whether these are lawful or unlawful.

Sins relating to the beginning of a thing are of three degrees. The most detestable sin is to eat the meat of a goat which has eaten ill-gotten grass. Less detestable than this is to use the water of a canal dug by a tyrant. And the least detestable sin is to restrain oneself from a lawful thing that has come through the hand of a tyrant.

Sins relating to a thing of exchange is also of different degrees. The most detestable is to purchase a thing on credit and to buy it with ill-gotten money. Less detestable is to sell grapes to a drunkard or instruments to a dacoits. The least detestable is to accept the price of an unlawful thing, such as wine.

4. Where there is a diversity of legal proofs for the lawfulness or unlawfulness of a thing. Doubt arises therefrom for three reasons: contradictory proofs of Sharī'ah, contradictory signs, and contradictory doubts.

With regard to the first reason, the verses of the Qur'an or the words of the Prophet (ṣ) contradict each other, thus creating doubt in the mind. In this case, what is strong prevails, and if any proof does not become strong, it reverts to its original proof. If the unlawfulness of a thing is not strong, it is lawful. If there is doubt, it is more pious to abstain from it. If it is subject to dispute between jurists and theologians, it is better to accept the opinion of a mufti who is well known in a locality for his knowledge and piety, just as it is better to go to a physician who is well known in a locality for his knowledge of medicine. If theologians are unanimous on a certain question, all should accept it. If any proof for the lawfulness of a thing is weak, one should abstain from it. There are three degrees with regard to this matter.

The first degree is to give up a matter which has a weak proof in favour of a matter which has a strong proof. The Prophet (ṣ) is reported to have said, "A believer sacrifices in the name of Allah, whether he utters 'In the name of Allah' or not." This is contradictory to a clear verse of the Qur'an and some traditions in which it is said that to say it at the time of slaughter is obligatory. So the former tradition will have to be disregarded.

The second degree is that it is almost a baseless conjecture, such as not eating the foetus of an animal after the latter is lawfully sacrificed. According to an authentic *ḥadīth*, the sacrifice of the mother includes that of its foetus. So the former conjecture is to be abandoned.

The third degree is that a thing becomes lawful by only one tradition. It is better not to reach a decision relying on only a single *ḥadīth* on a particular subject if there are differences of opinion. It is not unlikely that the narrator might have made a mistake in narrating it or hearing it. But there is no reason to oppose the tradition without a cause. For example, there is no mention of a grandson becoming an heir to his grandfather in the Qur'an, but the Companions were unanimous that a grandson becomes an heir to his grandfather in the absence of his father. When difficulty arises in these matters, one should rely on his conscience, as it does not dictate without truth. What is more, the Prophet (ṣ) instructed us to rely on our conscience to make a decision about doubtful things.

With regard to the second reason, if the proof of a thing's unlawfulness is stronger, it should be considered unlawful. Conversely, if the proof of its lawfulness is stronger, it should be considered lawful.

With regard to the third reason, if the proof of a thing's lawfulness is as strong as the proof of its unlawfulness, then doubt about each is equal. For instance, a man is to distribute some money among the poor, some of whom have some money, but are not rich. So there arises doubt whether such people are really fit for the acceptance of the money.

This is a very subtle question. In such a case, if the person possesses only necessary things, he can accept the charity, but if he possesses more than what is necessary for him, it is prohibited. There is also no limit to necessity. For this reason, the Prophet (ṣ) said, "Abstain from what raises doubt in your mind and keep to what is free from doubt." For this reason, it is written in the Psalms that Allah revealed to Dāwūd, "Tell the children of Israel, 'I do not look at your prayers and fasts. I look at the person who gives up a thing when doubt arises in his mind for My sake. I help him with My help and boast of him before My angels.'"

3

Arguments and questions

Know that every time a person receives food or a present or wishes to buy something or give a gift, he should not have doubts and say, "I shall not accept this as lawful until I enquire about it." But at the same time, one should not give up enquiry into some matters. In some cases, therefore, it is obligatory to enquire, in some unlawful, in some recommended and in some offensive. Cases which require enquiry are cases in which there is doubt, which has connections.

The first connection is with the ownership of a thing. It has three states. The first state comes when the owner is unknown, the second when there is doubt about the owner and the third is to know the condition of the owner by some sort of proof.

The first state occurs when a person enters an unknown town or place, meets strangers and unknown people, not knowing their character or conduct, and, as a result, entertains doubts about them. Yūsuf ibn Asbāṭ said, "For the last thirty years, I have ignored doubt whenever it arose in my mind." The rule is that if any of them gives him food or drink, he should enjoy it without doubting and should not entertain evil conjectures about him, as some conjectures are sinful. On the other hand, if there is sufficient cause of doubt, it is unlawful to enjoy the food or drink.

The Prophet (ṣ) used to accept any invitation without enquiry. Once, a tailor invited him and he accepted it. Another time, a Persian invited him, whereupon the Prophet (ṣ) asked him, "'Ā'ishah and I?" The Persian said, "You and not 'Ā'ishah." The

Prophet (ṣ) did not accept the invitation, but when he invited both, he did. Abū Bakr enquired about the earnings of a slave when a strong doubt arose in his mind. It is not good to ask where a thing has been procured, as it offends a Muslim. Allah says, "Avoid most of suspicion, for surely suspicion in some cases is a sin. And do not spy, nor let some of you backbite others" (Qur'an, 49:12). Once, the Prophet (ṣ) ate the food of Burayrah. When he was informed that it was *zakāh*, he said, "It was *zakāh* for her, but for us it is a present." So baseless doubt should be ignored.

The second state occurs when there is doubt about the owner because of proof. Proofs that a thing is unlawful include the character of the owner, his clothes and his actions, or the that he is a well-known dacoit, thief, or tyrant or that his actions are opposed to the fundamental principles of Sharī'ah. In such cases, two types of doubt arise in his mind. One type arises from the reality of the possession of a thing, which indicates the ownership of that thing. It is lawful to accept the thing from such a possessor. The second type of doubt arises strongly from an indication that a thing may be unlawful. In such a case, it is better to ignore. The Prophet (ṣ) said, "Leave what raises doubt in your mind for what does not raise doubt." This is recommended. He also said, "Doubt of the mind is a sin." He once enquired, because of doubt, whether a thing was *zakāh* or a present. And 'Umar enquired about milk, and Abū Bakr about the earnings of a slave.

The third state occurs when experience or news indicates that a thing is lawful or unlawful. If a man is honest, pious and trustworthy, his possessions can be considered lawful, even though it may be otherwise. In this case, it is unlawful to enquire about a thing in his possession. To eat the food of the pious was the rule of the Prophet (ṣ) and the friends of Allah. The Prophet (ṣ) said, "Do not feed anyone except the pious, and do not eat the food of anyone except the pious."

The second connection is with a mixture of lawful and unlawful things. In the market, where possessions gained by theft and dacoity are mixed with lawful possessions, a buyer should not enquire about their lawfulness. If, however, it is disclosed that most of the possessions of the market are unlawful, enquiry becomes compulsory. The Companions used to do this, and they did not enquire unless they had doubts.

Ibn Mas'ūd said, "You are the inhabitants of a town where there are the Zoroastrians also. So look at the meats of sacrificed animals and the hides of dead animals." So if most of the possession are unlawful, it is not lawful to buy them. If the meat of sacrificed animals is mixed with the meat of ten unsacrificed animals, it is obligatory to abstain from the meat. 'Alī said, "Take what a ruler gives you, as he generally gives from lawful things." Ibn Mas'ūd was asked about that and said, "He may ask." He was also asked, "Should I accept the invitation of a man who deals in usury?" He replied, "Yes."

'Alī did not accept anything from the state treasury. He had only one covering, and he washed it, he had nothing else to wear. Once, Abū Hurayrah produced before the caliph 'Umar abundant wealth of the state, and the latter enquired, "Is this lawful?" In a similar way 'Alī said, "There is nothing dearer to Allah than the justice and kindness of a leader, and there is nothing more detestable than the injustice and oppression of a leader."

4

Knowledge of the lawful and unlawful

If any man has in his possession a mixture of unlawful and lawful things, he should do two things:

First, he should separate the mixture, which can be of two types: a mixture of lawful and unlawful things of the same kind, such as crops, money and oils, or a mixture of unlawful things with different kinds of things, such as clothes and houses. In such cases, the quantity is either known or unknown. If, for instance, half is unlawful, it should be separated. It is lawful to keep doubtful things, but to abstain from it is better and pious. The repentance of a man is not accepted until what was wrongfully taken is returned to the rightful owner.

Second, he should know how to get rid of the unlawful things. It is obligatory to return the unlawful things to the rightful owner and, in his absence, to his heirs. It is also obligatory to return the income and profits arising out of these possessions to them. If the owner or his heirs are unknown, they may be given in charity to the poor.

The question might arise, How can an unlawful thing be given in charity when he has no right to do so? In support of this are traditions of the Prophet (ṣ). When cooked mutton was presented to the Prophet (ṣ), the mutton informed him that it was unlawful. The Prophet (ṣ) then ordered it to be given in charity saying, "Give it to the prisoners of war to eat." Once, Abū Bakr brought to the Prophet (ṣ) a thing won by gambling. The Prophet (ṣ) who said, "It is unlawful. Give it in charity." Ibn Masʿūd purchased a slave-girl, but he could not find her master in spite of continued searches. He eventually gifted her price to the poor on behalf of the master. Aḥmad ibn Ḥanbal and al-Ḥārith al-Muḥāsibī supported this view. So when the owner is not found, an unlawful possession is either destroyed or spent for the good of the people, the latter being better.

The Prophet (ṣ) said, "A cultivator or a planter of trees will get rewards for the crops and fruits which the people, birds and beasts eat." The rule is that only lawful things can be given in charity applies to cases in which we seek rewards for charity. When giving away unlawful things, we seek only salvation for ourselves. Further, the saying, "What we love for ourselves we should love for others" is true, but in the case of giving away unlawful things, it is unlawful for our enjoyment, but lawful for the poor. If the receiver of unlawful possessions is himself poor, and the owner is not traceable, he can lawfully use it to the extent that is necessary for himself and for his family members. The Qur'an also allows a person to consume unlawful foods such as wine when his life is in jeopardy.

5

Allowances and gifts from rulers and kings

When accepting allowances and gifts from rulers, a man is required to consider three things: the source of wealth, the right to acquire it and the quantity of lawful and unlawful things therein.

The ruler and his subjects have a right to reclaimed lands, booties gained in war and without war against the unbelievers, possessions which have no heirs and endowments which have no managers. Besides these, all other possessions are unlawful for him, including revenues, fines, taxes and other sources of income for the state.

Gifts and rewards the ruler gives to any man come from eight sources: poll taxes, heirless possessions, endowments, reclaimed lands, purchased goods, the revenue from Muslims, wealth from merchandise or specially fixed revenue.

With regard to poll taxes on unbelievers, four-fifths of it should be spent for the good of the people, and one-fifth only for special purposes. Heirless possessions should be spent for the good of the Muslims. Endowments should be spent for the purposes specified by donor. Lands reclaimed by the ruler can be given in any way he likes. Similarly, goods, clothes, horses and other things purchased by the ruler can be given in any way he likes. Taxes imposed on Muslims, booties, fines and so on are all unlawful to a ruler, except profits arising out of his personal business with others. Taxes specially imposed on a person are unlawful for a ruler as well.

The right to acquire it

Some of the scholars say that if it is not established that a possession is unlawful in any way, it may be accepted. In support they cite the following instances. There were many among the Companions who were alive during the time of tyrant rulers and used to accept wealth from them. Among them were Abū Hurayrah, Abū Sa'īd al-Khudrī, Zayd ibn Thābit. Abū Ayyūb al-Anṣārī, Jarīr ibn 'Abdullāh and Anas ibn Mālik. Some of them received wealth from the caliphs Marwān and Yazīd ibn 'Abd al-Malik, and some from the tyrannical governor al-Ḥajjāj. Imam al-Shāfi'ī once received from the caliph Hārūn al-Rashīd a thousand dinars. Anas ibn Mālik also received wealth from different caliphs.

'Alī said, "Whatever a ruler gives you he gives from lawful things." But he himself did not accept it out of a greater sense of piety. When al-Ḥasan ibn 'Alī came to the caliph Mu'āwiyah, the latter gave him four hundred thousand dirhams, which he accepted.

These sages used to accept the wealth of tyrannical rulers. The supporters of the above opinion say that some of the sages did not accept it out of a greater sense of piety and that it does not indicate its unlawfulness. Among such men were the rightly guided caliphs, Abū Dharr and other sages who renounced the world.

Four degrees of piety

There are four degrees of piety in relation to the acceptance of wealth from rulers.

First degree

In this degree, which is the highest, the rightly guided caliphs and a party of extremely pious men did not accept anything from the state treasury or rulers. The allowance which Abū Bakr received from the state treasury as a ruler amounted to six thousand dirhams, which he later returned to the treasury. Once, when 'Umar was counting the wealth of the state treasury, his young daughter concealed a dirham from him. When he found it, he returned it. Abū Mūsā al-Ash'arī found a dirham while sweeping the house of the treasury and gave it to the young daughter of 'Umar. The latter took it from her and returned it. 'Umar said in connection with the wealth of the state treasury, "In connection with this wealth, I see myself as the caretaker of an orphan's wealth. If I am well off, I refrain from taking anything from it. If I am in want, I enjoy from it in a just manner."

Second degree

A person can accept wealth from a ruler when he knows that his wealth is lawful, and is not accountable if it is disclosed afterwards that it was unlawful. This is supported by the Companions. The Companion Ibn 'Umar said about the tyrannical ruler al-Ḥajjāj, "I have not eaten to my satisfaction since he became the ruler." It is related that 'Alī had some wheat in a sealed cup, out of which he used to eat and drink. Upon being asked about it, he said, "I do not wish to fill my belly except with pure things."

Third degree

A person can accept gifts from a ruler and give them in charity to the poor or distribute them among those who are entitled to them, even if the ruler is a tyrant. For this reason, many people used to accept gifts from rulers. Whatever Ibn 'Umar received from rulers he distributed among the poor. One day he distributed sixty thousand dirhams among the poor. After this a poor man came to him and he gave him some dirhams after borrowing from a man. 'Ā'ishah would do the same. Imam al-Shāfi'ī accepted gifts from the caliph Hārūn al-Rashīd and distributed them among his relatives without keeping anything for himself.

Fourth degree

In this degree, the possessions of rulers have been established to be unlawful and therefore cannot be accepted, nor can they be given in charity. One should accept from rulers possessions which are mostly lawful.

These are the four degrees of piety. In our times, most of the possessions of rulers are unlawful because, although the Islamic state treasury used to consist of only *zakāh* and wealth gained by war and without war, nothing of these items is found in the present state treasuries.

Further, the people who received gifts from rulers in the past are different from the people who receive gifts now from the present rulers. The rulers of past ages used to give gifts to the learned and the sages who impressed them, while the present rulers give gifts to people who can flatter them with their lies.

The recipients of gifts should be qualified to receive them according to Sharī‘ah. For instance, there are people prescribed by the Qur’an to receive *zakāh*, war spoils, one-fifth of the wealth gained without war and heirless wealth. Wealth fixed for Muslims in general must be spent on them only, and it will be illegal to spend it on others. ‘Umar said, “Every Muslim is entitled to the treasury because he is a Muslim and this increases the population of Islam.”

The wealth of the treasury is for the good of the people. The good is connected with the religion and with the state. The religious scholars are the guards of the religion, and the soldiers are the guards of the state. The religion and the state are interconnected: One cannot be separated from the other. So religious scholars as well as soldiers of the state are entitled to receive wealth from the state treasury. The officers of the state fall under the same category as the guardians of the state and are as such entitled to it.

The rightly guided caliphs used to give to the Emigrants (*Muhājirūn*) and Madīnan Helpers (*Anṣār*) allowances from the state treasury. One day, Mu'āwiyah gave al-Ḥasan four hundred thousand dirhams. 'Umar fixed an annual allowance of twelve thousand dirhams for selected people including 'Ā'ishah, ten thousand for some people and six thousand for others; nothing remained after such distribution. Abū Bakr used to distribute equally. 'Umar amended it and used to give more or less as he wished. He used to give to 'Ā'ishah twelve thousand dirhams, Juwayriyah six thousand, Zaynab ten thousand and 'Uthmān five gardens. All the Companions agreed with the distribution of these two caliphs, as they believed in their sense of justice and sincerity.

6
Frequenting rulers

In this chapter, we will discuss when frequenting rulers is lawful and when it is unlawful. With regard to rulers, a person is in one of three circumstances: he frequents rulers, he is frequented by rulers or he keeps aloof from them.

Frequenting rulers

According to Sharīʿah, it is not recommended to frequent the rulers and administrators. A great deal of warnings to this effect have been given by sages and scholars of the religion.

Ḥadīth

The Prophet (ṣ) said:

> He who keeps away from them (tyrannical rulers) will get salvation. He who keeps separate from them will be safe or near safety. He who falls with them in their worldly passions will belong to them.
>
> There will be false and oppressive rulers after me. He who supports their falsehood as true and helps their tyranny does not belong to my followers, I am not of him and he will not be able to drink from my fountain.
>
> The learned man who frequents rulers is an object of Allah's hatred.
>
> Rulers who frequent scholars are good, and scholars who frequent rulers are bad.

> So long as scholars do not mix with rulers, they are the guardians of Allah's servants on behalf of the messengers. When they mix with them, they betray the messengers. So be careful of them and keep away from them.

Traditions from Companions and early Muslims

Ḥudhayfah said, "Be careful of ruinous places." He was asked, "What are those places?" He said, "The courts of rulers."

Abū Dharr said to Salmah, "Do not frequent the courts of rulers, as the religious harms will be greater than the benefits you get from them."

Sufyān said, "There is a valley in hell in which will live scholars who frequent rulers."

'Ubādah ibn al-Ṣāmit said, "If a pious scholar loves rulers, he commits hypocrisy, and if he loves the rich, he commits show."

'Umar ibn 'Abd al-'Azīz appointed an officer. He was then informed that he was an officer of the tyrant al-Ḥajjāj and dismissed him on this ground.

Al-Fuḍayl said, "The nearer a man becomes to rulers, the more distant he becomes from Allah.

From the above traditions and wise sayings, it appears that many dangers and difficulties arise out of mixing with rulers and frequenting their courts. He who frequents them faces sin, for by his actions, silence, words and invocations he commits disobedience to Allah. If he bows his head to a tyrannical ruler, or kisses his hand or does any similar actions, he sins. If he sees actions in the court of the ruler which are unlawful, he sins by his silence, as it is his duty to protest against such unlawful actions. If someone praises him and supports his unlawful actions, he sins. If he asks Allah to give a tyrant a long life, he sins. The Prophet (ṣ) said, "He who prays for a tyrant to have a long life loves sins"; "When any man praises a transgressor, Allah becomes angry"; "When a man honours a transgressor, Allah hates him"; and "When a man honours a transgressor, he helps the destruction of Islam."

Sa'īd ibn al-Musayyib was asked by caliph 'Abd al-Malik ibn Marwān to swear allegiance to his two sons al-Walīd and Sulaymān, he said, "I will never swear allegiance to them, as the Prophet (ṣ) prohibited allegiance to two people." As a result, he was flogged and made to wear a dress of disgrace.

Being frequented by rulers

There is no harm in saluting a tyrannical ruler and standing up in his honour, as a disturbance may occur among his subjects if a person does not. Thereafter, he should speak with him, giving him sound advice and informing him of the injunctions and prohibitions of Sharī'ah. Once, Muḥammad ibn Sulaymān went to Ḥammād ibn Salamah, who had before him a mat for sitting, a copy of the Qur'an, a bag for keeping books and a pot for ablution. The caliph said, "Whenever I see you, my heart is filled with fear. What is the reason?" Ḥammād said, "The reason is the tradition of the Prophet (ṣ) 'Everything fears a man who seeks Allah's pleasure with his knowledge.'" The caliph then placed before him forty thousand dirhams as a gift, which he refused to accept.

Keeping aloof from rulers

Scholars should not frequent the courts of rulers. If a person is reminded of the rewards and presents of a ruler, he should recall the words of Ḥātim al-Aṣamm, who said, "There is a difference of only one day between me and the rulers. They did not get the joys of yesterday, and they and myself have the fear of tomorrow. Only today remains. And what may happen today?"

Once, the caliph Hishām ibn 'Abd al-Malik went to Makkah for pilgrimage. When he entered the sanctuary of the Ka'bah, he called for Ṭāwūs al-Yamānī. When he came to him, he took off his shoes and kept them by the side of the royal carpet. He said, "O Hishām, peace be on you," sat beside him and asked him, "O

Hishām, how are you?" At this conduct of the sage, the caliph was about to kill him, but as he was in the sanctuary, he was not killed. The caliph asked Ṭāwūs, "Why have you treated me like this? You have placed your shoes by my carpet, have not kissed my hand, have not addressed me with "O Commander of the Faithful," have taken your seat by me without my permission and have asked me how I am doing, addressing me by name?" Ṭāwūs replied, "Regarding the placing of my shoes by your carpet, I take off my shoes five times a day when I go to my Lord for prayer, and He does not punish me for it. As for the kissing of your hand, I heard 'Alī say, 'Let nobody kiss anyone's hand, except for a man's kissing his wife's hand out of passion and his kissing his parents' hands out of reverence.' As for addressing you as the Commander of the Faithful, the people are not satisfied with your rule, and I do not wish to tell lies. Regarding my addressing you by your name, Allah addressed even His dear friends and prophets by their names. As for my sitting by your side, I heard 'Alī say, 'If you wish to see an inmate of hell, look at someone who sits while people stand around him.'" Then Ṭāwūs went away from him.

Sufyān al-Thawrī said, "I went once to the caliph Abū Ja'far al-Manṣūr and said to him, "You have reached this honour by the help of the Emigrants and Madīnan Helpers, but their descendants are dying of starvation at present, so fear Allah and give them what they are entitled to."

Ibn Abī Shumaylah went once to the court of the caliph 'Abd al-Malik ibn Marwān, who said to him, "Speak." He said, "Nobody will get salvation from the severe chastisement of Resurrection Day, except those who gain the pleasure of Allah, causing displeasure to their baser selves." 'Abd al-Malik wept and said, "I will keep this advice before my eyes until my death."

Once, the caliph Sulaymān ibn 'Abd al-Malik came to Madīnah and called for Abū Ḥāzim. When he came to him, he said, "O Abū Ḥāzim, why is death so detestable to me?" He said, "It is because you have destroyed your hereafter and adorned your world with numerous adornments." The caliph said, "How shall we approach Allah?" He said, "O Commander of the Faithful, the pious will return to their families in happiness like someone who has been absent, and the sinners like a fugitive slave to his master." The caliph then burst into tears and said, "What will be my condition?" Abū Ḥāzim said, "Look at this verse 'Most surely the righteous are in bliss, and most surely the wicked are in burning fire' (Qur'an, 83:13-14)." Sulaymān asked, "Where is the mercy of Allah?" He said, "Near the pious." The caliph asked, "Who among Allah's servants is the most honourable?" He said, "The pious and the God-fearing." The caliph asked, "Who among the believers is the wisest?" He said, "The believer who obeys the religion of Allah and calls the people towards it."

The caliph 'Umar ibn 'Abd al-'Azīz once said to Abū Ḥāzim, "Give me advice." He said, "Place death near your head when you go to bed and then look at what you love; you will then give up what you do not like."

Once, a desert Arab came to the caliph Sulaymān ibn 'Abd al-Malik, who said to him, "Give me some advice." On being assured of his safety, he said, "O Commander of the Faithful, there are some men among your special friends who have adopted dishonest ways and purchased the world with their next world and seek your pleasure by incurring the displeasure of their Lord. They fear you concerning Allah, but do not fear Allah concerning you. You are on good terms with the world after forgetting the next world. You have not given security to people from what Allah has given you security from. They are in dire want and need. You will be asked for what they do and will not do good to your world by selling your hereafter, as he who sells his hereafter for his world is a fool." Sulaymān said, "O desert Arab, beware, as the sharpness of your tongue is more than that of your sword." He said, "O Commander of the Faithful, that is true, but it is for you and not against you."

Once, Abū Bakr said to Mu'āwiyah, "O Mu'āwiyah, fear Allah, and know that the day which leaves you and the night which comes take you away from this world and take you closer to the hereafter. Behind you is a seeker from whom you can never save yourself. You have a fixed limit which you cannot cross, and as soon as you reach it, the seeker will arrest you. The possessions we have will all pass away, and what we send forward will remain. Stick to what is good and give up what is bad."

The Prophet (ṣ) said, "This community will not cease to be in the help and protection of Allah so long as the reciters of the Qur'an are not attracted to rulers." Allah says, "Do not incline to those who are unjust. In other words, "Do not remain satisfied with their actions."

Sufyān said, "Do not mix with the rulers and do not mix with those who mix with the rulers. The owners of pens, the owners of ink and the owners of paper are partners." What he said is true, as the Prophet (ṣ) cursed ten people in connection with wine.

Ibn Mas'ūd said, "Those who devour interest, those who give interest, those who are witnesses to it and those who write it are all cursed by the tongue of the Prophet (ṣ)."

Allah's words "Those whom the angels cause to die while they are unjust to themselves" (Qur'an, 16:28) were revealed in connection with those Muslims who increased the numbers of polytheists by mixing with them. It has been related that Allah revealed to the prophet Joshua, "I will destroy from among your followers forty thousand good people and sixty thousand other people." He asked Allah, "What sin have the good people committed?" Allah said, "They do not become displeased with actions which displease Me, and they eat and drink with unbelievers." This proves that to love for Allah and to hate for Allah is obligatory. The Prophet (ṣ) said, "Allah cursed the children of Israel for living with transgressors."

7

Miscellaneous issues

The Prophet (ṣ) said, "Give presents to one another and you will beget love for one another" Any present is lawful provided nothing is expected in return. If a present is given to a man knowing that he is a poor man, but in fact he is not poor, the latter's acceptance of the present is unlawful. So is the case in all similar matters. If a present is given to a person with administrative or official power, such as a judge, magistrate, *zakāh* collector, revenue collector or tax collector, it will be considered a bribe, as it was given for a special purpose.

Two sons of 'Umar accepted some loans from the state treasury. 'Umar took the profits of the loans from them and deposited them in the treasury saying, "These loans have been given to you because you are the sons of the caliph."

The wife of Abū 'Ubaydah ibn al-Jarrāḥ sent a casket of attar as a present to the queen of Byzantium. In return, the queen sent him a valuable necklace decorated with jewels. 'Umar took it from her and deposited it in the state treasury after giving the price of the casket to her.

When the caliph 'Umar ibn 'Abd al-'Azīz returned his present, it was said to him that the Prophet (ṣ) used to accept presents. He said, "It was a present for the Prophet (ṣ), but it is a bribe to us."

The Prophet (ṣ) sent a man to collect *zakāh* from the tribe of al-Azd. When he collected *zakāh* and returned it to the Prophet (ṣ), he kept something which was given to him as a present. The Prophet (ṣ) then said to him. "Tell me truthfully whether it would have been given to you if you kept seated in your parents' house. By Him in whose hand is my life, let nobody take from you except what is due to him. Beware, he will come to Allah with the thing he accepts. Let nobody come on Resurrection Day bearing a squealing camel on his back, a bellowing cow or a sounding goat." Then he raised his hands so high that the whiteness of his armpit was visible and said, "O Allah, have I communicated Your message?"

Book 5
Love and brotherhood

Introduction

Love for one another and friendship and brotherhood between one another is the best way to draw near to Allah. We shall describe in this chapter love and friendship for Allah and its conditions and rules; the duties of companionship and its rules and duties to Muslims, relatives, neighbours and rulers.

1

The merits of friendship and brotherhood

Know, dear readers, that friendship is the result of good love for one another, and bad conduct is the root of hatred, envy and enmity. The result of good conduct is praiseworthy, and its merits in religion are no secret. Allah praised His Prophet (ṣ), saying, "And most surely you conform (yourself) to sublime morality" (Qur'an, 68:4).

The Prophet (ṣ) said:

> The attributes which will take the majority of people to paradise are God-fearingness and good conduct.
>
> Upon being asked what good attribute man has been given, he said, "Good conduct."
>
> I have been sent to perfect good conduct.
>
> What will be the heaviest in the balance is good conduct.
>
> Allah has not made the conduct and constitution of people such that fire will burn them.

In other words, the fire of hell will not be able to burn someone whose character and constitution are beautiful.

> "O Abū Hurayrah, you should have good conduct." Abū Hurayrah asked, "O Messenger of Allah, what is good conduct?" He said, "Keep the tie of relationship with whoever cuts it off, forgive whoever oppresses you and give charity to whoever deprives you."

Some traditions have come in praise of friendship. When the tie of friendship is love for Allah, its merits are great, as the Qur'an and traditions attest.

The Qur'an

Showing how kind He is to all creatures, Allah says, "Had you spent all that is in the earth, you could not have united their hearts, but Allah united them" (Qur'an, 8:63) and "By His favour, you became brethren" (Qur'an, 3:103). Condemning separation and disunity, He says, "Hold fast by the covenant of Allah all together and be not disunited" (Qur'an, 3:103).

Ḥadīth

The Prophet (ṣ) said,

> The best of you in good conduct is nearest to me.
>
> A believer loves and is loved. There is no good in someone who does not love and is not loved.
>
> Allah gives a friend to someone who is good. If he forgets, he reminds him. If he does not remember, he helps him.
>
> If two brothers meet, they are like two hands, one of which clears the dust off the other. If two believers meet, Allah benefits one through the other.
>
> If a man creates brotherhood for Allah, Allah will increase his rank in paradise and will not reduce anything from his actions.
>
> "Chairs will be placed around the Throne for a party of men. Their faces will be like the full moon. People will be afraid, but they will not. People will be perturbed, but they will not. They are the friends of Allah and will not have any fear or sorrow." He was asked, "O Messenger of Allah, who are they?" He answered, "Those who love one another for Allah."
>
> "There are pulpits of light around the Throne. A party of men will be seated therein. Their dress will be of light. They are not

prophets or martyrs, but prophets and martyrs will envy their rank." It was said to him, "O Messenger of Allah, tell us about their qualities." He said, "They love one another for Allah, sit together in an assembly for Allah and meet one another for Allah."

Concerning two men who love each other for Allah, "The one more beloved to Allah is the one who loves his friend more. Allah says, 'I shall make their children attached to them, and nothing will be reduced from their actions.'"

Allah says, "My meeting with those who meet one another for Me becomes sure. My love for those who love one another for Me becomes sure. My help to those who help one another for Me becomes sure."

Allah will say on Resurrection Day, "Where are those who loved one another for Me? There is no shade today except My shade. I will give them My shade."

On the day when there will be no shade except the shade of Allah, Allah will place seven people under His shade: a just ruler; a young man engaged in worship; a man who is attracted to the mosque after he leaves it; two people who love each other for Allah, meet each other for Allah and keep the company of each other for Allah; someone who remembers Allah when he is alone and as a result his eyes shed tears; a man who does not respond to the evil temptation of a beautiful woman coming from a respectable family, saying, "I fear Allah"; and a charitable person who keeps his charity so secret that his left hand does not know what his right hand gives.

When a man meets another out of love for Allah and hoping to meet Him, an angel proclaims from behind him, "You are blessed, your foot steps are blessed, paradise for you is blessed."

Once, a man wished to meet his friend for Allah. Allah secretly sent to him an angel who asked him, "What do you intend?" He said, "I intend to meet my brother." The angel asked him, "Do you need anything from him?" He said, "No." The angel said, "Has he benefitted you?" He said, "No." The angel said, "Then why are you going to meet him?" He said, "I love him for the sake of Allah." The angel said, "Allah sent me to tell you that He loves you as you love him, and that paradise is sure for you."

Love for Allah and hate for Allah are the firmest faith. For this reason, a man should have enemies so that he may hate them, and should have friends so that he may love them.

O Allah, let no sinner benefit me, as my love may grow for him.

The most beloved of you to Allah are those who love and are loved, and the most hated of you to Allah are those who roam with slander and create disputes among brethren.

There is an angel of Allah half of whose body was created of fire and the other half of which was created of ice. He says, "O Allah, just as You have created a tie between fire and ice, create love in the hearts of Your pious servants."

If a man makes a friendship for Allah, He creates for him a rank in paradise.

Those who love each other for Allah will live on long pillars of red emeralds. On each pillar will be seventy thousand rooms, and from them they will see the inhabitants of paradise. The brilliance of their look will illuminate the inhabitants of paradise as the rays of the sun illuminate this world. The inhabitants of paradise will say to one another, "Take us to see those who loved one another for Allah." On their foreheads will be written, "Lovers for Allah."

Once Allah revealed to a prophet, "You have hastened the happiness of paradise because of your renunciation of the world. You are honourable to Me for having renounced the world to come to Me. Have you made an enemy for My sake? Have you made a friendship for My sake?"

Allah revealed to 'Īsā, "If you only perform the devotions of the inhabitants of the heaven and the earth but do not love for Me and hate for Me, it will do you no benefit." 'Īsā said, "Be dear to Allah by having enmity towards sinners. Be near to Allah by keeping away from them. Seek the pleasure of Allah by displeasing them." He was asked, "O Spirit of Allah, whose company shall we keep?" He said, "People who remind you of Allah when you see them, whose words increase your good deeds and who arouse in your mind eagerness for the actions of the next world when you see them."

Once, Allah revealed to Mūsā, "O son of 'Imrān, if your heart is awake, seek friends. A friend who does not meet you for My pleasure is your enemy."

Allah revealed to Dāwūd, "O Dāwūd, why are you alone?" He said, "O Allah, I have adopted loneliness for You." He said, "O Dāwūd, seek friends for yourself and do not make friends with those who do not help you for My pleasure: they are your enemies and will make your heart hard and keep you far from Me." Dāwūd once said to Allah, "O Lord, how is it possible that everyone will love me and obey the message of the religion?" It was said, "Treat people according to their nature, and make good what is between you and Me." In another version says, "Treat the people of the world according to the nature of the world, and treat the inhabitants of the next world according to the nature of the next world."

Traditions from Companions and early Muslims

'Alī said, "You should make friends, for they will be counted in this world and in the next. Have you not heard the words of the inhabitants of hell 'We have no intercessors, nor a true friend' (Qur'an, 26:100-101)."

'Abdullāh ibn 'Umar said, "By Allah, if I fast all days, pray all nights, spend all my wealth in the way of Allah without account and then die not loving those who obey Allah and not hating those who disobey Allah, none of that will be of use to me."

Al-Ḥasan said, "O children of Adam, do not be deceived by the words 'He who loves someone will be with him,' because one cannot earn the rank of the pious without doing their actions. Jews and Christians love their prophets, but they do not act according to their injunctions. This shows that mere love without actions will be of no use."

Al-Fuḍayl said in one of his sermons, "It is strange that you wish to live in the highest part of paradise and in the neighbourhood of the Merciful with prophets, those with great faith, martyrs and pious men. What actions have you done for it? What passions have you given up for it? What tie of relationship have you united after it was severed? What faults of your brother have you forgiven? What distant people have you brought near to Allah?"

Allah revealed to Mūsā, "What actions have you done for My pleasure?" He said, "O Lord, I have prayed to You, fasted and given charity and *zakāh*." He said, "Prayer is a clear proof for you, fasting is a shield for you, charity is your shade and *zakāh* is your light; but what actions have you done for Me?" Mūsā said, "O Lord, show me an action which will be only for You." Allah said, "O Mūsā, have you made a friend for My sake? And have you made any enemy for My sake?" Then Mūsā came to know that the best action is love for Allah and hatred for Allah.

Al-Ḥasan said, "To hate the sinners is a means of nearing Allah."

A man once said to Muḥammad ibn Wāsiʿ, "I love you for Allah." He said, "He loves you for whom you love me." Then he said, "O Allah, I seek refuge in You from a person who loves me for You, as I do not know your love."

ʿUmar said, "When one of you gets love from his brother, let him stick to it, for such a man is rarely found."

Mujāhid said, "When two lovers meet and express gratitude, their sins fall from them as the leaves of trees fall in winter."

Al-Fuḍayl said, "If a man looks at his brother with affection and kindness, it becomes his devotion."

The difference between love for Allah and love for the world

Know, dear readers, that love for Allah and hate for Allah are subtle, and what we will discuss will lift the curtain therefrom.

Friendship is either out of love for Allah or out of love for the world. It is not love for Allah if there is love for a neighbour, for reading together, for trading in the same market or for travelling together on a journey. It is love for Allah when the intention is love for Allah, for, undoubtedly, there is no merit unless an action is done willingly.

Either a thing is loved for itself and not so that an object of love or a goal can be reached, or it is loved so that a goal can be reached thereby. This goal is not confined to this world alone, but is also connected with the next world or with Allah. Thus love is of four kinds.

The first is loving a thing for itself. It is possible for a man to become someone's object of love in a natural way, when he sees him, knows him and thinks him good after seeing his character and conduct. Everything beautiful is an object of pleasure to a man who loves beauty. Love can also be for internal qualities. The Prophet (ṣ) said, "Souls are the arrayed soldiers. Those of them who know one another, love one another, and those who do not know one another have differences of opinion." The cause of their differences is ignorance of one another, and the cause of their love is knowledge of one another, as love grows out of acquaintance. In another version, the Prophet (ṣ) said, "Souls are arrayed soldiers. One soul meeting with another in the horizon becomes near." Some scholars explain this by saying that Allah, after creating souls, released them into the air and they roamed around the Throne. The souls which knew one another in the air meet one another in the world and love one another.

The Prophet (ṣ) said, "The souls of two believers meet with each other from a distance of a day's journey, though neither of them has seen the other." He also said, "When a believer enters an assembly of a hundred hypocrites and only one believer, he will sit near the believer. If a hypocrite enters an assembly of a hundred believers and one hypocrite, he will sit near the hypocrite." It is evident from this that similar natures are attracted to one another, even if they are unacquainted with one another.

Mālik ibn Dīnār said, "Two out of ten people cannot agree, but if the nature of the two is the same, they agree." This proves that a man loves another man of the same nature not for gaining any benefit or acquiring wealth, but because their natures and internal qualities are the same.

The second kind of love is for the sake of gaining the love of another. The means to a dear thing is also dear. For this reason, gold and silver are dear to men, although they have no attribute of their own, as they cannot be eaten or used as clothes, but they are the means of getting these things. Similarly, there are men who are loved like gold and silver, as they are the means of reaching a destination or goal, and thereby wealth, a name and fame are earned.

The third kind of love is not for the sake the good of this world but for the good of the hereafter. This is evident, not hidden, as in the case of a person's love for a spiritual guide who becomes the means of gaining spiritual knowledge; his object is to succeed in the next world. 'Īsā said, "He who acquires knowledge, acts on it and teaches it to others is called noble in the spiritual world." And as teaching is not complete without students, they are a teacher's means to perfection.

Likewise, he who spends his wealth on his friend, clothes him, feeds him, gives him a home and helps him in all his affairs, and whose object in doing these things is to give him leisure for devotions, is beloved to Allah. In the days of yore, a party of rich men used to supply food to religious men and loved them. And he who marries with the object of getting a son who will pray for him and for that he loves his wife is beloved to Allah as well. For this reason, there are ample rewards for spending money on family members, even for a morsel of food which a husband puts into the mouth of his wife.

'Īsā said in a supplication, "O Allah, do not allow my enemies to become pleased with me, do not create trouble in my religion, do not make the world a great object of my anxiety and remove the pleasure of my enemies from the wealth of the world." He did not pray, "Do not make the world the root of my anxiety." Rather, he said, "Do not make the world a great object of my anxiety."

The Prophet (ṣ) said in a supplication, "O Allah, I pray for Your mercy, so that I may gain the glory of Your honour in this world and in the next." He also prayed, "O Allah, save me from the calamities of this world and the next." "This world" and "the next world" refer to two states, one of which is nearer than the other. So if a man does not love the happiness of today, how can he love the happiness of tomorrow? Surely he should love the happiness of tomorrow as tomorrow will turn into a lasting state. So it is necessary to enquire into the lasting state.

The pleasures of this world is of two kind. One kind is opposed to the pleasure of the next world and is a stumbling block to it. The prophets and friends of Allah were careful of this kind of pleasure. Another kind of pleasure is not opposed to that of the next world and was not prohibited for them. It includes marriage, lawful eating and the like.

The fourth kind of love is for the sake of Allah. It is selfless and disinterested love. This is the highest, most secret and subtlest kind of love. Love of this kind is possible, for if this love exceeds limits, it spreads towards the things which are connected with the beloved. A lover even loves the things of the beloved, loves those whom the beloved loves, loves those who praise and glorify the beloved and loves those who try to please the beloved. Baqiyyah ibn al-Walīd said, "When a believer loves a believer, he even loves his dog." In this connection, the madman of Banī 'Āmir said, "When I went to the house of Laylā, I kissed its wall. My love was not for the wall, but for its owner." If love is strong, it spreads more. And love for Allah is similar. When love for Allah envelopes the heart, it rules the heart and spreads over everything, with the result that the lover sees His power in everything.

He who loves a man loves his handicrafts, his letters and all his actions. For this reason, when a fresh fruit was brought to the

Prophet (ṣ), he placed it on his eyes, honoured it and said, "It has become with the help of my Lord." A lover reduces the pangs of a lover. The love of a party of men reaches such a degree that they say, "We do not distinguish between sorrow and happiness, as all come from Allah; we feel happiness at His pleasure." Samnūn said, "I find no delight in anyone but You so test me as You wish!"

He who loves a king, loves also those people whom the king loves and even his servants. A sage said, "When pain gives pleasure, can the pangs of a wound remain?" The extent of a person's love for someone is proportionate to the extent he gives up what is dear to him. The reason is that when love for a person envelopes his entire heart, love for other things does not remain in it. Therefore, a friend of Allah gives everything he has in charity in order to please Allah. For this reason, Abū Bakr left nothing for his family when the Prophet (ṣ) called for charity. He even sacrificed his little daughter for the Prophet (ṣ).

Ibn 'Umar said, "Once, the Prophet (ṣ) was seated with Abū Bakr, who put on a long shirt with a bell tied on the chest. Jibrīl descended and said to the Prophet (ṣ), 'O Prophet of Allah, why shall I see Abū Bakr covered with a long shirt?' He said, 'Because before the conquest, he gave all his wealth in charity.' Jibrīl said, "Greet him on behalf of Allah and tell him that his Lord is saying to him, 'Are you satisfied or dissatisfied with Me?' The Prophet (ṣ) turned to Abū Bakr and said, 'O Abū Bakr, he is Jibrīl, and He greets you on behalf of Allah because of your want.' He said, 'Then Abū Bakr wept and said, 'I am satisfied with my Lord.'"

Hatred for Allah

He who loves Allah has no alternative but to hate for Allah, because someone who loves a man for any of his good works hates him for any act contrary to it. These two things—love and hatred—are connected with each other and cannot be separated. When they are expressed in words, they are named friendship and enmity. Allah said to Mūsā, "Have you made friends and enemies for My sake?"

One loves a person about whom nothing has been disclosed except his obedience, and one hates a person about whom nothing has been disclosed except his sins and bad conduct. A person may have different characteristics, for some of which he is loved and others hated. A beautiful wife who is a sinner, for instance, is loved for her one attribute by her husband and hated for another. A Muslim can be loved for his religion Islam, and can be hated for his sins.

Hate should be expressed by words and actions. If hate is expressed by words, one stops talking with a sinner and sometimes uses harsh words. If hate is expressed by action, one sometimes harms a sinner and destroys his evil design; this occurs in proportion to his sins. When he is repentant, one keeps his sin secret. When one loves a person, one hates him also for his faults by protesting against his evil actions, leaving him, not looking at him. These are expressions of anger so far as action is concerned.

Misṭaḥ ibn Uthāthah once spread slander against the character of 'Ā'ishah. Abū Bakr used to help him by giving him charity. When he heard what he had done, he stopped he promised to stop helping him, whereupon this verse was revealed: "Let not those of you who possess grace and abundances wear against giving to the near of kin and the poor and those who have fled in Allah's way, and they should pardon and turn away. Do you not love that Allah should forgive you?" (Qur'an, 24:22). Though the sin of Misṭaḥ was great, Abū Bakr felt restless because of what he had done. It is the habit of those with great faith to forgive oppressors.

Sinners are either those who have no faith or those who commit sins by their actions. Those who have no faith are either unbelievers or innovators. Innovators either promote views opposed to Sharī'ah or remain silent. Further, those who remain silent are either compelled to do so or do so willingly. So there are four kinds of sinners.

1. An unbeliever. If he is at war with Muslims, he can be killed or made a slave. There is no other punishment except these

two for him. A *dhimmī* (non-Muslim subject of an Islamic state) cannot be given trouble, but if he protests against Islam, he can be given trouble. To humiliate him is to constrict his livelihood, not to salute him first, not to mix or trade with him and not to take part in enjoyments with him as one does with friends. Allah says, "You shall not find a people who believe in Allah and the latter day befriending those who act in opposition to Allah and His Messenger, even though they were their (own) fathers or their sons or their brothers or their kinsfolk" (Qur'an, 58.22). The Prophet (ṣ) said, "O those who believe, do not take my enemy and your enemy as friends."

2. An innovator who encourages innovation. If innovation leads to infidelity, the punishment is severer than that of a *dhimmī*, as he cannot be given the advantage of a *dhimmī*. If it does not lead to infidelity, the punishment is lighter. An innovator promotes misguidance because he believes his views to be correct. So his evil is also unlimited. The best way to express hate for him is to leave his company and rebuke him for his innovation. The Prophet (ṣ) said, "Whoever rebukes an innovator, Allah fills his mind with peace and faith." Thus, whoever disgraces an innovator, Allah will keep him safe on the most grievous day.
3. An ordinary innovator. If people do not follow him, or if he is unable to convince them of his views, his affair is easy. It is better to treat him harshly at the onset, and it is better to advise him first with humility. If this is ineffective, it is better to turn away from him.
4. Someone who disobeys the injunctions of Allah by his actions and not by his faith. This kind of sinner is of two kinds: a sinner who troubles another by such acts as oppression, misappropriation, false evidence, slander and backbiting, and a sinner who does not trouble another by such actions. The latter either invites others to sinful acts or does not invite others, as in the case of a man drinks wine but does not

encourage others to drink it. Such sinners, then, are of three kinds.

The sinners of the first kind commit sins which are injurious to a great extent, such as backbiting, false evidence and oppression. It is better not to mix or transact with sinners of this kind, who are of three kinds: those who murder men, those who wrongfully take the chattels of men and those who wrongfully take the real estate of men. It is better not to mix with such people.

Sinners of the second kind create disturbances and facilitate the means to them. They do not trouble mundane people, but injure their religion by their actions. Such sinners should be humiliated, and ties with them should be cut off..

Sinners of the third kind are those who commit such great sins as drinking wine, shirking religious obligations and doing unlawful things. If a man sees him commit such sins, it is obligatory for him to prohibit him, be it by beating him or otherwise, because it is obligatory to prohibit an evil action. If he is habituated to doing it, he should be advised if there is a possibility that he will cease. Moreover, if there is benefit in treating him harshly, it should be done. If it is useless to give him advice, one should be led by his conscience to take a suitable measure against him. It has been related that a drunkard was beaten several times before the Prophet (ṣ), but still he did not give up drinking wine. One of the Companions said, "Allah's curse be on this drunkard." Thereupon, the Prophet (ṣ) said, "Do not help the Devil against your brother," meaning "The Devil is sufficient for the man; you should not rebuke him."

Conditions of friendship

Know, dear readers, that not every man is fit for friendship. The Prophet (ṣ) said, "A man follows the religion of his friend, so let him consider whom he befriends." When a person wishes to establish a friendship, he looks for qualities he would like in a friend, qualities which will benefit him worldly or religiously. Worldly benefits include wealth, name and bargain; but these are not our objects. Religious benefits include acquiring knowledge and good deeds; saving oneself from name and fame, which perturb the heart; gaining wealth to maintain oneself; seeking help in necessary actions, in dangers and difficulties and in many other actions in life; getting the blessings of the invocations of a friend; and hoping for the intercession of a friend in the next world. A sage of yore said, "Increase the number of friends, as every believer has the right of intercession, and you may hope to be included in the intercession of your friend." Regarding Allah's words "He answers those who believe and do good deeds, and gives them more out of His grace" (Qur'an, 42:26), there is a *ḥadīth* which says that believers will intercede for their friends, and Allah will admit them into paradise along with them. It has also been said, regarding the verse, that when a man is forgiven, he will have the right to intercede for his friends.

These benefits have some conditions. A man with whom companionship is to be kept should have intellect and good conduct, and should not be a sinner, an innovator or a man addicted to the world.

Intellect

Intellect is the root of wealth, and there is no good in the company of fools and the illiterate. 'Alī said in a poem, "Do not keep the company of fools; break your friendship with them. When a wise friend remains patient, an illiterate friend becomes impatient. When a wise friend is in danger, an illiterate friend leaves him in disaster. Though he wants to do good, he will do you harm, as he is ignorant." Al-Thawrī said, "It is a sin to look at the face of a fool." An intelligent man is he who understands the reality of things, and a fool is he who has no sense of right and wrong and who does not understand it even it is dictated by others.

Good conduct

A friend should have good conduct because, although many intelligent men often understand things as they truly are, when they get angry, sexual passion, miserliness and cowardice gain supremacy, and he conducts himself according to his whims and acts contrary to his wisdom. There is no good in having such friends.

Religious nature

A friend should have a religious nature in order to benefit. There is no good in keeping the company of a sinner. He who fears Allah cannot be engaged in great sins. If a man does not fear Allah, one cannot be safe from his harms and cannot trust his words. He changes when the need arises. Allah says, "Do not follow him whose heart We have made unmindful to Our remembrance, and he follows his low desires" (Qur'an, 18:28); "Therefore let not him who believes not in it and follows his low desires turn you away from it" (Qur'an, 20:16); "Therefore turn aside from him who turns his back upon Our reminder and does not desire anything but this world's life" (Qur'an, 53:29); and "Follow the way of one who turns to Me" (Qur'an, 31:15). It is understood from this that it is lawful to turn away from great sins.

Innovation

It is one's duty to have no connection with an innovator. What benefit can his help bring? 'Umar encouraged befriending someone with a religious nature, saying, "You should befriend the truthful, for if you do, you will live under their care and they will increase your happiness in times of joy and remove your difficulties in times of sorrow. Bear well the affairs of your friends, keep your enemy distant and warn your friend. But do not keep a trusted man of a people distant. He who does not fear Allah is not a trustworthy man. Do not keep the company of a great sinner, nor tell him your secrets. And regarding your affairs, consult with those who fear Allah."

'Alqamah al-'Uṭāridī advised his son at the time of his death, "Dear son, if you see the need to befriend a man, befriend a man who will save you if you save him, who will increase your beauty if you keep his company, who will help you when you are in trouble, who he will extend his hand of good towards you if you extend your hand of good towards him, who will help you in any good act you undertake, who will remove any evil he sees in you, who will give you if you want something from him, who will initiate conversation when you are silent, who will be sorry when any disaster befalls you and gives you pain, who will believe what you say, who will advise you when you intend to do an action and who will prefer your opinion when there arises differences of opinion among you."

Ja'far al-Ṣādiq said, "Do not keep the company of four people: a liar, because he will deceive you and make the distant near and the near distant; a fool, because you will not get any benefit from him, and he will do you harm if he tries to benefit you; a miser, because he will forsake you when you are in dire need; a coward, because he will flee after surrendering you to the enemies; and a great sinner, because he will sell you for a morsel of food or a thing of lesser value."

Al-Junayd said, "The friendship of a transgressor with good conduct is dearer to me than that of a learned man with bad conduct."

Bishr said, "Friends are three: a friend for your next world, a friend for your present world and a friend to console your heart."

Al-Ma'mūn said, "Friends are of three kinds: those who are like food—there is no alternative but to get their help; those who are like medicine—their help is necessary at times—and those who are like an epidemic disease—they are never needed."

It is said that a party of men are like trees which have shade but no fruits. These trees are like those people who are useless for the next world but not this world, the benefits of which disappear as quickly as the disappearance of shade. Among them are trees which have fruits but no shade. These are like those people who are useless for the good of this world but not the next. Some trees have both fruits and shade, and some trees have neither fruits nor shade, like *umm ghīlān*, whose thorns pierce clothes and which has neither taste nor drink; these are like snakes and rats."

Abū Dharr said, "Loneliness is better than a bad companion, and a good companion is better than loneliness. Allah's words "When the ignorant address them, they say, 'Peace'" (Qur'an, 25:63) means "We are safe from your sins, and you are safe from our evil."

'Alī said, "If a man gives life to your devotions, keep your religion alive by keeping his company." Luqmān advised his son, "O dear son, keep the company of the learned, as the heart is enlivened with wisdom as land is enlivened with rainwater."

2

The duties of friendship and brotherhood

The tie of friendship and brotherhood is like the tie between a husband and wife. Just as some duties arise out of wedlock, so also they arise out of the tie of friendship and brotherhood. These duties are eight.

First duty

The first duty concerns wealth and possessions. The Prophet (ṣ) said, "Two friends are like two hands, one of which washes the other." Similarly, friendship is complete when one of them keeps the other, as if they are one and the same, and they share each other's enjoyments. There are three degrees of self-sacrifice for each other.

The lowest degree is to bring down a friend to the level of a servant and give him, charity from one's surplus when he is in need, without obliging him to ask. Obliging him to ask is the ultimate shortcoming in friendship.

The second degree is to bring a friend down to one's level and be content to have him as a partner in one's possessions. One will also come down to his level to the point of sharing it equally with him. Al-Ḥasan said, "Once, a friend divided his shirt into two portions and gave one portion to his friend."

The third degree is to place the needs of a friend above ones own needs. This is the rank of those with great faith, is the highest degree of friendship and its fruit is self-sacrifice. It has been reported that a party of wicked people defamed a party of religious men. As a result, the caliph ordered execution of the religious men, among whom was Abū al-Ḥasan al-Nūrī. Before all of them, he advanced towards the gallows and said, "Hang me first." Upon being asked why he desired to die, he said, "I wished that my brothers, rather than I, should have that moment to live." This was the cause of their lives being saved. Maymūn ibn Mahrān said, "He who is pleased with not putting his brother first might as well be a brother to the people of tombs."

As for the lowest degree, it is displeasing to religious men. It is said that 'Utbah al-Ghulām once went to his friend's house and said, "I need four thousand coins of your wealth." He said, "Take two thousand coins." He declined, saying, "You have preferred this world to Allah. Do you not feel ashamed that you claim friendship for Allah but place the love of the world over friendship?" Abū Ḥāzim said, "When you have a friend for the sake of Allah, do not engage him in your worldly affairs."

As for the highest degree, this corresponds to Allah's description of true believers when he said, "Their rule is to take counsel among themselves, and who spend out of what We have given them" (Qur'an, 42:38). In other words, they mixed their wealth and did not distinguish it. If any of them said, "This is my shoe," they would not keep his company, as he attributed it to himself.

It is said that Fatḥ al-Mawṣilī once went to his friend's house in his absence and said to his maid-servant, "Take to me the cash box of your master." When she brought it to him he took therefrom some coins necessary for him. The maidservant informed her master about it and he said, "If you speak the truth, I set you free, because what you have informed me of is good news."

One day a man came to Abū Hurayrah and said, "I wish to befriend you for the sake of Allah. Abū Hurayrah said, "Do you know the rights of a friend?" The man said, "One of the rights of friendship is that your right regarding your possessions and wealth is not more than that of mine." Abū Hurayrah said, "I have not yet reached that level." The man said, "Then go away."

'Alī ibn al-Ḥusayn said to a man, "Does any of you place his hand in the pocket of his friend or in his purse and take what he needs without permission?" The man said, "No." 'Alī said, "Then you are not friends."

A party of men came to al-Ḥasan and said, "O Abū Sa'īd, have you prayed?" He said, "Yes." They said, "The market folk have not yet prayed." He said, "And who takes his religion from the market folk? I know that none of them gives charity."

As Ibrāhīm ibn Adham was leaving for Jerusalem, a man said to him, "I wish to go there with you." Ibrāhīm said to him, "On condition that I have greater right to your money." The man said, "No." Then Ibrāhīm said, "I admire your truthfulness."

Whenever Ibrāhīm had a companion with him, he never acted contrary to his companion's wishes; he never accepted anybody as his companion if he did not agree with him. Once, he gifted an ass belonging to this friend without his permission. When his friend returned, he said nothing and did not disapprove.

Ibn 'Umar said, "Once, a man presented a companion with a fried goat's head. The latter sent it to his friend, as he was in greater need. The latter again sent it to another man. Thus it went through seven people and returned to the first."

It is related that Masrūq owed a heavy debt, and his friend Khaythamah also had debts. Masrūq paid off the debts of the latter without his knowledge. In return, Khaythamah also paid off the debts of Masruq without his knowledge.

When the Prophet (ṣ) witnessed the brotherhood between 'Abd al-Raḥmān ibn 'Awf and Sa'd ibn al-Rabī', the former said to the latter, "Allah has given me abundant wealth. So take therefrom whatever you wish." Sa'd had the quality of equality, and 'Abd al-Raḥmān had the quality of self-sacrifice, which is better than equality.

'Alī said, "To spend twenty dirhams on a friend for the sake of Allah I consider better than to give in charity a hundred dirhams to the poor."

One should follow the Holy Prophet (ṣ) in the matter of self-sacrifice. He once entered a jungle with some of his Companions and took two tooth sticks, one straight and another crooked. He gave the straight one to a Companion, who said, "O Messenger of Allah, by Allah, you are simpler than I, so you are more entitled to the straight tooth stick than I." The Prophet (ṣ) said, "If anybody keeps the company of a man for a portion of the day, he will be asked whether he fulfilled the duties of companionship."

Once, the Prophet (ṣ) went out to a well for a bath. His Companion Ḥudhayfah screened him with a cloth until he finished his bath. After his bath, the Prophet (ṣ) was going to screen Ḥudhayfah when he said to the Prophet (ṣ), "O Messenger of Allah, may my parents be sacrificed for you. Do not do it." Yet the Prophet (ṣ) insisted on screening him while he washed, and said, "If two men keep company each other's company, he who is kinder to his companion is dearer to Allah."

It is reported that Mālik ibn Dīnār and Muḥammad ibn Wāsi' went to the house of al-Ḥasan in his absence. Muḥammad took out a cup of food which was under his bed and began to eat. Mālik said, "Hold out your hand until the owner comes." Suddenly al-Ḥasan came and said, "O Mālik, we used to trouble one another in this way. Allah ordered us to treat our friends well, saying, "Or your friends' (houses)" (Qur'an, 24:61). At that time, a friend handed over his house key to his friend who had the option of doing whatever he wished. His friend, however, refrained from eating, until Allah revealed this verse.

Second duty

The second duty is to help a friend, before asking, in times of need. This help has different degrees.

The lowest is to fulfil with pleasure and kindness the needs of a friend when he asks. A wise man said, "When a man asks his friend to fulfil a need, and the latter does not do so, let him remind him a second time. If he does not fulfil it without delay, let him recite the verse "(As to) the dead, Allah will raise them" (Qur'an, 6:36), meaning that he and the dead are equal. A sage of yore maintained the family members of his friend for forty years following his death. The Prophet (ṣ) said, "Surely, Allah has cups in the world, which are hearts. And the dearest of hearts to Allah is the cleanest and softest of them." "Clean" means clean from sins, and "firm" means firm in religion and soft means kind to friends and relatives.

In short, a person should consider the needs of his friend as his own or even greater. As his friend is not indifferent to his needs, so he should not be indifferent to his friend's needs. Instead, he should relieve his friend from asking him to fulfil his needs. He should try to remove his friend's difficulties and dangers.

Al-Ḥasan said, "My friends are dearer to me than my wife and children, as my family reminds me of this world." He also said, "If a man spreads the fame of his friend for the sake of Allah, Allah will send His angels of the Throne on Resurrection Day to spread his fame in paradise."

A *ḥadīth* says, "If a man meets with his friend for the sake of Allah, an angel calls out from behind him, 'You have done well, and it will be well for you in the garden of paradise.'"

'Aṭā' said, "Ask about your friends once every three days. If they are ill, visit them. If they are busy, help them. If they forget, remind them."

The Prophet (ṣ) once said to Ibn 'Umar, "If you love someone, ask him his name, his father's name and his address. If he is ill, visit him. If he is busy, help him."

Once Ibn 'Abbās was asked, "Who is the dearest to you?" He said, "My friend." He also said, "If a man comes to my assembly thrice without any necessity and does not get any benefit from me, I know that his aim is not the world."

Sa'īd ibn al-'Āṣ said, "I have three duties to my friend. When he comes, I should entertain him. When he speaks, I should face him. When he sits, I should give him a good place."

Allah says, "Compassionate among themselves" (Qur'an, 48:29).

Third duty

The third duty concerns the tongue. Sometimes a person will talk with a friend, and sometimes he will not. He should not disclose any secret which his friend tells him, even to his close friends, and even if they are separated, as it is sign of bad conduct. He should not speak ill of his friends, wives or children. Anas said, "The Prophet (ṣ) never faced anyone with something displeasing to him, for the hurt comes immediately from the informant and only indirectly from the original speaker."

Furthermore, he should not hide any praise he may hear, for this is considered envy. Nor should he backbite his friend or any member of his family. Ibn al-Mubārak said, "A believer searches for excuses, and a hypocrite searches for faults." Al-Fuḍayl said, "It is the rule of religion to pardon the faults of a friend." The Prophet (ṣ) said, "I seek refuge in Allah from a bad neighbour. If he sees any good, he keeps it secret, and if he sees any bad, he discloses it."

There is no man who cannot be considered good in some respects and bad in others. A *ḥadīth* says that once a man praised another before the Prophet (ṣ). On the following day, he began to defame him. Then the Prophet (ṣ) said, "You praised him yesterday, but are defaming him today." The man said, "By Allah, I told the truth about him yesterday and have not lied about him today. He pleased me yesterday, so I told the best I knew of him. But today he angered me, so I spoke the worst I knew of him." The Prophet (ṣ) said, "There is certainly sorcery in oratory." In another *ḥadīth*, he said, "Oratory and harshness are two branches of hypocrisy." And in another, "Allah hates argumentation for you—all argumentation." Imam al-Shāfi'ī said, "There is no Muslim who obeys Allah and at the same time does not obey Him. And there is no Muslim who disobeys Allah and at the same time does not disobey Him. He whose virtues are more than his sins is righteous." He, moreover, should not be suspicious about his friend, because this is the backbiting of the heart, which is prohibited. The Prophet (ṣ) said, "Allah made unlawful four things for a believer—to shed the blood of a believer, to destroy his properties, to mar his honour and to harbour evil conjectures against him. The Prophet (ṣ) said, "Beware of suspicion, because suspicion is the most untruthful report, and it leads to prying and spying." He also said, "Do not disclose each other's secrets, do not seek out each other's secrets and do not cut off each other's ties, but unite the servants of Allah in brotherhood." Allah is content with someone who imbues himself with divine attributes, as He is the Keeper of secrets, Pardoner of sins and Kind to His servants. So how can you fail to be indulgent towards someone who is above you or who is lower than you?

ʿĪsā said to his disciples, "What do you do when the wind blows off the clothes of your friends in his sleep and makes him naked?" They said, "We screen his private parts." He said, "Rather, you uncover his private parts." They said, "Glory to Allah, who would do such a thing?" He said, "When any you hears a secret about his brother, he adds to it other words and discloses it in an exaggerated form."

Know that the faith of a man is incomplete until he loves for others what he loves for himself. The lowest degree of friendship is where one treats one's brother as one would like to be treated. Allah says, "Woe to the defrauders, who, when they take the measure (of their dues) from men take it fully, but when they measure out to others or weigh out for them, they are deficient" (Qur'an, 83:1-3).

The Prophet (ṣ) said, "If a man conceals the faults of his brother in this world, Allah will conceal his faults in the next." And in another version, "… it is as if he restores the life of a baby girl buried alive." He also said, "The discussions of all assemblies are confidential except for three assemblies: an assembly where unlawful murders are committed, an assembly where fornication is made lawful and an assembly where wealth is unlawfully used." The Prophet (ṣ) said, "The consultations of two friends are like a trust. It is unlawful to disclose to another what they do not like."

A wise man was asked, "How can you keep a secret?" He said, "I am their tomb." A saying goes, "The heart of a fool is in his tongue, and the tongue of a wise man is in his heart." That is, a fool cannot keep secret what is in his heart, but discloses it where he does not know.

Al-'Abbās said to his son 'Abdullāh, "I see 'Umar preferring you to the elderly Companions. So remember five pieces of advice from me: do not disclose secrets to him; do not vilify in his presence; do not give currency to a lie about him; do not disobey his orders; and do not let him not see you committing any act of treachery." Al-Sha'bī said, "Every word of these five is better than a thousand."

Ibn 'Abbās said, "Do not argue with a fool lest he give you trouble. And do not argue with a wise man, lest he envy you." The Prophet (ṣ) said, "If a man refrains from disputing over something insignificant, a house will be built for him in a corner of paradise. If a man refrains from disputing over a matter when he is in the right, a house will be built for him in a lofty place in paradise." The Prophet (ṣ) said, "Do not envy one another, nor cut off ties with one another, but establish brotherhood among the servants of Allah. A Muslim is a brother to another Muslim. He does not oppress him, deprive him or dishonour him." Abū Umāmah al-Bāhilī said, "The Prophet (ṣ) once came to us while we were arguing with one another. He got enraged and said, 'Give up arguing, as there is little good in it. Give up dispute, as it has little benefit and it creates enmity between two friends." A wise man said, "If a man disputes with his friends, he loses his chivalry and honour." The Prophet (ṣ) also said, "Do not dispute with your brother, do not ridicule him and do not break promises with him." He also said, "You give in charity ample wealth to people, but it is not given cheerfully and with proper manners."

The fourth duty is to treat a friend well in word and deed. Just as brotherhood required silence about unpleasant things, so it calls for speaking of favourable things. One should use words of love and share one's sorrows and happinesses. The Prophet (ṣ) said, "When one of you loves his brother, he should tell him" because it increases love. If a friend knows that one loves him, he will surely reciprocate that love. And when one comes to know that one's friend also loves one, one's love for him will increase. So love will increase from both sides.

The existence of love among believers is the object of Sharī'ah and religion. Thus, presents should be given to one another. In this connection, the Prophet (ṣ) said, "Give presents to one another and you will love one another." The Prophet (ṣ) compared two friends to two hands, one of which works for the other. In other words, one friend helps another in all his affairs. The Prophet (ṣ) said, "A Muslim is a brother to another Muslim. He does not treat him badly; he does not forsake him or betray him."

In addition, one should not backbite one's friend, as Allah likens backbiting to eating the flesh of a dead brother: "Does one of you like to eat the flesh of his dead brother?" (Qur'an, 49:12). The angel who provides sensory representation of what the soul has learnt from the Guarded Tablet symbolises backbiting in the form of eating carrion. Thus, if someone has such a dream, it means that he roams about backbiting. Mujāhid said, "Do not backbite your friend, as you wish that nobody would backbite you."

The Prophet (ṣ) said, "Treat your neighbour well and you will be a good Muslim." Treat your companion well and you will be a believer." He also said, "A believer is the mirror of another believer. The substance of this *ḥadīth* is that one should conduct oneself in such a way that one's friend may correct himself by looking at one's actions. Mus'ir was asked, "Do you love someone who tells you your faults?" He said, "If he advises me with regard to the faults that are in myself and him, it is good, but when he defames me before a party of men, it is not good." What he said is true, because to advise him before others is ignominy. The saint Dhū al-Nūn said, "Do not keep the company of Allah without obeying His commands; the company of people without advising one another; the company of your passion without opposing it; and the company of the Devil without being his enemy." 'Umar said, "If a man holds out the faults of his brother before him, Allah will show kindness to him." For this reason, 'Umar said to Salmān, "What actions of mine do you disapprove of?" Since he insisted, Salmān said, "I heard that you have two shirts, one of which you wear during the day and the other at night. I heard also that two kinds of curries are served before you at the same time." 'Umar said, "Neither of these is true. Have you heard any other thing?" Salmān said, "No." Ḥudhayfah al-Mar'ashī wrote to Yūsuf ibn Asbāṭ, "I heard that you sold your religion for two grams. You said to the milkman, 'What is its price?' He said, 'One sixth.' You pressed for a lower price until the milkman said, 'Let it be so.' The man was cognisant of your God-fearingness and so he sold the milk to you at a reduced price. Uncover your head from the screen of passion and give up the urge of passion."

The fifth duty is to forgive the faults of friends. If a friend commits a sin and persists in it, one should advise him with kind words. If he desists, it is better. If he does not, one should cut off relations according to Abū Dharr. According to Abū al-Dardā', relations with him should not be cut off, as he walk sometimes on a straight path and at other times on a crooked path. Ibrāhīm al-Nakha'ī said, "Do not cut off relations with your friend and do not leave him when he commits a sin, as he may commit a sin today and give it up the following day." A *ḥadīth* says, "Fear the slip of a scholar. Do not boycott him, but hope for his return."

A friend of 'Umar went to Syria and stayed there for a long time. 'Umar was informed of this by a man from Syria. He also said to 'Umar, "He has become the brother of the Devil and begun to drink wine." 'Umar wrote to him, "In the name of Allah, the Beneficent, the Merciful. Ḥā Mīm. The revelation of the Book is from Allah, the Mighty, the Knowing. The Forgiver of the faults and the Acceptor of repentance, Severe to punish" (Qur'an, 40:1-3), rebuked him with this verse. When his friend read it, he wept and said, "Allah speaks the truth. 'Umar advised me truly. He then repented and came back."

It has been related that one of two friends fell in love with a woman and told the other friend, who said, "If you wish, you may cut off relations with me." He said, "Should I lose a friend on account of this one sin?" Then he promised that he would fast until his friend fell out of love with the woman. He fasted for forty days, as a result of which his friend's love for the woman left his heart. Then he ate and drank again.

It has also been related that two friends of the children of Israel were performing acts of worship on a hill. One day, one of them got down and went to a market to buy meat. He saw there an unchaste woman and fell in love with her. He took her to a private place and satisfied his lust. This continued for three days. His friend on the hill came down to search for him and found him following a woman. He embraced and kissed his friend and said, "I have come to know of your condition. Now let us go to the hill to worship." Repentant, his friend went with him to the hill.

One should not cut off relations with a relative who is seen engaged in a sin. Allah said to His Prophet (ṣ) in connection with his relatives, "But if they disobey you, then say, 'Surely I am clear of what you do'" (Qur'an, 26:216). He did not order the Prophet (ṣ) to say, "I am clear of *you*." When Abū al-Dardā' was asked, "Why do you not hate your friend who is doing this sin?" He said, "Surely, I hate his sin, but how can I hate him when he is my brother in religion?" The brotherhood in religion is firmer than brotherhood in kinship." A wise man was asked, "Who is dearer to you, a friend or a brother?" He said, "If my brother is my friend, he is dearer to me."Al-Ḥasan said, "Many a friend was not born of your mother."

It has therefore been said that kinship needs love, but love does not need kinship. Ja'far al-Ṣādiq said, "A day's love is a connection, a month's love is a kinship and a year's love is a blood tie. If anyone cuts it, Allah will cut him off." It is compulsory, then, to keep the tie of friendship. One should not, however, befriend a great sinner from the outset. But if one does, one should not cut him off. The Prophet (ṣ) said, "The worst of Allah's creatures are those who roam with slander, separating friendships." Once, a man committed a sin, and his friend rebuked him. The Prophet (ṣ) then said to him, "Stop, do not rebuke him. Do not aid the Devil against your friend." So it is better to keep away from great sinners from the start than to sever the friendship after. Imam al-Shāfi'ī said, "If a man is provoked but does not get angry, he is an ass." If a man has cause for pleasure but is not pleased, he is a devil." So do not be an ass or a devil. Rather, be your friend's deputy and be pleased with yourself. And beware of being a devil by not accepting it. A wise man said, "I never rebuked anybody, because if an honourable man rebukes me, I pardon his fault, as it is pardonable. But if a dishonourable man rebukes me, I save myself from his attack without replying to his rebuke." And whenever a friend offers an excuse, one should accept it, be it true of false. The Prophet (ṣ) said, "He who does not accept the excuse of his friend commits a sin like that of the tax collector in the street."

The Prophet (ṣ) also said, "A believer suddenly gets angry, but his anger is soon appeased." He did not say that he does not get angry. Similarly, Allah says, "Those who restrain (their) anger" (Qur'an, 3:134), not, "Those who *lose* their anger." To remove anger from the soil of heart is not possible, as it is an essential attribute of man. But to appease it and to act contrary to its nature is possible. To act in agreement with anger is to take retaliation. The Prophet (ṣ) said, "Be moderate in loving your friend; he may become your enemy someday. Be moderate in getting angry at your enemy; he may become your friend someday." 'Umar said, "Let not your love exceed the limit, and let not your hatred lead you to the path of destruction."

The sixth duty is to pray for one's friend in his lifetime and even after his death. Just as one likes to pray for oneself and one's family members, so one should pray for those whom one's friend had ties with after his death. The Prophet (ṣ) said, "If a man prays for his friend in his absence, the angels says, 'A similar prayer for you.' In another version, the words are '... Allah says, O My servant, I begin with you My slave.'" A *ḥadīth* says, "A man's prayer for his friend is better accepted than his payer for himself." The Prophet (ṣ) said, "If a man prays for his friend in his absence, it is not rejected."

After your death, a good friend will follow one with the angles, as there is a *ḥadīth* which says, "When a man dies, the people say, 'What possessions has he left behind?' but the angels say, 'What has he achieved?' They rejoice in his achievements, ask about his condition and intercede for him." He also said, "A dead man in a grave is like a drowning man in water. Just as a drowning man catches whatever he gets to save his life, so a dead man remains anxious to receive the supplication of his father, children, brothers, friend and near relatives." The prayer of a living man enters into the grave of a dead man like a hill of light. A sage said, "The prayer of a living man for the dead is like a present. The angel takes a tray of light to the dead man and says, 'This is a present to you from your friend so-and-so. This has come from your relative so-and-so.' He then rejoiced in it as a living man rejoiced in a present."

The seventh duty is loyalty and sincerity. Loyalty means to remain steadfast in friendship, to keep it until the death of one's friend and after his death with his wife, children, friends and relatives and to take care of them. Sincerity means to fulfil selflessly the duties of friendship for the sake of Allah, the object of which is to gain benefit in the next world. The Prophet (ṣ) said that seven people will be shaded under the shade of the Throne on Resurrection Day. Two of them are men who love each other for the sake of Allah. It is also related that a woman once came to the Prophet (ṣ), who showed respect to her. Asked why, the Prophet (ṣ) said, "This woman used to come to our house during the lifetime of Khadījah. Honouring the right of friendship appertains to faith."

Satan exerts himself to spoil what is between two brothers joined in brotherhood and love for the sake of Allah. Allah says, "Say to My servants (that) they speak that which is best; surely Satan sows dissensions among them" (Qur'an, 17:53). He also says in the story of Yūsuf, "After Satan had sown dissensions between me and my brothers" (Qur'an, 12:100).

Friendship becomes lasting when it is done for the sake of Allah. If one establishes friendship for a certain purpose, it ends when the purpose is fulfilled. The result of friendship for Allah is that envy, whether temporal or spiritual, cannot exist with it. Allah says of this love for Him, "(They) do not find in their hearts a need of what they are given and prefer (them) before themselves" (Qur'an, 59:9). Finding a need here means envy.

The eight duty is not to trouble a friend. One should not ask for any his wealth or possessions, hope to get any benefit from his name and fame or tell him, "Take care of me and fulfil your duties to me." One should rather hope for the rewards of his prayer, meet with him, help in his religious duties and seek the nearness of Allah by fulfilling one's duties to him. A wise man said, "A friend who places his honour above the honour of his friend and thinks himself superior to his friend, commits a sin and allows another to commit it. The man who considers his friend as his equal suffers mental agony. The man who considers himself inferior to his friend keeps himself and his friend safe." 'Ā'ishah said, "A believer is a brother to another believer. He neither plunders him, nor embarrasses him.

Al-Junayd said, "I kept the company of four classes of Sufis, thirty men in each class: al-Ḥārith al-Muḥāsibī and his class, al-Ḥasan al-Masūḥī and his class, al-Sarī al-Saqaṭī and his class, Ibn al-Karībī and his class. Those of them who made friends for the sake of Allah did not trouble one another and did not keep the company of one another without any reason." A sage said, "Behave politely with the people of this world. Behave wisely with the people of the next world. Behave as you wish with the God-fearing."

Know, dear readers, that there are three classes of people: one from whom a person can benefit; one whom he can benefit, but who will harm him and from whom he cannot benefit; and one whom he cannot benefit, but who will harm him, namely fools and ill-tempered people. He should not avoid the second class of people, as they will benefit him in the next world by their intercession and invocation. Allah revealed to Mūsā, "If you obey Me, you will have many friends." In other words, "If you show sympathy to them, suffer them and do not hate them and you will have many friends." A wise man said, "The love of someone who is not ostentatious is lasting." A Companion said, "Allah curses those who trouble others." The Prophet (ṣ) said, "I and the God-fearing men of my followers are free from troubling others." A wise man said, "When a man does four things in the house of his friend his love becomes complete: if he eats with him, uses his toilet, prays and sleeps." He also said, "A man is on a par with the religion of his friend. And there is no good in keeping the company of a friend who does not consider good for his friend what he considers good for himself."

A person should look at his friend with the look of love, so that he can know your love, and he should look at his good deeds and not his faults. It has been related that the Prophet (ṣ) showed his face to whoever sat with him, and each man thought that the Prophet (ṣ) honoured him the most. His sitting, his hearing, and his kind enquiring were all for his Companion. His assembly was that of shame, humility, modesty and trust. He wore a smile before his Companions and was satisfied with what the Companion was satisfied with.

Summary of duties to friends

If you want good company, meet your friends and enemies with a smiling countenance and do not dishonour them, without undue humility or fear, with dignity free of arrogance and with modesty short of abjection. Adopt a middle course in all your dealing, as both extremes of conduct are blameworthy.

Do not keep turning this way and that. Do not look at anything for a long time. Do not keep standing in the assembly of many men. When you sit, sit comfortably and do not make sounds with your fingers, play with your beard or ring, pick your teeth or nose, spit much, blow your nose much, drive away flies much and yawn much in people's faces during prayer and at other times.

Let your sitting be still and your speech orderly. Use good words with someone with whom you are having a discussion, without showing too much astonishment. Do not ask him to repeat himself.

Be silent near those who arouse laughter and tell stories. Do not talk about your satisfaction with your children, servants, poetry, composition, books and other things.

Do not engage yourself in telling stories like servants and slaves. Do not use oil or antimony in great quantity.

Do not relieve yourself off and on. Do not call an oppressor "brave."

Do not keep your wife and children informed of how much wealth you have because if they consider it small, you will feel humiliated, and if they consider it much, you will not be able to satisfy them. Put them in fear without being harsh, and be gentle to them without weakness.

Do not joke with servants or else you will lose their respect. Be honourable during disputes, and beware of your ignorance. Give up haste and consider your proof. Do not gesture much with your hand or look at those behind you. Do not sit on your knees. Speak when anger has subsided.

If a ruler appoints you as one of his near advisers, be with him as if on the tip of a spear. If he laughs with you, you have no guarantee that he will not turn against you. Treat him like a boy, and say things to please him, provided they are not sinful. If he shows kindness to you, do not treat his wife and children unjustly.

Be careful of a fair-weather friend, as he is the greatest enemy.

Do not honour your wealth more than yourself.

When you enter an assembly, salute them first. Do not go in front of someone who goes forward. Sit wherever you find a space. Greet those who come to you when you sit. Do not sit in the middle of the pathway. When you sit, close your eyes, help the oppressed and the weak, direct the misguided, return greetings, give charity to beggars, enjoin good and forbid evil, spit in its proper place, not towards the direction of prayer or to the right or left, but under your left foot.

Do not sit with kings and rulers. If you do, avoid backbiting and falsehood, guard secrets, speak very little to them about your needs, speak to them with using the words of a gentleman and mention their qualities. Do not joke with them, nor fear them too much. If their love for you is expressed, it is better. Do not yawn before them and do not pick your teeth after a meal. Hear every word they have to say, but do not divulge secrets or attempt to impress his entourage.

Do not sit with people in general. If you do, avoid useless talks and be indifferent to their evil words. Meet with them rarely, even in times of necessity.

Joke neither with the intelligent nor with fools, as the former will hate you and the latter will oppose you. When you jest, fear departs, honour is lost, hatred increases, the sweetness of affection goes away, the wisdom of the wise becomes marred, fools become bold, your standing with the wise lowers, the God-fearing dislike it, the heart dies, you become distant from Allah and you become careless. The Prophet (ṣ) said, "If a man sits in an assembly where much useless talks are held and says before he gets up therefrom, 'Glory to Allah. O Allah, Yours is all praise. I bear witness that there is no deity but You. I seek Your forgiveness and turn to You,' Allah will forgive him for the sins he committed in that assembly."

3

Duties to a Muslim

The following duties have come in the Qur'an and Ḥadīth.

The first duty is that, when you meet a Muslim, greet him; when he invites you, accept his invitation; when he sneezes, bless him; when he falls ill, visit him; when he dies, join his funeral prayer; when he seeks your advice, give him advice; and when he is absent, guard his possessions. Love for him what you love for yourself; do not love for him what you do not love for yourself The Prophet (ṣ) said, "You have four duties: to help the pious, to seek forgiveness for sinners, to pray for the welfare of the unfortunate and to love those who repent." Explaining Allah's words "Compassionate among themselves" (Qur'an, 48:29), Ibn 'Abbās said, "The pious among them seek forgiveness for the sinners. When a sinner among the Muslims looks at a pious man, the latter should say, 'O Allah, bless him in the good of which you have decreed for him, keep him firm over it, and benefit him thereby.' When a pious man looks at a sinner among them, he should pray for him thus: 'O Allah, give him guidance, accept his repentance, and forgive his sins.'"

The second duty is to love for the believers what you love for yourself, and dislike for the believers what you dislike for yourself. The Prophet (ṣ) said, "The Muslim society is like a body in respect of mutual love and sympathy. If a limb of the body suffers pain, the whole body responds to it by sleeplessness and fever." He also said, "A believer is like a building to another believer, a building whose portion strengthens another portion."

The third duty is not to trouble a Muslim by word or deed. The Prophet (ṣ) said, "A Muslim is he from whose tongue and hands other Muslims remain safe." In a long sermon in which he advised people to do good deeds, he said, "If you are unable to do that, then advise people to give up evil, because this will be considered an act of charity for you." He once asked, "Do you know who a Muslim is?" The Companions replied, "Allah and His Messenger know best." He said, "A Muslim is he from whose tongue and hands other Muslims are safe, and a believer is he in whose hand the lives and possessions of believers remain safe." The Companions asked, "Who is a refugee?" He said, "He who gives up sin." A man once asked, "What is Islam?" The Prophet (ṣ) replied, "That you surrender your heart to Allah, and that Muslims remain safe from your tongue and hands." The Prophet (ṣ) said, "I saw a man loitering freely in paradise as a reward for cutting a tree which was obstructing the path of Muslims." One day, Abū Hurayrah asked the Prophet (ṣ), "O Messenger of Allah, give me some advice which will benefit me." The Prophet (ṣ) answered, "Remove injurious things from the path of Muslims." Similarly, the Prophet (ṣ) said, "If a man removes an injurious thing from the path of Muslims, Allah writes for him a virtue, and paradise is sure for someone for whom Allah writes a virtue." He also said, "It is unlawful for a Muslim to give another Muslim a look which troubles his heart," "It is unlawful for a Muslim to threaten another Muslim with fear," and "Allah does not like that believers be troubled."

The fourth duty is to be modest towards every Muslim, not to treat him harshly, and not to be arrogant towards him, as Allah does not love the arrogant. The Prophet (ṣ) said, "Allah revealed to me, 'Be modest towards one another and do not be arrogant towards one another.'" If anybody shows you pride, keep patient. Allah ordered the Prophet (ṣ), "Take to forgiveness and enjoin good and turn aside from the ignorant" (Qur'an, 7:199). The

Prophet (ṣ) was modest towards every Muslim, was not harsh to them, and did not dislike to do the necessary tasks of the poor and the widows.

The fifth duty is not to listen to backbiting and not to spread it. The Prophet (ṣ) said, "A backbiter will not enter paradise."

The sixth duty is to give up disputes and quarrels. When you get angry with another, do not ignore him for more than three days, for the Prophet (ṣ) said, "It is unlawful for a Muslim to remain aloof from his brother for more than three days, and he should not turn away his face from him if both of them meet. The better of the two is he who greets first." He also said, "If a man pardons the faults of a Muslim, Allah will forgive his faults on Resurrection Day. 'Ā'ishah said, "The Prophet (ṣ) never took revenge for personal wrongs." The Prophet (ṣ) said, "Wealth does not decrease by charity. Allah does not increase someone who pardons except in honour. Allah raises a man who becomes modest for the sake of Allah."

The seventh duty is to do good to everyone, be he deserving or undeserving. The Prophet (ṣ) said, "Do good to everyone, pious or impious." If you do good to someone who is fit to receive it, it is good. If he is not fit to receive it, you are fit to do good. The Prophet (ṣ) also said, "The root of wisdom after religion is to love men and to do good to everyone, pious or impious." Abū Hurayrah said that the Prophet (ṣ) did not withdraw his hand from another till the latter withdrew his own hand.

The eighth duty is to treat everyone well and speak to everyone according to his intellect. If you meet an illiterate person with words of wisdom and with theology and dispute with fools, you will get trouble.

The ninth duty is to honour the dead and show affection to the youth. The Prophet (ṣ) said, "He who does not show affection to our youth is not of us." He also said, "To honour an aged Muslim is to honour Allah." The honour of an aged man does not become complete if someone talks with others of the party without his permission. Jābir said, "A deputation of the Juhaynah tribe once came to the Prophet (ṣ). A young man among them stood on their behalf to talk to the Prophet (ṣ). The Prophet (ṣ) said, 'Stop! Where is your aged man?'" The Prophet (ṣ) said, "If a young man shows an aged man honour, Allah will create for him in his old age someone who will show him honour." This means that he will live to be old. So if you show the aged honour, Allah will prolong your life. The Prophet (ṣ) said that the Hour will not come until a son gets angry at his parents, there is profuse rain, backbiters emerge from every place, the honourable will be unseen, the youth will not show the aged honour, and the wrongdoers do not wrong the honourable. So treat boys affectionately, as was habit of the Prophet (ṣ). Whenever the Prophet (ṣ) returned from a journey, boys used to meet him, and he would wait for them, standing before them. He, moreover, used to sit some boys in front of him and some behind him, and he used to put on his lap little children, some of whom urinated on his clothes.

The tenth duty is to live among men with a smiling face and a kind heart. The Prophet (ṣ) said, "Do you know for whom hell has been made unlawful?" The Companions said, "Allah and His Messenger know best." He said, "Those who are modest, simple, and neighbours of Allah." Similarly, he said, "Allah loves the simple and those having smiling countenances." A man once asked the Prophet (ṣ), "O Messenger of Allah, show me an action which will send me to paradise." He said, "To greet and to speak kind words are causes for forgiveness." Similarly, he said, "Save yourself from the fire of hell by giving charity, even if only half a dried-grape seed. If you cannot, save yourself with a kind word." He also said, "There are rooms in paradise whose inner sides can be seen from the outer sides." A desert Arab asked, "O Prophet of Allah, for whom are these rooms ?" He said, "For those who use kind words, give food and remain busy with prayers when the people are asleep." The Prophet (ṣ) advised Mu'ādh ibn Jabal, saying,

"Fear Allah, tell the truth, fulfil promises, do not break trusts, take care of neighbours, show kindness to orphans, be modest in talk, greet with *al-salām* and spread peace." Anas said, "A poor woman came to the Prophet (ṣ) and said, 'I need something from you.' Some companions were then present there. He said, 'Sit down in this lane; I shall also sit with you.' She sat down, and the Prophet (ṣ) also did so. She then said to the Prophet (ṣ) what she had to say."

The eleventh duty is to fulfil promises with Muslims. The Prophet (ṣ) said, "Promises are like charity." He also said, "The signs of a hypocrite are three: when he promises, he breaks it; when he speaks, he speaks lies; and when he is entrusted with a thing, he does not return it." Likewise, he said, "He who has these signs is a hypocrite, even if he prays and fasts."

The twelfth duty is to do justice to the people willingly and give them what they love. The Prophet (ṣ) said, "Whoever does not have these three qualities, his faith is incomplete: to spend till he becomes poor, to do justice to himself, and to greet with *al-salām*." He also said, "He who hopes to keep Hell distant and to enter paradise should testify at the time of death that there is no deity but Allah and Muḥammad is the messenger of Allah, and he should treat people in the same way he wants them to treat him." Similarly, he said, "O Abū al-Dardā', treat your neighbour well and you will be a believer; love for men what you love for yourself and you will be a Muslim." Mūsā asked Allah, "O Lord, who is the justest among Your servants?" He said, "That servant who is the justest to himself."

The thirteenth duty is to honour those to whom honour is due. Honour someone who is understood to be honourable in rank from his nature, conduct, appearance, and dress. It is reported that when 'Ā'ishah was in her tent during a journey, a beggar came to her when food was served to her and begged for some food. 'Ā'ishah said, "Give him a piece of bread." Thereafter, a man came to her riding a horse. 'Ā'ishah said, "Invite him to this feast." She was asked, "You gave bread to the beggar, while you called the horseman to a feast. What is the reason?" 'Ā'ishah said, "Allah has given different people different ranks. We should entertain them according to their ranks. This poor man will be pleased with a piece of bread, but to give to this rich man a piece of bread is a breach of etiquette." It has also been reported that the Prophet (ṣ) once entered a room, and the people came there, filling up the room. Then Jarīr ibn 'Abdullāh, the chief of the tribe, came there, but finding no place to sit, he sat by the door. When the Prophet (ṣ) gave him his shirt to sit on, he began to kiss it and then handed it over to the Prophet (ṣ), saying, "May Allah honour you, as you have honoured me." The Prophet (ṣ) said, "Whenever an honourable man of a people comes to you, honour him." The foster mother of the Prophet (ṣ) once came to him, and the Prophet (ṣ) gave her his own shirt to her to sit on, saying, "Mother, you are welcome. Your intercession will be accepted, and you will be given what you want." She said, "I intercede for my own people." The Prophet (ṣ) said, "You are the owner of my dues and the dues of the people of the Hashemite dynasty." Then he gave to her the entire booty gained in the battle of Ḥunayn, which she sold to 'Uthmān ibn 'Affān for a hundred thousand dirhams.

The fourteenth duty is to settle disputes among Muslims if you are able. The Prophet (ṣ) said, "Shall I not inform you of a rank greater than that of prayer, fasting and *zakāh*?" The Companions answered, "Indeed." The Prophet (ṣ) said, "It is to settle disputes, which, between two people, is destructive. He also said, "To settle a dispute between two people is the best charity"; "Fear Allah and settle disputes among you and He will settle disputes among believers; "He who settles a dispute between two people is not a great liar"; and "Every lie is recorded except three: the lie of a man in war, as it is deception; the lie of a man to settle a dispute between two people; and the lie of husband to please his wife."

The fifteenth duty is to keep the secrets of Muslims secret. The Prophet (ṣ) said, "If a man keeps the faults of a Muslims secret,

Allah will keep his faults secret both in this world and in the next"; "If a man keeps the sin of a man secret in this world, Allah will keep all of his sins secret on Resurrection Day"; and "If a believer keeps the fault of his brother secret, he will enter paradise." When Mu'ādh ibn Anas disclosed his fornication to the Prophet (ṣ), the latter said, "Had you kept it concealed under your cloth, it would have been better." Abū Bakr said, "If I see a drunkard, I hope in my heart that Allah will keep his sin secret." One night, 'Umar went out in the city in disguise and saw a man and a woman fornicating. In the morning, he told the people, "What is your opinion about a leader who sees a man and a woman committing fornication and then metes out to them the punishment prescribed in the Qur'an?" They said, "You are a ruler. You have freedom in this action." 'Alī said, "Punishment in this case is unlawful. In fact, you are to suffer a punishment for this slander, for the punishment for fornication cannot be meted out without the evidence of four people." After this, 'Umar kept silent for some days. Again, he questioned them, and they replied as before. He eventually became inclined towards the opinion of 'Alī and decided not to mete out the punishment. This is a good proof that the sins of Muslims should be kept secret and that four eyewitnesses are necessary for capital punishment for fornication, which is practically impossible in the case of sexual intercourse.

The Prophet (ṣ) said, "If Allah keeps a sin of a person secret in this world, He is more generous than to disclose it in the next world." 'Abd al-Raḥmān ibn 'Awf said, "One night, we went out with 'Umar secretly to travel in the city of Madīnah. We saw a light in a house and proceeded towards it. When we came near, we found that, behind a closed door Rabī'ah ibn Umayyah was intoxicated from drinking wine. I said, 'Do not spy.' So 'Umar desisted." The Prophet (ṣ) said to Mu'āwiyah, "If you enquire into the secrets of people, you will ruin them." He likewise said, "O people who have faith by tongue but in whose hearts the light of Islam has not yet entered, do not backbite Muslims and do not roam about enquiring into their secrets, for he who roams about enquiring into the secrets of his brother, Allah will enquire into his secrets, and he whose secrets He follows, He humiliates, even if he remains in his house." Abū Bakr al-Ṣiddīq said, "If I see anybody commit an offense, I will not arrest him, nor will I tell anybody to arrest him until someone else is with me." A wise man said, "As I was sitting with ʿAbdullāh ibn Masʿūd one day, a man brought another man to him, saying 'This man is a drunkard.' ʿAbdullāh said, 'Smell his mouth.' They smelled his mouth, and it was found that he drank wine. After arresting and whipping him, ʿAbdullāh asked the man who brought him, 'Is this man your relative?' to which he replied, 'I am his uncle.' ʿAbdullāh said, 'You have neither taught him good manners, nor kept his sin secret. When any sin of a person is mentioned to a ruler, he has no other alternative but to punish him. Allah is forgiving and loves forgiveness.' Then he recited, 'They should pardon and turn away' (Qur'an, 24:22) and said, 'I shall tell you about a thief who was brought to the Prophet (ṣ) for the first time. He ordered the severing of his hands, and they were cut off. But then the colour of his face changed at this. The Companions asked, 'Are you dissatisfied with the severing of his hands?' He said, 'Why should I not be? Do not be helpers of the Devil against your brothers.' The Companions asked, 'Then why have you not forgiven him?' He said, 'When a man is brought to a ruler for committing a crime, it becomes compulsory for the ruler to inflict the prescribed punishment on him. Allah is forgiving and loves forgiveness.' Then he recited, 'They should pardon and turn away. Do you not love that Allah should forgive you? And Allah is Forgiving, Merciful' (Qur'an, 24:22)."

One night, while ʿUmar was going to the city, he heard the sounds of songs in a house. He scaled over the wall and found that there was a woman with them and a pot of wine near a man. He said, "O enemy of Allah, did you think that Allah would keep your sin concealed?" He said, "O Commander of the Faithful, you have come yourself! Do not be hasty in judgement. I committed one sin this time, but you have committed three sins. Allah says, 'Do not spy' (Qur'an, 49:12), but you have spied, thus committing a sin. Allah says, 'It is not righteousness that you should enter the houses at their backs' (Qur'an, 2:189), but you have scaled the wall, thus committing another sin. Allah says, 'Do not enter houses other than your own houses until you have asked permission and saluted their inmates' (Qur'an, 24:27), but you have entered my house without permission and greeting." 'Umar said, "If I pardon you, will it do any good to you?" He said, "By Allah, O Commander of the Faithful, it will do me good. If you pardon me, I will never do it again." So he pardoned him and went away.

The Prophet (ṣ) said, "Allah will take a believer near Him, spread His mercy on him and keep his faults secret on Resurrection Day. He will say, 'O My servant, I have kept them secret for you in the world and wish to pardon you today.' Then the book of good deeds will be given to him." He also said, "Every one of my followers will be forgiven except he who commits sins and then discloses them" and "If a person secretly hears the news of a people secretly, and the latter dislike this, molten brass will be put into their ears on Resurrection Day."

The sixteenth duty is to keep away from places of slander and backbiting so that people's minds remain free from evil ideas about you. Allah says, "Do not abuse those whom they call upon besides Allah, lest exceeding the limits they should abuse Allah out of ignorance" (Qur'an, 6:108). The Prophet (ṣ) said, "Do you see a man who insults his parents?" The Companions said, "Is there anybody who insults his own parents?" He said, "Yes. A person insults the parents of others, who in turn insult his parents." In order to avoid the suspicion of others, one should not even talk with his wife on a public pathway. 'Umar once passed by a man who was talking with a woman on the road. When 'Umar was about to whip him, he said, "She is my wife." 'Umar said, "Why have you not talked with her in a place where people will not see you?"

The seventeenth duty is to intercede for everyone. With someone in authority, intercede to fulfil the needs of a Muslim. The Prophet (ṣ) said, "If any of you seeks something from me, I wish to give it to him at once, but if any of you remains near me, I like that he should intercede for him, as he gets rewards for that. So intercede and you will receive a reward. Allah does through His Prophet (ṣ) what He loves." Similarly, he said, "Intercede with me and you will get rewards. I delay doing something I wish to do, so that you may receive rewards by interceding for it." He also said, "No charity is better than oral charity?" He was asked, "What is oral charity ?" He said, "A just pleading which saves the life of a man, benefits him, or saves him from a calamity."

The eighteenth duty is to greet every Muslim before talking and to shake his hand when you greet him. The Prophet (ṣ) said, "Do not respond to someone who begins talking before greeting you until he greets you." A wise man said, "I once went to the Prophet (ṣ), but did not greet him and did not seek permission. The Prophet (ṣ) said, 'Go back and say, 'Peace be on you' and then enter.'" The Prophet (ṣ) said, "When you enter your house, greet its inmates, for when one of you greets, the Devil does not enter his house." Anas said, "I have been serving the Prophet (ṣ) for the last eight years. One day he said to me, 'O Anas, perform ablution well and your life will be prolonged. Greet any of my followers you meet and your rewards will increase. Greet the inmates of a house when you enter it, as that will be good for you.' He also said, 'When two believers meet and shake hands, seventy virtues are divided among them. Whichever of the two has a smiling, countenance will get sixty-nine of those virtues."

Allah says, "When you are greeted with a greeting, greet with a better (greeting) than it or return it" (Qur'an, 4:86). The Prophet (ṣ) said, "By Him in whose hand is my life, you will not enter paradise until you believe, and you will not believe until you love one another. Shall I not inform you of an action which will cause you to love one another?" The Companions said, "Yes,

O Messenger of Allah." He said, "Spread greetings among you." Likewise, he said, "When a Muslim greets another Muslim, and the latter answers it, the angels bless him seventy times." He also said, "Someone who is riding should greet someone who is sitting. When one of a party greets, it is sufficient for them."

It is recommended to shake hands when greeting. A man came to the Prophet (ṣ) and said, "Peace be on you." The Prophet (ṣ) said, "For him ten rewards have been written." Another man came and said, "Peace be on you, and Allah's mercy." The Prophet (ṣ) said, "For him twenty rewards have been written." Another came and said, "Peace be on you, and Allah's mercy and blessings." The Prophet (ṣ) said, "For him thirty rewards have been written." Anas used greet boys when passing by them.

The Prophet (ṣ) said, "Do not greet Jews and Christians first. If one of you meets any of them on a path, lead him to the narrow corner of the path." He also said, "Do not shake hands with non-Muslim subjects of the Islamic state (*ahl al-dhimmah*), nor greet them first. When you meet any of them, take him to a corner of the pathway." 'Ā'ishah said, "A party of the Jews came to the Prophet (ṣ) and said, 'Death be on you,' to which he replied, 'And on you.' I said, 'And on you be death and curses!' The Prophet (ṣ) then said, 'O 'Ā'ishah, Allah loves kindness in everything.' I said, 'Have you not heard what they said?' He said, 'I also said, 'And on you.'" The Prophet (ṣ) said, "The rider greets a pedestrian; a pedestrian greets someone who is seated; a small group greets a large group; and the young greet the old." He also said, "Do not follow Jews and Christians, because the greeting of Jews is a finger gesture and the greeting of Christians is clapping." Moreover, he said, "When a man reaches an assembly, he should greet them. When he deems it good to sit, he should sit. And when he leaves, he should greet them. The first man has no greater right than the last."

'Umar said, "I heard the Prophet (ṣ) say, 'When two Muslims meet, and one of them greets the other and shakes hands with him, a hundred mercies are showered on them, ninety for the one who greeted first and ten for the one who shakes hands.'" Al-Ḥasan said, "Shaking hands increases love." The Prophet (ṣ) said, "Handshakes among you completes greetings." He also said, "A handshake is akin to a Muslim's kissing his brother." There is no harm in kissing the hand of a religious man and an honourable man out of respect. Ibn 'Umar said, "We used to kiss the hands of the Prophet (ṣ)." A desert Arab once said to the Prophet (ṣ), "O Messenger of Allah, give me permission to kiss your head and hands." Upon being given permission, he kissed his head and hands."

Al-Barā' ibn 'Āzib said that when he had greeted the Prophet (ṣ) while the latter was performing ablution, he did not respond until he had finished his ablution. After the Prophet (ṣ) returned his greeting and shaking his hand, al-Barā' said, "This is the practice of foreigners," to which the Prophet (ṣ) replied, "When two Muslims meet and shake hands, their sins fall."

It is unlawful to bow the head when greeting. Anas said, "We asked the Prophet (ṣ), 'O Messenger of Allah, should we bow our heads to one another?' He said, 'No.' We asked, 'Should we kiss one another?' He said, 'No.' We asked, 'Should we shake hands with one another?' He said, 'Yes.'" Abū Dharr said, "Whenever I met the Prophet (ṣ), he shook hands with me. Once, during my absence, he enquired about me. When I heard of this, I went to him and found him sitting on a bed. He got up and embraced me." This shows that embracing is good. It is offensive to stand up for a man, thinking him great; but it is not offensive to stand in his honour." Anas said that nobody was dearer to the Companions than the Prophet (ṣ). When they saw him, they would not stand up, because they knew that the Prophet (ṣ) disliked it. The Prophet (ṣ) once said to them, "When you see me, do not stand up as foreigners do." He also said, "Let he who is pleased with the standing of others for him seek his abode in hell." Furthermore, he said, "Let nobody take the seat of another person after asking him to get up. Rather, he should make it spacious." Similarly, he said, "When any of you meets his brother, let him say, 'Peace be on you, and Allah's mercy.' If he does not find a place to sit after greeting, let him not leave, but rather take a seat behind the rows." Finally, he said, "If two Muslims shake hands with each other after meeting, Allah forgives them before they part."

The nineteenth duty is to help the distressed. Protect your Muslim brother's honour, wealth, and life from being oppressed by others and help him, because it is binding on you on account of the brotherhood of Islam. Once, a man abused another before the Prophet (ṣ), then another man defended him. Thereupon, the Prophet (ṣ) said, "If a man defends the honour of his Muslim brother, it screens him off from hell." Similarly, he said, "If a Muslim defends the honour of another Muslim, it becomes the duty of Allah to defend him from the fire of hell on Resurrection Day." The Prophet (ṣ) also said, "If a Muslim is mentioned before his brother, and the latter does not help him in spite of being able to do so, Allah will arrest him in this world and the next. If a Muslim is mentioned before his brother, and the latter helps him, Allah will help him in this world and the next." He likewise said, "If a Muslim keeps alive the honour of his Muslim brother in this world, Allah will send to him an angel on Resurrection day to save him from the fire of hell." He also said, "If a Muslim helps his Muslim brother when his honour is at stake, Allah will help him when he depends on Him for His help. On the other hand, if a Muslim is about to disgrace his Muslim brother, and if another Muslim does not help him to the extent of his ability and shows no sympathy, Allah will disgrace and dishonour him in a situation in which he requires help."

The twentieth duty is to respond to someone's sneezing. The Prophet (ṣ) said, "Someone who sneezes should say, 'Praise to Allah in all circumstances.' Someone who hears this should say, 'Allah have mercy on you.' The one who sneezed should then say, 'Allah guide you and rectify your condition.'" Once, the Prophet (ṣ) replied to a person who sneezed, but did not reply to another. When asked the reason, he said, "One praised Allah, and the other remained silent." The Prophet (ṣ) said, "When a Muslim sneezes thrice, respond to him. If he sneezes more than three times, it is a disease." When the Prophet (ṣ) sneezed, he would cover his mouth with his hand or cloth. The Jews once sneezed before the Prophet (ṣ) with the hope of getting the reply "Allah have mercy on you." But he would say, "Say, 'Allah guide you.'" The Prophet (ṣ) said, "Sneezing comes from Allah, and yawing from the Devil. So when any of you yawns, let him place his hand over his mouth." Mūsā said, "O Lord, are You near me, so that I may engage in intimate discourse with You? Or are You distant, so that I may speak loudly to You?" Allah said, "I am with whoever remembers Me." Mūsā said, "We are sometimes in such a condition that to remember You is impertinence, such as when we are impure or relieving ourselves." Allah said, "Remember me at all times."

The twenty-first duty is to help in times of distress and in calamities. Allah says, "Repel evil by what is best" (Qur'an, 23:96) and "They repel evil with good" (Qur'an, 28:54). Explaining this evil, Ibn 'Abbās said, "Those who repel harm and harsh treatment with peace and modesty." Regarding Allah's words "Were it not for Allah's repelling some men with others" (Qur'an, 2:251), Ibn 'Abbās said that the meaning of 'others' is a people with hope, fear, modesty, and humble behaviour. The Prophet (ṣ) said, "O 'Ā'ishah, the worst man on Resurrection Day will be a man whom the people forsook for fear of his harm." He also said, "If a man keeps patient to save his honour after hearing abusive words, it will be an act of charity for him."

The twenty-second duty is to avoid the company of the rich and be in the company of the poor and show kindness to the orphans. The Prophet (ṣ) said, "O Allah, let me live as a poor man, let me die as a poor man, and resurrect me with the poor." Whenever Sulaymān saw a poor man, he sat with him and said, "A poor man is sitting beside a poor man." It has been reported that nothing could please 'Īsā more than being addressed as a poor man. Al-Fuḍayl said, "I heard that a prophet said, 'O Lord, how can I know that You are pleased with me?' He said, 'Look for it when the poor are satisfied with you.'" The Prophet (ṣ) said, "Beware of the assemblies of the dead." He was asked, "O Messenger of Allah, who are the dead?" He said, "The rich." Mūsā asked Allah, "O Lord, where shall I search for You?" He said, "Near the broken-hearted." The Prophet (ṣ) also said, "Do not be envious of the fortunes of sinners, as you do not know what will be their condition. Behind them is someone who enquires of them with haste."

With regard to orphans, the Prophet (ṣ) said, "Paradise is sure for someone who maintains an orphan until he comes of age after taking him from Muslim parents." The Prophet (ṣ) also said, "I and the care taker of an orphan will be in paradise like these two fingers," joining his two fingers. He also said, "He who out of sympathy passes his hand over the hair of an orphan will get rewards to the number of hairs over which his hand passed" He likewise said, "The best house of Muslims is one in which an orphan is well treated, and the worst is one in which an orphan is badly treated."

The twenty-third duty is to give advice to every Muslim. The Prophet (ṣ) said, "A believer should love for another believer what he loves for himself." Similarly, he said, "None of you can be a believer until he loves for his brother what he loves for himself." He said, "Each of you is like a mirror to other. If he sees anything wrong in him, he should remove it from him." He said, "He who fulfils the needs of his Muslim brother, it is as though he served Allah his whole life." He said, "If a man destroys the honour of a believer, Allah will destroy his rewards on Resurrection Day." He said, "If a man spends one hour of the day or night trying to relieve the sufferings of his Muslim brother, it is better than two months of seclusion in a mosque, whether his sufferings are relieved or not." Likewise, he said, "If a man removes the anxieties of a believer or helps an oppressed person, Allah forgives seventy-three of his sins." He said, "Help your Muslim brother, be he oppressed or an oppressor." He was asked, "How can he help an oppressor?" He replied, "He stops him from oppression." He said, "Among the most beloved acts to Allah is to make happiness enter the heart of a believer, to pay off his debt, and to satisfy his hunger by giving him food."

The Prophet (ṣ) said, "If a man saves a believer from the deceit of a hypocrite, Allah will send him an angel to protect his flesh from the fire of hell on Resurrection Day." He said, "The two most evil sins are to ascribe associates to Allah and to oppress Allah's servants. The two best virtues are to have faith in Allah and to do good to Allah's servants." He also said, "He whose heart is not moved by the suffering of Muslims is not of them." Maʿrūf al-Karkhī said, "Whoever says daily, 'O Allah, show mercy to the followers of Muḥammad,' Allah will include him as one of the *Abdāl*." In another version, "If a man recites thrice every day, 'O Allah, make the followers of Muḥammad good. O Allah, relieve the suffering of the followers of Muḥammad,' Allah will include him as one of the *Abdāl*."

The twenty-fourth duty is to visit the ill. If a Muslim falls ill, visit him and nurse him. Among the manners you should observe are to sit for a short while before the patient, ask him few questions, be compassionate, and pray for his recovery. The Prophet (ṣ) said, "A perfect visit to a patient is that one of you place his hand on the patient's forehead or hand and ask him about his illness. And a perfect greeting is to shake his hand." He said "He who meets with a patient, sits beside paradise. When he returns, he is entrusted with seventy thousand angels who pray for him until night." He said, "When a man goes to see a patient, he remains immersed in mercy. When he sits by his bed, it becomes permanent." He said, "When a Muslim visits his brother, whether he is sick or not, Allah says, 'Blessings on you. Your steps are good." The Prophet (ṣ) said, "When a man falls ill, Allah sends to him two angels and says to them, 'See what he says to the patient.' When he comes to him and praises Allah, they take it up to Allah and praise Him. Allah says, 'If I cause the death of this servant, I will admit him into paradise. If I cure him, I will give him better flesh than this flesh, better blood than this blood, and forgive his sins. The Prophet (ṣ) said, "Allah gives disease to a man He loves." The Prophet (ṣ) once came to see a patient and said, "In the name of Allah, the Beneficent, the Merciful. I protect you from the evil I see to by placing you under the wing of Allah, the Unique, who is free from want, who did not beget, who was not begotten, and whom there is none like." The Prophet (ṣ) said, "Visit a patient on alternate days and be modest towards him."

The twenty-fifth duty is to join the funeral prayer of a Muslim. The Prophet (ṣ) said, "He who follows a bier will get a *qīrāṭ* of reward. If he stands until he is buried, he will get two *qīrāṭ*s of reward." According to a tradition, "One *qīrāṭ* is like Mount Uḥud." The Prophet (ṣ) also said, "Three things follow a dead man, two of which return and one does not: his relatives and wealth return, but his actions do not."

The twenty-sixth duty is to visit the graves of the dead. The object is to pray, to take lessons and to soften the heart. The Prophet (ṣ) said, "I have not seen a more horrible sight than a grave." He once went to the grave of his mother Āminah and said, "I sought Allah permission to visit her grave, and He gave me permission. I sought His permission to ask for her forgiveness, but He refused." The Prophet (ṣ) said, "The grave is the first station of the next world. If its inmate gets relief from it, what occurs after it will be easy. If he does not get relief from it, what occurs after it will be severe." Abū al-Dardā' used to sit by graves. Asked why, he said, "I sit with people who remind me of the next world. And when I leave them, they do not backbite me." The Prophet (ṣ) said, "There is no night in which a proclaimer does not proclaim, 'O inhabitants of graves, whom do you envy?' They say, 'We envy the people of the mosque, as they fast, but we do not; they pray, but we do not; they invoke Allah, but we do not.'" Sufyān said, "He who remembers the grave much will find it to be one of the gardens of paradise. He who does not remember the grave will find it to be one of the pits of hell."

4

Duties to neighbours

Just as a Muslim has rights over you, so does a neighbour. The Prophet (ṣ) said, "Neighbours are three: a neighbour with one right, a neighbour with two rights, and a neighbour with three rights. The neighbour with three rights is a Muslim neighbour who is a relative. He has the right of being a neighbour, of being a relative, and being a Muslim. The neighbour with two rights is a Muslim neighbour. He has the right of being a Muslim and of being a neighbour. The neighbour with only one right is a non-Muslim or polytheist." The Prophet (ṣ) said, "Treat your neighbour well and you will be a Muslim." He said, "Jibrīl kept ordering me concerning the neighbour until I thought that he would give him the right of inheritance." He said, "Let him who believes in Allah and the next world honour his neighbour."

The Prophet (ṣ) said, "He from whose harms his neighbour is not safe is not a believer." He said, "The first two who will come as disputants on Resurrection day will be neighbours." He said, "When you throw a stone at the dog of a neighbour, you trouble his heart." It was once said to the Prophet (ṣ), "A man fasts all day and prays all night, but he troubles his neighbour" to which he replied, "He is in hell." At another time, a man complained about his neighbour to the Prophet (ṣ), who said, "Have patience." When he repeated his complaints three or four times, the Prophet (ṣ) said, "Throw your goods on the pathway." When he threw them, people asked him, "What is the matter with you?" They were told that his neighbour was giving him trouble. They began to say,

"Allah's curse on him." His neighbour then came to him and said, "By Allah, I will no longer treat him in such a manner."

The Prophet (ṣ) said, "Consider forty surrounding houses to be the houses of neighbours." He said, "Fortune and misfortune lie in women, houses and conveyances. A woman is a cause of fortune when her dowry is little, her marriage is easily performed, and her character and conduct are good. The cause of her misfortune occurs when her dowry is heavy, her marriage is solemnised with difficulty, and her character and conduct are bad. Fortune regarding a house occurs when it is spacious and its neighbour is good, and misfortune comes when it is narrow and its neighbour is bad. Fortune regarding a horse comes when it becomes submissive and has a good figure, and misfortune comes when it is disobedient and has an ugly figure."

In short, your duties to your neighbour are to greet him first, not to talk with him long, not to ask about his condition long, to call on him when he is ill, to show sympathy in his distress, to be sorry in his sorrows, to be happy in his happiness, to pardon his faults, not to look at the inner side of his house from the top of your roof, not to trouble him by placing your rafters on his wall, not to let water flow down into his courtyard, not to shut the outflow of the water of his house through your boundary, not to make the path to his house narrow, to cover his fault if it disclosed, to try to remove his distress as soon as possible, to take care of his house in his absence, to not listen to his backbiting, to talk with his sons and daughters with affection, and to guide him with regard to his ignorance of worldly and religious matters.

The Prophet (ṣ) said, "Do you know your duties to your neighbour? Help him if he seeks your help; give him a loan if he wants it; satisfy his wants if he is in want; follow his bier when he is dead; give him joy if he receives good news; show him sympathy and express sorrow if he is in danger; do not, without his permission, make your house higher such that it blocks the wind to him; and do not trouble him. If you purchase some fruits, give him some. If you do not, take them secretly to your house. Do not allow your children to go out with them, as it may displease his children. Do not trouble him with the smoke of your cooking shed. There is no harm in sending food cooked in your cooking shed to your neighbour's house." He then said, "Do you know the rights of a neighbour? By Him in whose hand is my life, only he whom Allah shows mercy can fulfil these duties to neighbours." Al-Ḥasan used to offer sacrificial meat to his Jewish and Christian neighbours. Abū Dharr said, "My friend, the Prophet (ṣ), instructed me, 'When you cook curry, increase its soup and send some of it to your neighbour.'" 'Ā'ishah said to the Prophet (ṣ), "O Messenger of Allah, I have two neighbours. The house of one is near my house, and the house of another is distant. Whose right is greater?" He said, "The right of the one whose house is nearer."

'Ā'ishah said, "An honourable man has ten habits. They may be found in a man, but may not be found in his father. They may be found in his servant, but may not be found in his master. Allah gives them to whoever He loves. They are to speak the truth, to treat people well, to give charity to beggars, to help in domestic tasks, to treat relatives well, to protect trusts, to fulfil the duties to a neighbour, to maintain friendship, to entertain guests, and to be modest, which is the foundation for all the qualities." Abū Hurayrah related that the Prophet (ṣ) said, "O Muslim women, do not deem it insignificant to give your neighbours only a goat's cooked hoof." The Prophet (ṣ) said, "The fortune of a Muslim is in a spacious abode, a good neighbour, and a satisfactory conveyance." 'Abdullāh said, "A man asked the Prophet (ṣ), 'O Messenger of Allah, how can I know whether a man is good or bad?' He said, 'When you hear your neighbour say, 'He is good,' he is really good. If you hear say, 'He is bad,' he is really bad.'" Jābir related that the Prophet (ṣ) said, "If a man owns a share of a wall, he should not sell it without asking his co-partner." Abū Hurayrah related that the Prophet (ṣ) said, "A neighbour can place his rafter on the wall of his neighbour, whether he is willing or not." Similarly, Ibn 'Abbās related that the Prophet (ṣ) said, "Let none of you prevent his neighbour from placing his rafters on his wall." The Prophet (ṣ) said, "Allah gives sweetness to whomever He wishes good." He was asked, "What is the meaning of 'sweetness'?" He replied, "He makes him dear to his neighbour."

5

Duties to relatives

The Prophet (ṣ) said, "Allah says, 'I am the Beneficent (*Raḥmān*), and 'kinship' (*Raḥīm*) is derived from my name. I keep attached to whoever maintains its ties, and I keep aloof from whoever severs its ties." He said, "If any man wishes to prolong his life and have ample sustenance, let him fear Allah and maintain the tie of kinship." He was once asked, "Who is the best person?" He replied, "He who fears Allah most, keeps the best connection with his relatives, gives much advice concerning good deeds, and prohibits bad deeds." Abū Dharr said, "My friend, the Prophet (ṣ), advised me to keep good relations with relatives, even if they treat me badly. And he ordered me to speak the truth, though it may be bitter." The Prophet (ṣ) said, "Kinship hangs from the Throne. The real protector of kinship is not he who maintains its tie, but rather he who joins it after it is severed." He said, "The rewards of keeping a good relationship with relatives are found more hastily than other rewards. His wealth and possessions increase in spite of the inhabitants of his house being sinners, and their numbers increase when they keep the relationship intact."

When the Prophet (ṣ) started for the conquest of Makkah, a man came to him and said, "If you wish to marry a beautiful woman and to get a camel of red hue, start a campaign against the tribe of Banū Mudlij. The Prophet (ṣ) replied, "Allah prohibited me from waging a campaign against them because of my relationship with them." The Prophet (ṣ) said, "Charity to a poor man has one reward, and charity to a poor relative has two. Abū Ṭalḥah was greatly satisfied upon hearing the words of Allah "By no means shall you attain to righteousness until you spend (benevolently) out of what you love" (Qur'an, 3:92) and wished to give in charity his garden of dates, saying, "O Prophet of Allah, I have given this garden in charity to the poor and destitute." The Prophet of Allah answered, "Your reward from Allah has become sure. Distribute it among your near relatives." The Prophet (ṣ) also said, "The greatest reward is of that charity which you give to your relative who is in dispute with you." This can be understood from the *ḥadīth* of the Prophet (ṣ) "If a man joins the tie of kinship after it was severed, and gives charity to a man who deprives him, he will get the greatest rewards." 'Umar sent this order to his governors: "Order relatives to meet one another."

Duties to parents and children

The nearer the relation is, the greater are the duties to him. Parents are the nearest to a man, and so the duty to them is the greatest. The Prophet (ṣ) said, "A son cannot fulfil his duties to his father. He can, however, fulfil a part of it if he sees his father as a slave and liberates him." He said, "To treat parents well is better than prayer, fasting, the greater pilgrimage, *zakāh*, the lesser pilgrimage, and jihad in the way of Allah." He said, "If a man arises in morning pleasing his parents, two doors of paradise are opened for him. If he gets up at dusk, he gets similar rewards. If he pleases one of them, one door is opened for him, even if they both oppress him, even if they both oppress him, even if they both oppress him. If a man gets up at dawn displeasing his parents, two doors to hell are opened for him. If a man does this at dusk, he will receive a similar punishment. If he displeases one of them, one door is opened for him, even if they both oppress him, even if they both oppress him, even if they both oppress him." He said, "The fragrance of paradise will be smelt for the distance of five hundred years' journey. Neither he who is disobedient to his parents, nor he who severs the tie of relationship, will be able to smell it." He said, "Obey your mother, then your father, then your sister, then your brother, then your nearest relatives, then near relatives."

Allah said to Mūsā, "O Mūsā, if a man obeys his parents, but commits sins, I record that he is obedient to his parents. If a man disobeys Me, but is obedient to his parents, I record that he is obedient to his parents." It has been reported that when Ya'qūb went to Yūsuf, the latter did not stand in his honour. Allah then revealed to him, "Have you not stood up in your father's honour? By My glory, I will not make any of your descendants prophets."

The Prophet (ṣ) said, "When a man wishes to give charity for his Muslim parents, his parents get the rewards without any reduction." A man once asked the Prophet (ṣ), "O Messenger of Allah, do any duties to parents remain after their death?" He said, "Yes. To supplicate for them, to seek forgiveness for them, to fulfil their promises, to honour their friends, and to maintain the tie of their relatives." The Prophet (ṣ) said, "The best duty is to maintain, after their death, ties with those who were dear to them."

The Prophet (ṣ) said, "The right of a mother is double that of a father." He said, "The supplication of a mother for her child is soon accepted." Asked why, he said, "She is more affectionate than the father. And the supplication of relatives does not go unanswered."

A man once asked the Prophet (ṣ), "To whom shall I do good?" The Prophet (ṣ) answered, "Do good to your parents." The man said, "I have no parents." The Prophet (ṣ) said, "Then to your children. Just as you have duties to you parents, so also you have duties to your children." The Prophet (ṣ) said, "May Allah show mercy on the father who helps his children to obey him." In other words, he does not help them to become misguided by his evil actions. He said, "Treat your children equally with regard to charity." It has been said that a child is your flower, and until he reaches the age of seven, you will enjoy his fragrance. When he is seven years old, he becomes your servant. Thereafter, he becomes either your enemy or sharer in your tasks.

The Prophet (ṣ) said, "Seven days after a child is born, perform a sacrifice for him (*'aqīqah*), give him a name, and remove from him uncleanliness. When the child is six years old, teach him good manners; nine years old, give him his own bed; thirteen years old, impose prayer on him; sixteen years old, get him married. Then, holding his hands, say to him, "I have taught you good manners, educated you, and gotten you married. Now I seek refuge in Allah from your dangers and difficulties and your punishment in the next world." The Prophet (ṣ) said, "The right of a son over his father is that his father teach him good manners and give him a good name." A man once complained about his son to the Prophet (ṣ), who asked him, "Have you supplicated against him?" He said, "Yes." The Prophet (ṣ) said, "You have ruined him."

It is recommended to show kindness to a child. Al-Aqra' ibn Ḥābis saw the Prophet (ṣ) kissing his grandson al-Ḥasan and said, "I have ten children, but never kissed any of them." The Prophet (ṣ) replied, "He who is not kind will not be shown kindness." Once, the Prophet (ṣ) was in prostration, leading a prayer, when al-Ḥusayn got on the Prophet's shoulder. The Prophet (ṣ) prolonged the prostration so much that the Companions thought that revelation was coming to him. When he finished the prayer, the Prophet (ṣ) said, "Al-Ḥusayn made me his conveyance, and I did not like to put him aside until he finished what he was doing."

The Prophet (ṣ) said, "The fragrance of a child is the fragrance of paradise." A man once came from Yemen to join jihad with the Prophet (ṣ), who asked him, "Do you have parents?" He said, "Yes." The Prophet (ṣ) asked, "Have they given you permission for jihad?" He said, "No." The Prophet (ṣ) said, "Go to your parents and get their permission. If they do not give permission, serve them to your utmost, because after belief in Allah's oneness, the best merit with which you will meet Allah is in the service of parents." At another time, a man sought the advice of the Prophet (ṣ) about joining jihad. The Prophet (ṣ) asked him, "Do you have a mother?" He said, "Yes." The Prophet (ṣ) said, "Stay with her, as paradise lies under her feet." At another time, a man came to give allegiance to the Prophet (ṣ) and said, "My parents were weeping when I was leaving them." The Prophet (ṣ) said, "Go back and give them joy, as you have made them weep." He also said, The right of an older brother is like the right of a father over his son."

6

Duties to slaves and servants

The last advice that the Prophet (ṣ) gave was regarding slaves: "Fear Allah. Give them of the food you eat, give them of the clothes you wear, and do not give them more work than they can bear. If you do not wish to keep them, ask them to go. And do not inflict punishment on the servants of Allah. Allah has placed them under your control. If He wishes, He may place you under their control." He said, "Give the slaves food and clothes justly, and do not engage them in tasks beyond their capacity." He said, "Those who cheat, the proud, those who break trusts, and those who ill-treat slaves will not enter paradise." A man once asked the Prophet (ṣ), "How many times should I forgive the faults of a servant?" The Prophet (ṣ) remained silent for a while and then said, "Forgive him seventy times a day."

Once, a Companion of the Prophet (ṣ) beat a slave, who began to raise a loud cry. On seeing the Prophet (ṣ) coming he stopped the beating. The Prophet (ṣ) said, "Why did you not pardon him before? But you have restrained your hand when you saw me." He said, "O Messenger of Allah, I manumit him for the pleasure of Allah." The Prophet (ṣ) said, "Had you not done it, hell would have blackened your face."

The Prophet (ṣ) said, "When any slave serves his master and serves Allah well, a double reward is written for him." He said, "The first three people who will enter paradise and the first three people who will enter hell were presented to me. The first three people who will enter paradise are a martyr, then a slave who worshipped well and served his master, then a needy man who refrained from begging, even though he had a large family. The first three people who will enter hell are a tyrannical ruler, then a person of wealth who did not give Allah his due, then a proud, poor man." Abū Mas'ūd al-Anṣārī said, "When I was beating my slave, I heard behind me, "O Abū Mas'ūd." Upon turning around, I found the Messenger of Allah. Immediately I threw the stick which was in my hand, and he said, "By Allah, Allah has more power over you than your power over this slave."

The Prophet (ṣ) said, "When any servant comes to any of you with food, let him ask him to sit and eat with him. If he does not, let him give him a morsel of food." In another version, "When a slave prepares food for you and gives you relief from it, the vapour of that food and his labour are sufficient for you. Make him sit near you and eat with him. If he does not, allow him to take some food therefrom and using his hand, or place some food in his hand and tell him, 'Eat.'" He said, "He who takes care of his female slave and gets her married after setting her free will get double rewards." He said, "Every one of you is a king and will be asked about his subjects."

The sum total of your duties to servants and slaves are to share your food and clothes with him, not to give him work beyond his strength, not to regard him with an eye of hate and contempt, to pardon his faults and remember, when you are angry with him, that Allah has power to punish you for your sins and faults—more power than you. The Prophet (ṣ) said, "Do not ask about three people: a person who destroyed unity, a person who disobeyed his leader and died a sinner, and a woman whom her husband left behind after relieving her from worldly needs and who, after that, shows her external beauty. Three people will not be called to reckoning: a person who vied with Allah for his mantle—his mantle is haughtiness and his garment is glory and honour; a person who doubted the existence of Allah; and a person who despaired of the mercy of Allah."

Book 6
The rules of living in seclusion

Introduction

There are differences of opinion regarding living in seclusion and living in society among people. Those who supported the former were Sufyān al-Thawrī, Ibrāhīm ibn Adham, Dāwūd al-Ṭā'ī, al-Fuḍayl ibn 'Iyāḍ, Sulaymān al-Khawwāṣ, Yūsuf ibn Asbāṭ, Ḥudhayfah al-Mar'ashī, Bishr al-Ḥāfī and others. The majority of those who personally learned from one or more of the Companions (*tābi'ūn*) advocated living in society because a person could do good to others; he could establish brotherhood, love, and friendship among believers; and people could help one another in religion. Those who supported this view were Sa'īd ibn al-Musayyib, al-Sha'bī, Ibn Abī Laylā, Hishām ibn 'Urwah, Ibn Shabramah, Shurayḥ, Sharīk ibn 'Abdullāh, Ibn 'Uyaynah, Ibn al-Mubārak, al-Shāfi'ī, Aḥmad ibn Ḥanbal and others.

'Umar said, "Loneliness is like worship." Al-Fuḍayl said, "I am satisfied with Allah as an object of love, with the Qur'an as a companion, and with death as an admonisher." Dāwūd al-Ṭā'ī said to Abū al-Rabī' al-Zāhid, "Fast from the temptations of the world and break it in the next world. Flee from society as you flee from a tiger." Al-Ḥasan said, " I have remembered from the Torah, 'You will be free from depending on men if you are satisfied with little. You will be safe if you keep distant from society; you will get the pleasure of freedom if you give up sexual passion; manliness will manifest if you give up hatred;

and you will get everlasting happiness if you can refrain from temporary greed."

Wuhayb ibn al-Ward said, "I have heard that wisdom has ten parts, nine of which are in loneliness." Yūsuf ibn Muslim said, "I used to mix in society, but did not talk with people." Sufyān al-Thawrī said, "The present time is the time of loneliness and staying in a corner of the house." Ibrāhīm al-Nakha'ī said, "Acquire knowledge and adopt loneliness." Al-Rabī' ibn Khuthaym said that Mālik ibn Anas used to attend funeral prayers, nurse the sick and pay the dues of friends. Eventually, he gave up everything." Sa'd ibn Abī Waqqāṣ and Sa'īd ibn Zayd used to live at al-'Aqīq near Madīnah. They did not come to Madīnah for the Friday prayer, or for any other thing, and died in al-'Aqīq."

Sufyān al-Thawrī said, "Loneliness has become lawful now." Bishr ibn 'Abdullāh said, "Become acquainted with few people, as you do not know what will happen on Resurrection day. If you are disgraced, few people will know you." A ruler asked Ḥātim al-Aṣamm, "Do you need anything?" Ḥātim said, "Yes." The ruler asked, "What is it?" Ḥātim said, "Do not meet me, and I shall not meet you. Nor be acquainted with me."

A man asked Sahl, "I want to keep your company." Sahl said, "When one of us dies, with whose company will he keep?" The man said, "Allah's." Sahl said, "Then it is better at present to keep Allah's company." Al-Fuḍayl said, "The more a man is acquainted with people, the less his wisdom is." Ibn 'Abbās said, "Your assembly within your house is the best assembly. You will not find anybody there, and nobody will find you." These are the words of those who love loneliness.

Those who advocate living in society present the following evidence. Allah says, "Be not like those who became divided and disagreed ..." (Qur'an, 3:105) and "He united your hearts" (ibid.). These verses speak of unity on the grounds of love and speak of differences regarding the Book of Allah.

The second proof is said to be the words of the Prophet (ṣ) "A believer loves an object of love, and there is no good in someone who does not love or have love. In this *ḥadīth*, the Prophet (ṣ) condemns bad conduct, as it is a hindrance to love.

Another *ḥadīth* says, "He who separates from the (Muslim) community even half a span removes the tie of Islam from his neck." He said, "He who keeps separate from the united body dies the death of the days of ignorance." These are weak proofs of mixing in society. They speak of allegiance to one ruler, but there is no mention of loneliness therein.

The fourth proof cited is that the Prophet (ṣ) prohibited ignoring a Muslim brother for more than three days. This proof is also weak because what is meant is ignoring your brother after a quarrel.

The fifth proof cited is that the Prophet (ṣ) said, "The patience of one of you in some of the lands of Islam is better than his worship of forty years in a lonely place." This speaks of the time when Islam was in danger. At another time, when a Companion liked a lonely place where there was a current of water, the Prophet (ṣ) said, "Do not do it, because the rank of one of you in the way of Allah is better than his divine service of sixty years. Do you not love that Allah should forgive you and that you should enter paradise? Engage in jihad in the way of Allah, as someone who fights in the way of Allah, even for a short time, Allah will admit him into paradise."

Another proof is this *ḥadīth* "The Prophet (ṣ) said, 'The Devil in men is like a tiger among a flock of sheep. The tiger attacks near and distant ones. Beware of hillocks and stick to the united body, mosques and ordinary people." This means that loneliness is prohibited before the completion of knowledge.

1

Merits and demerits of secluded living

That seclusion is good or bad depends on the circumstances of each man. It is good for some people and bad for others.

Benefits

The benefits are either worldly or religious. Benefits that are derived from loneliness are engagement in divine service, leisure for meditation or religious thought, and relief from prohibited sins, such as ostentation, backbiting, and being in the bad company of sinners and transgressors. The benefits in this world are that a person can carry out his worldly matters with peace of mind. Thus, there are six benefits of loneliness.

The first benefit is that a person can have sufficient leisure for divine service and deep contemplation of Allah's glory. The greatest meditation on divine matters is meditation on the wonderful creations of Allah and of His sovereignty and power. In society, that benefit cannot be availed of. A wise man said, "It is not possible for anybody to take to seclusion unless he holds firmly the Qur'an of Allah." Those who hold the Qur'an firmly can enjoy the comforts of the material and spiritual worlds. Those who remember Allah live in His remembrance, die in His remembrance, and meet Him in His remembrance. The reason why the Prophet (ṣ) was always thinking of Allah, even when he was among people, was before his mission he had been immersed in deep meditation in the cave of Ḥirā'.

Al-Junayd said, "For the last thirty years, I have been speaking to Allah, but people have been thinking I was speaking to them." A sage was asked, "How can you keep patient in solitude?" He said, "I am not alone; Allah is my companion. When I want to speak to Him secretly, I observe prayer." Another sage was asked, "What benefit have you derived from renouncing the world?" He replied, "Allah's love." Once, al-Ḥasan asked a sage, "What prevents you from mixing with people?" The sage said, "I enter the morning and evening between blessings and sins. I remain busy thanking Allah for the blessings and ask His forgiveness for the commission of sins." Dhū al-Nūn al-Miṣrī said, "The joy and taste of a believer lies in his supplicating his Lord." A wise man said, "Love for people is a sign of bankruptcy in religion."

The second benefit is that a man can avoid the sins which are committed in societal life. These sins are four kinds: backbiting and listening to it, not enjoining good deeds and not prohibiting bad deeds, working for show, and entertaining bad conduct and evil deeds. Except those with great faith, nobody can be safe from backbiting. Enjoining good deeds and prohibiting evil deeds is the basic principle of religion and an obligation. In a sermon, Abū Bakr said, "O people, you need this verse of Allah, 'O you who believe, take care of your souls; he who errs cannot hurt you when you are on the right way' (Qur'an, 5:105). But you do not use it in the appropriate place. I have heard the Prophet (ṣ) say, 'If a man does not remove an evil deed of another man after seeing it, Allah sends a punishment for it to all.'" The Prophet (ṣ) said, "Allah will take account of a servant, even asking him, 'When you saw an evil deed being done, why did you not prevent it?' When Allah shows proof to His servant, the latter will say, 'O Lord, I feared men and hoped for your pardon.'"

The third benefit concerns show. Show is an incurable disease, and to remove it is very difficult for religious and pious men. Positive feelings need to be maintained in a society in which a person feels inclined to show off his character and conduct. The

Prophet (ṣ) said, "The worst man is he who has two faces. He comes with one face to one people and with another face to another people." A wise man said, "If Allah loves a man, He wishes that his fame does not spread. Ṭāwūs once went to the caliph Hishām and said, "O Hishām, how are you?" Hishām became displeased with him and said, "Why have you not addressed me as 'Commander of the Faithful'?" Ṭāwūs said, "The Muslims are unanimously against you. I fear that if I addressed you as 'Commander of the Faithful,' I would be a liar." There is no fear for such a man to mix in society. Some people once asked 'Īsā, "How are you?" to which he replied, "I do not have in my possession what I hope, nor do I have power to remove what I fear. I am busy with my affairs. All deeds are in the hand of another. There is nobody more in want than myself." A man asked Abū al-Dardā', "How are you?" He said, "I am well, provided I am saved from hell." Uways al-Qarnī was asked, "How are you?" He answered, "How is a man who does not know whether he will live to the next morning when evening comes, or to the evening when dawn comes.'

The fourth benefit concerns imitating the behaviour of others, as people imitate what they see. This is a subtle disease from which even the wise are not safe, not to speak of the heedless. If a person constantly sees major sins being committed around him, he begins to regard them as inconsequential. Thus, if you always look at the gifts of the rich, you will consider your own gifts little. For this reason, you should keep the company of the poor, look at the conduct and character of the religious, not of those who are irreligious and commit sins and transgressions. The Prophet (ṣ) said, "Mercy descends when pious people are mentioned." "Mercy" means to be able to reach paradise and see Allah. So the beginning of mercy is good deeds, the beginning of good deeds is desire, and the beginning of desire is discussing the character of the pious. "Curse" means to remain distant from Allah, the roots of which are sins. The cause of being cursed is to leave the remembrance of Allah and be busy with the worldly comforts.

If such is the effect of discussing the lives of the pious and sinners, then what would the effect of meeting the pious and sinners be? The Prophet (ṣ) said, "A bad friend is for you like the hammer of a blacksmith. If the spark of the fire of heated iron does not touch you, its vapour touches you just as its vapour touches you even when you do not know." He also said, "A good companion is like a seller of perfume. If he does not give you perfume, you get its fragrance." Hence, it is unlawful for a man to disclose the faults of a scholar for two reasons. The first is that it is backbiting, and the second is that people are apt to commit the sins of the scholar when they see that he has always committed them. This is of the machinations of the Devil. Allah says with regard to those who oppose the Devil, "Those who listen to the word, then follow the best of it" (Qur'an, 39:18). The Prophet (ṣ) gave an example of wicked people, saying, "A man who hears words of wisdom and does not act but on what is evil is like a man who says to a shepherd, 'Give me a stout and strong sheep from your flock.' The shepherd then says, 'Choose the best one from the flock.' Then the man takes the sheepdog by its ear from the flock." Thus is he who seeks out the faults of a leader. His seeing his bad deeds constantly, his heart is unaffected.

The fifth benefit is relief from quarrels and disputes and safety from useless talks. The Prophet (ṣ) said, "When you see people breaking their promises and trusts, and when they become such (he thrusts the fingers of one hand into the fingers of the other), they will engage in quarrels and disputes." A man asked, "What will we do then?" to which the Prophet (ṣ) replied, "Stay in your own houses, keep the tongue under control, accept what you know, give up what you do not know, be busy with your own affairs, and give up the affairs of others." The Prophet (ṣ) also said, "The wealth of a Muslim in the near future will be goats and sheep. He will roam in the caves of hillocks and places of water. Because of calamities, he will shift from one place to another with his religion." Similarly, he said, "In the near future, there will be a time when it will be difficult for a man to preserve his religion. To do so, he will flee like a jackal from one cave to another and from one hillock to another." Asked, "O Prophet of Allah, when will it occur?" he answered, "When you will not be able to earn a livelihood without sin. When that time comes, a man will be ruined at the hands of his parents; if he has no parents, then at the hands of his wife and children; if he has no wife or children, then at the hands of his. relatives." They asked him, "O Prophet of Allah, how will they treat him?" He said, "They will abuse him for his poor condition. The parents will ask what is beyond the capacity of their son, ruining him."

Sufyān said, "Now seclusion has become lawful." Sa'd did not join the party of Mu'āwiyah or the party of 'Alī when they were fighting for the caliphate. It has been related that when al-Ḥusayn was proceeding towards Iraq, Ibn 'Umar prevented him on the grounds that he had with him a letter of allegiance from the Iraqi people. Ibn 'Umar then recited the *ḥadīth* which said that Jibrīl once came to the Holy Prophet (ṣ) and asked him to choose this world or the next, whereupon he chose the latter. You are a piece of flesh of the Holy Prophet (ṣ). "By Allah," 'Ibn 'Umar said, "None of you will be the ruler of this material world which has been kept separate from you." In spite of this advice. Al-Ḥusayn refused to turn back. He started with ten thousand men, but there were no more than forty with him at the time of the battle.

Ṭāwūs remained in his own house. Being asked the reason, he said, "The dangers and calamities of this age and the oppression of the leaders compelled me to remain in the house." When 'Urwah erected a house at al-'Aqīq to live in and stopped going to the Prophet's mosque, he was asked why. He replied, "Upon seeing your mosques as places of sport and jest, your bazaars as places of useless talks, and your lanes as places of obscene acts, I chose to stay in the house, where there is peace."

The sixth benefit is that a person can save himself from the harms of others. 'Umar said, "Loneliness is better than a bad companion." Al-Sammāk said, "One of our friends said, 'Men used to be like medicine which treated disease. Now, men have turned into a disease for which there is no cure. Flee from them as you flee from a tiger.'" Al-Ḥasan said, "Thābit al-Bunānī was a friend of Allah. When I intended to make the pilgrimage, he wanted to accompany me. I said, 'If we live together, we may treat each other such that we end up hating one another.'"

Another benefit is that a man can hide matters of religion, manliness, character and conduct, poverty, and other internal qualities. Allah praised such a man: "The ignorant man thinks them to be rich on account of (their) abstaining (from begging)" (Qur'an, 2:173). Abū al-Dardā' said, "Before, man was a leaf without thorns, but now he is a thorn without leaves." This was at the end of the first century; imagine the state of man now.

Sufyān ibn 'Uyaynah said, "In his life time and after his death in a dream, Sufyān al-Thawrī said to me, 'Become acquainted with few people, as it is difficult to save oneself from them.' I do not think I saw anything I disliked except from an acquaintance." A man was asked, "Why have you abandoned society?" He said, "I feared that my religion would be robbed in my absence." Abū al-Dardā' said, "Fear Allah and fear society, for when they ride on a camel, they wound it, they whip a horse when they ride it, and they harm the mind of an unbeliever." A wise man said, "Become acquainted with few and your religion and heart will remain safe and your duties will be less: The more the acquaintances, the more the duties."

The seventh benefit is that people's expectations of you, and your expectations from them, will vanish, as it is impossible to please everyone. So it is better to remain busy purifying one's own character and conduct. Al-Shāfi'ī said, "To benefit sinners is the root of every opposition." If one does not see the fineries of the world from the beginning, greed does not grow in him. For this reason, Allah says, "Do not strain your eyes after what We have given certain classes of them to enjoy" (Qur'an, 15:88). The

Prophet (ṣ) said, "Look at those who are below you in respect of wealth, nor look at those who are superior to you in wealth. Otherwise, you will consider the gifts of Allah to you insignificant." 'Awn ibn 'Abdullāh said, "I was at first in the company of the rich. I saw their dress better than mine, their conveyances better than mine. Then I kept company of the poor and got peace of mind."

The eighth benefit is that if the idle and the foolish take to loneliness, they get security from foolishness and heinous character. To meet with an idle man is akin to becoming blind. Al-Aʻmash was asked, "How have you lost your sight?" He said, "By seeing the idle." Once, Abū Ḥanīfah came to al-Aʻmash and said, "The Prophet (ṣ) said, 'If Allah robs the sight of two eyes of a man, He gives him better than them in exchange.' What thing has He given you in exchange of the loss of your eye sight?" Al-Aʻmash said jokingly, "Allah has given me in its exchange the sight of the idle, and you belong to that class." The sage Galen said, "Everything has a fever, And the fever of the soul comes at the sight of the idle." Al-Shāfiʻī said, "If I sit beside an idle man, the side of my body nearest to him becomes heavier to me than the opposite side."

2

Benefits of society

Know, O dear readers, that there are some religious acts which cannot be performed without becoming part of society. The benefits which are gained by mixing with society are not gained by loneliness. The benefits of society are as follows.

The first benefit is to teach and gain religious knowledge, which is the best act of worship in this world. Learning has a greater scope. Some learning is obligatory, and some optional. If loneliness is adopted without gaining obligatory knowledge, it is a sin. If you can become an expert in a branch of knowledge, loneliness is harmful. For this reason, Ibrāhīm al-Nakha'ī and other sages said, "First acquire religious knowledge, then seek solitude." If one spends the whole day in devotions without having acquired sufficient knowledge, his mind and body are not free from conceit and deceit. So education is the root of religion.

The second benefit is to benefit, and derive benefit from, people by trading with them. Without mixing with society, this is impossible. If you are obligated to earn a livelihood, it is obligatory to become a member of society. To benefit means to help people at the cost of life and wealth and to satisfy the wants of Muslims.

The third benefit is to struggle and gain the attribute of patience. By mixing with society, man can acquire the quality of patience by bearing the harms and injuries others inflict.

The fourth benefit is to give and receive love. The Prophet (ṣ) said, "Allah is not vexed with you until you become vexed." Loneliness is not without undisturbed peace. The Prophet (ṣ) said, "This religion is firm, so take it with kindness." Ibn 'Abbās said, "Had I not feared random thoughts, I would not have mixed with society." He also said, "Who injures man except man?" The Prophet (ṣ) said, "A man follows the religion of his friend, so let him consider whom he befriends."

The fifth benefit is to reap religious rewards. In society, a man is required to be present at funeral prayers, visit the sick, attend the *'Īd* prayers, and so on.

The sixth benefit is to acquire modesty and humility, which cannot be acquired in solitude, which sometimes breeds pride. An Israeli tradition tells of a man who wrote nearly three hundred and sixty books on wisdom and thought that he acquired some rank with Allah for this. Allah then revealed to the prophet of that age, "Tell the man, 'You have filled up the world with hypocrisy; I will not accept any portion of your hypocrisy.'" He then gave up writing books and took refuge in a grave, thinking, "I have now gained the pleasure of Allah." Allah then revealed to His prophet, "Tell him, 'You cannot gain My pleasure until you mix with society and bear their harms and troubles.'" Afterwards, he mixed with society, and Allah revealed to His prophet, "Tell him, 'Now you have gained My pleasure.'"

'Alī used to carry the daily necessities of the family from the bazaar, saying, "The perfection of a perfect man is not reduced if he carries something for his benefit." Abū Hurayrah, Ḥudhayfah, Ubayy, Ibn Mas'ūd, and others used to carry firewood and foodstuffs on their backs. When Abū Hurayrah was the governor of Madīnah, he would say while carrying loads of firewood, "Give way to your ruler. The Prophet (ṣ) also used to carry his necessities from the bazaar." Some Companions asked him, "Give me the load to bear," to which he replied, "The owner of the load has a right to carry it."

Al-Ḥasan ibn 'Alī would sit with the poor, who would say to him, "O descendant of the Messenger of Allah, eat with us. He would then get down from his conveyance and eat with them, saying, "Allah does not love the proud." Another reason is that someone who remains busy pleasing others falls into error. Because if he knows Allah perfectly, he understands that there is no good in the pleasure of people without the pleasure of Allah, that all harms and benefits are in the hand of Allah, and that there is no benefactor or destroyer except Him. He who incurs the pleasure of men by incurring the displeasure of Allah, Allah becomes displeased with him and keeps people dissatisfied with him. If the object is only to gain the pleasure of people, it is not fulfilled. Allah is the object of love.

Al-Shāfi'ī said, "There is not a man without friend and foe, so keep the company of the pious." Mūsā supplicated Allah, "O Lord, save me from the tongues of people." Allah answered, "O Mūsā, I am also not free in this matter. So how can I make you free from their tongues?" Allah revealed to 'Uzayr, "I will not record you as one of the humble ones near Me if you do not remain satisfied with the chewed matter in the mouths of chewers."

The seventh benefit is to gain the experience which is gained by mixing with society. Loneliness does not suit someone whose natural intellect cannot understand the good of the material and spiritual worlds. If a boy without experience adopts loneliness, he will be misguided. He should therefore remain busy educating himself. Every experience of loneliness is secret. Those who walk in the path of the next world seek to purify their hearts and allow themselves in the fiery tests. If they feel pride in their hearts, they try to remove it. Some of them carry waterskins, bundles of firewood, or necessary articles from the markets. Thereby they gain experience and pride goes away. So the great benefit of mixing with society is the elimination of one's faults. For this reason, it has been said that a journey discloses the character and conduct of a man, as it is a result of mixing with society.

So from what has been described above about the benefits and harms of seclusion, it is clear that loneliness is sometimes good and sometimes bad, depending on the individual's circumstances and surroundings, which depend on his friends and companions. A wise man said, "To keep separate from society is a cause of enmity, and to mix with society sometimes means keeping the company of bad people. So do not be separate, nor mix. Rather, adopt the path of loneliness in society."

3

Rules and regulations of secluded living

A person should:

- intend by loneliness to save himself from the harms of others
- seek safety from the harms of others
- intend to be free from faults by fulfilling his duties to Muslims
- intend to prefer loneliness for worship
- engage in learning, invocations, contemplation, and other acts of worship
- not allow people to mingle with him
- not allow others to put questions to him
- not ask about any place or any man
- be satisfied with little
- be patient with the harms of his neighbours, if any
- be deaf to the praise of others
- know the merits of the path of the next world. That is, he should humbly follow the rules and regulations of invocations; ponder on the wonderful creations of Allah, the heaven, earth, sun, moon and stars and of the sovereignty of Allah; and think about life and death and the conditions in the grave after death.

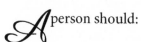

It you do not give up the passions and temptations of the world, your patience in seclusion will not be complete. The heart cannot be cleansed of impurities making short your hopes and passions, as you have no power to prolong life. Tell yourself, after getting up from bed in the morning, that you will not be able to reach the evening. This way you will be able to curtail your hopes and check your passions. Know for certain that he who cannot earn the love of Allah in his mind and His remembrance will not be able to bear loneliness after death. He who earns this attribute will be able to bear it, as death cannot destroy the place of Allah's love and remembrance. He will live in the midst of the mercy of Allah. For this reason, Allah says about martyrs, "Reckon not those who are killed in Allah's way as dead; nay, they are alive (and) are provided sustenance from their Lord" (Qur'an, 3:169).

Book 7
Rules and regulations of travelling

Introduction

Travelling is a means of warding off undesirable things or of acquiring objects of love, and is of two kinds: physical travelling from one's home to a distant country, and mental or spiritual travelling to Allah in heaven. The latter is better, but is fraught with dangers and difficulties, and the path is unknown. Travellers are indifferent to the wealth of this path. Hence, travellers of this path are few.

Allah says about this path:

> *We will soon show them Our signs in the universe and in their own soul.* (Qur'an, 41:53)

> *In the earth there are signs for those who are sure. And in your own souls (too).* (Qur'an, 51:20-21)

In the following verse, whoever keeps away from this journey Allah declares an unbeliever:

> *Most surely you pass by them in the morning and at night; do you not then understand?* (Qur'an, 37:137-138)

> *How many a sign in the heaven and the earth which they pass by, yet they turn aside from it.* (Qur'an, 12:105)

He who is satisfied with this journey, cheerfully roams in a paradise which extends across the heaven and the earth, though his body remains in his house.

1

Rules of travelling, from beginning to end

Travelling means to go from one place to another and has harms and benefits. One is to shift from his place of residence on account of religion or seeking livelihood. There are, then, two kinds of objects the traveller seeks: worldly and other-worldly. Name and fame, wealth and riches, power and influence, and so on are worldly objects. An other-worldly object is acquiring knowledge, which is also of two kinds: travelling to acquire religious knowledge and to correct one's character and conduct, and travelling to acquire knowledge of the wonderful creations of Allah, such as the journey of Dhū al-Qarnayn. Travelling to perform an action is of two kinds as well: travelling to visit holy places such as Makkah, Madīnah, and Jerusalem, and travelling to defend the frontiers of an Islamic state. Travelling is also for visiting the holy shrines of religious leaders, friends of Allah, and religious people who are still living. Thus, there are different purposes for travelling.

The first purpose is to acquire knowledge. Travelling for knowledge is either obligatory or optional. When acquiring knowledge is obligatory, travelling for it is also obligatory. When it is optional, travelling is optional. The Prophet (ṣ) said, "Whoever leaves his house to acquire knowledge remains in the path of Allah until he returns." He also said, "If a man crosses a path in search of learning, Allah makes his path to paradise easy. Sa'īd ibn al-Musayyib travelled many days in search of one *ḥadīth*. Al-Sha'bī said, "If a man travel's from Syria to the most distant part of Yemen to hear a sermon, his journey will not be fruitless." Jābir ibn 'Abdullāh travelled from Madīnah to Egypt for one month and heard a *ḥadīth* from 'Abdullāh ibn Unys al-Anṣārī.

The second purpose is to rectify one's character and conduct. To tread the path of the next world is impossible without character and conduct. He who does not enquire into his hidden faults cannot purify his heart. The word 'travelling' means to turn away from the bad characters and conducts of people. Because of it, Allah reveals the secrets of the heaven and the earth. Thus, while travelling, a man's character is disclosed. When a witness was brought before 'Umar, the latter asked him, "Were you with someone on a journey as a result of which you came to know of his character?" The man said, "I was not." 'Umar said, "Then I think you do not know him." Bishr said, "O learned men, if you travelled, you would have been purified, for if water is logged in a place, it becomes polluted, and if it flows, it is made pure. In short, if a man remains confined at home, his character and conduct keep confined there, and his bad character is undisclosed, as no opportunity arises to see things he is not accustomed to."

The third purpose is to see the wonderful creations of Allah, which offer food for thought. There is nothing in the world, mountains, seas, heaven or other creations which do not testify to the unity of Allah. He who appreciates them can see and hear them, and he who does not pay attention to them cannot appreciate them. By "hearing" we mean the hearing of the heart, for the ear cannot hear without sound, and it appreciates the present condition. It is just like the words of a man telling the story of the wall and the nail. The wall says to the nail, "Do not trouble me." The nail says, "Ask the one which beats me. The rod which is behind me beats me. Why does he not leave me alone?"

There is no sign in the heaven or earth which does not bear testimony to the uniqueness and unity of Allah. Various kinds of things glorify His name, but nobody understands their glorification, as nobody undertakes the mental journey. If this was impossible, Sulaymān could not have understood the words of birds, nor Mūsā the speech of Allah, in spite of their lacking words and sound, respectively. The signs of writing that are on the backs of lifeless things can be appreciated by a man of deep insight. His outward journey is not required, but his mental journey is. Such a man derives joy from hearing. He can command the sun, moon, and stars, which roam in the cycle of time once, twice, or many times in the course of months or years. Were a man to go round a mosque other than the Ka'bah, round which he has been ordered to go, his act would be considered wonderful. If someone who has been ordered to roam round the sky roams round the earth, his action will be considered wonderful as well. So a sojourner who cannot roam in the material world remains within the station of his own house without crossing the various stations to reach Allah. For this reason, a pious man said, "Man says, 'Open your eyes, and you will see the wonderful creations of Allah.' But I say, 'Close your eyes and you will see them.'" Both views are true. The first man is talking about the first station near the house, and the second man is talking about the news of the distant stations. Without the satisfied soul of the sojourner, the distant stations cannot be crossed. Sometimes he roams for many years in one station. Sometimes Allah's grace shows him the straight path, but there are few who can receive this favour. Those who cross these stations can, by the light of Allah's grace, gain lasting fortune.

The sovereignty of the spiritual world is like that of this world. Firstly, those who seek it are few, and among them many remain in the face of destruction and decrease considerably when the goal is reached. Cowards cannot attain this sovereignty. In order to attain a high rank, one has to labour and pass many sleepless nights. Allah does not give it to those who are idle and cowardly.

Second kind of travelling

It is travelling for divine service, such as pilgrimage, jihad, and visiting the shrines of prophets, their companions, and other sages. The merits gained by calling on living sages can be obtained by visiting their graves. Travelling for such purpose is allowed, and the following *ḥadīth* is not an obstacle to that. The Prophet (ṣ) said, "Do not tie your camel at any place except at three mosques: this mosque of mine, the mosque of the Ka'bah, and the distant mosque." Besides these three mosques, all other mosques are equal in rank. The merits of meeting living sages are greater than those of visiting dead sages. There is written in the Torah, "Meet with your Muslim brother for the sake of Allah even if you have to walk four miles."

We have been informed about the merits of visiting the mosque of Madīnah and the Ka'bah. But the merits of visiting Jerusalem are also great. Ibn 'Umar once travelled from Madīnah to Jerusalem and prayed five times in the mosque. Sulaymān invoked Allah, "O Lord, if a man wishes to visit the mosque only to pray therein, do not avert your gaze from him as long as he remains therein. When he leaves, take him out of his sins as on the day his mother gave birth to him." Allah accepted his invocation.

Third kind of travelling

It is good to travel to become free from obstructions to one's religion. It is the way of the Prophet (ṣ) to flee for freedom from work beyond one's capacity. It is also obligatory to flee away for freeing the mind from engagement in actions, name and fame, and power. Unless the mind is freed from things other than Allah, one's religion does not become complete. If it is impossible, the more one becomes free from troubles, the better it is for the mind to be free from such thoughts.

The mind can be made light or heavy. Those who can increase them are ruined. It is unsafe for a worldly man to get relief from anxieties unless he travels to a distant place and frees his mind from all sorts of worldly anxieties. The mind does not have space for both the Creator and the created. There are some men, like the Prophet (ṣ) and sages, who are mentally strong in the same way some people are physically strong. There are differences even in their physical strength. How many people there are who can carry two and a half maunds of loads, which a weak man cannot carry. The strength can be increased by gradual and constant efforts. Similar is the condition of mental strength. In order to reach a high spiritual stage, continued and sustained efforts are necessary. Thus, the early sages used to stay far away from their own houses. Sufyān al-Thawrī said, "The present time is very perilous. When unknown people suffer loss at present, what is the state of those who have name and fame?" So present people should change their residences so that people do not know them. Abū Nu'aym said, "I once saw once Sufyān al-Thawrī with a pitcher in one hand and a bag of leather full of articles in another. Upon being asked where he is going, he said, 'I am going where commodities are cheap. Live where these things are cheap, as it is safer for your religion and less stressful.'" Al-Khawwāṣ would not reside in any place for more than forty days.

Fourth kind of travelling

There is no fault in travelling to another place to save oneself from epidemic diseases such as small pox, cholera, and plague, or where commodities are cheap. Sometimes such travelling becomes obligatory and sometimes commendable. If there is an outbreak of an epidemic disease in a certain locality, people should not move to another place, as the Prophet (ṣ) said, "Some people were punished with epidemic disease before you. It remained in the world after that. It comes sometimes and goes away sometimes. When it breaks out in any place, do not go near it. When it breaks out where you live, do not flee from it." Similarly, he said, "My people will be destroyed by attacks and epidemic diseases." 'Ā'ishah asked, "What is an 'attack'?" He said, "It is an epidemic disease like the plague of camels. It grows in their sinews. He who dies of this disease dies a martyr. He who stays therein is like a prisoner in the way of Allah. He who flees from it flees as it were from jihad." The Prophet (ṣ) said to one of his Companions, "Do not ascribe associates to Allah, even if you are punished and threatened. Obey your parents. If they tell you to leave everything you own, do so. Do not give up any prayer willingly. He who gives up a prayer willingly becomes free from the security of Allah. Do not drink wine, as it is the key to all sins. Give up sin, as it displeases Allah. Do not flee from jihad. If an epidemic disease afflicts the people among whom you live, stay with them. Spend from your wealth for your family. Do not lift your stick from them, and generate fear in them." It appears from this *ḥadīth* that it is prohibited both to flee from and to go to an epidemic disease.

In conclusion, travelling could be either good, bad, or permissible. What is bad becomes sometimes unlawful, such as the fleeing of a slave or of a rebel. What is bad is fleeing from epidemic diseases. What is good is sometimes obligatory and sometimes recommended. Travelling for pilgrimage and learning are obligatory, and for meeting sages and visiting their graves recommended. What is permissible depends on the intention. If one travels to earn money by abstaining from begging, to protect the honour of oneself and of one's family, or to give charity, it is lawful, as these are actions of the next world. The Prophet (ṣ) said, 'All actions are judged by intentions." This *ḥadīth* is applicable to obligatory, recommended and permissible travels. A wise man said, "Allah appoints to travellers angels who observe their intentions, and they are given blessing according to their intentions."

2

Rules of travelling

The first rule is to return ill-gotten gains, to pay off debts, to provide for your dependents, and return trusts. Take lawful and good things for the journey, and take sufficient money, so that you may also help others with their needs. Ibn 'Umar said, "To help a traveller with lawful money is to honour him." So treat your fellow travellers well. Give them food and disclose your good conduct to them, as travelling discloses the hidden faults of the heart. A wise man said, "If a man is praised by his fellow trader or fellow sojourner, there is no doubt that he is a good man." Another wise man said, "Three men cannot be blamed for their anxiety: a fasting man, a patient man, and a traveller." The good character of a fellow traveller becomes complete if he treats his fellow travellers well, helps them with their needs, shows them sympathy, and helps them with their loading and unloading luggage and loads.

The second rule is to take along a good travel companion, one who will help you with your actions and religion—when you forget, he will remind you, and when you want help, he will help—as every man follows the religion of his friend. The Prophet (ṣ) prohibited travelling alone. He said, "Three people form a congregation." He also said, "When three of you form a company on a journey, choose one of you as a leader." The Companions would do so, saying, "This man is our leader." The Prophet (ṣ) would then appoint him as leader.

Appoint as leader he who is the best among you in character and conduct, is the kindest to his companions, and places the needs of companions before his own. The affairs of the world are best done if one is entrusted with one manager, just as one God manages the affairs of the universe. Had there been two Gods, they would have quarrelled and all the affairs of the world would have been mismanaged. The duties of a leader should be learnt from the following examples.

Two friends, 'Abdullāh al-Marwazī and Abū 'Alī al-Ribāṭī, started on a journey. 'Abdullāh said to al-Ribāṭī, "You are my leader," and al-Ribāṭī said to 'Abdullāh, "You are my leader." 'Abdullāh was made leader of the two and thereafter carried on his back his own luggage and the luggage of al-Ribāṭī. One night, it rained hard, so 'Abdullāh held a blanket over his companion for the whole night. Whenever al-Ribāṭī said, "Do not do this," 'Abdullāh would reply, "Have you not selected me as your leader? So do not order me and do not do other than what I order you to do." Thereupon al-Ribāṭī said, "I wished then that I were dead and that I should not have said to him, 'You are my leader.'" This should be the duty of a leader of a journey or in administration.

The Prophet (ṣ) said, "It is better to have four companions when you travel." There is surely some good in the words of the Prophet (ṣ) "A traveller has two duties: to protect luggage and to go for taking necessary things." These can well be done if there are four people together on a journey.

The third rule is to bid farewell to relatives and friends. Upon starting, say, "I entrust to Allah your religion, your trust, and the results of your action." The Prophet (ṣ) used to say that. The Prophet (ṣ) said, "When anyone of you wishes to travel, he should pray for his friends because Allah gives good to them on account of his prayer." He also said, "When you bid any man farewell, say, 'May Allah provide you with God-fearingness, forgive your sins and give you good wherever you go.'" Whoever stays at home should say that to the traveller. Mūsā ibn Wardān said, "One day, I intended to go on a journey and went to bid farewell to Abū Hurayrah, who said, 'O cousin, should I not teach you what the

Prophet (ṣ) taught me about bidding farwell?' I said, 'Yes.' He said, 'I entrust you to Allah, who does not break His trust.'" One day, a man came to the Prophet (ṣ) and said, "I intend to travel, so give me advice." The Prophet (ṣ) said to him, "In the protection and care of Allah. May Allah supply you with piety, pardon your sins and direct you to good wherever you are."

When you entrust to Allah, entrust everything to Him and not only a particular thing. The result of entrusting a particular thing is illustrated in the following story. A man with his son came to 'Umar as the latter was distributing money among people. 'Umar said to him, "The appearance of the boy is exactly like yours. I have never found such similarity." The man said, "O Commander of the Faithful, I will tell you his story. When he was in his mother's womb, I was on a journey. When starting, I said to his mother, 'I am entrusting the child in your womb to Allah.' Then I went abroad. When I returned, I saw that my wife had died. When I went to her grave, I found a fire burning over her grave. I asked the people, 'What is this fire?' They said, 'This is the grave of your wife. Every night we see this fire.' I then dug her grave and found a burning lamp with which a child was playing, and I heard a voice from the heaven say, 'You have entrusted this child to Me. Had you entrusted his mother also to Me, you would have found her after your return.'"

The fourth rule is to pray the guidance prayer (*istikhārah*) before starting. A man came to the Prophet (ṣ) and said, "I have made a vow for a journey, but have written a will. Tell me with whom I should keep it. My son, father, or brother?" The Prophet (ṣ) replied, "If a man prays four units in his house before starting on a journey, he cannot leave anything better than it. After putting on his travel clothes, he should pray these four units, reciting therein Sūrah al-Ikhlāṣ (Qur'an, 112), and then say, 'Allah, with this prayer I am seeking Your nearness, so make this prayer my successor with my family and wealth.' Then the prayer becomes his successor with his family and wealth and guards his house until he returns."

The fifth rule is to recite this invocation at the door of the house as you are exiting your house to set off on the journey: "In the name of Allah. I depend on Allah. There is no might or strength except in Allah. O Lord, I seek refuge in You from being misguided or misguiding others, from slipping or making others slip, from oppressing or being oppressed, and from acting ignorantly or being acted on ignorantly." When you start walking, say, "Allah, I have come out with Your help. On You I depend. I consider You my protector, and to You I turn my face. O Allah, you are my object of trust, and you are my hope. You are sufficient against what troubles me and what you know of me. It is glory to live in Your neighbourhood, and Your presence suffices. There is no deity but You. O Allah, increase my piety, pardon my sins, and guide me towards good wherever I go."

The sixth rule is to set off in the morning. The Prophet (ṣ) set off in the morning for Tabūk and said, "O Allah, bless my people on Thursday morning." It is also recommended to end one's travels on Thursday morning. The Prophet (ṣ) seldom ended his travels on other days. He also said, "Bless my people on Saturday morning." When he sent any expedition, he would do so in the early part of the day. He said, "Bless the morning for my people." One should not, however, travel on Friday morning. The Prophet (ṣ) said, "To take a few steps with warriors in the way of Allah and take care of their conveyances morning and evening are dearer to me than the world and its riches."

The seventh rule is to alight only at midday, which is recommended. Most of the Prophet's journeys were at night. The Prophet (ṣ) said, "You should travel during the night because the earth is not as straitened in day as at night." When you alight at a station, pray two units and say, "O Allah, I seek refuge in Your perfect words from the evils You have created."

The eighth rule is not to wander from the crowd, as you may be murdered. There should be a guard when you sleep at night. When the Prophet (ṣ) slept in the first part of the night, he spread out his hands, and when he slept in the latter part of the night, he placed his head on his hand. He would do that to prevent oversleeping. If there are two companions, one should guard the other.

The ninth rule is to show mercy to a riding animal and not to load it beyond its capacity. Do not beat its face, as this is prohibited. Also, do not sleep on its back, as this troubles it. The Prophet (ṣ) said, "Do not make the backs of your riding animals seats for comfort." It is recommended to alight from the animal in the morning and evening, allowing it to rest.

The tenth rule is to take six things. 'Ā'ishah related that when the Prophet (ṣ) travelled, he would take with him five things: a mirror, antimony, scissors, a toothstick and a comb. According to another version, he would take six things: a mirror, a urinal, a toothstick, scissors, antimony and a comb. Umm S'ad said, "The Prophet (ṣ) would always take a mirror and antimony with him on his journey. The Prophet (ṣ) said, "When you go to bed, you should use antimony, as it strengthens eyesight and makes hair grow." It has been related that the Prophet (ṣ) would apply antimony thrice in each eye.

The eleventh rule pertains to one's return. Whenever the Prophet (ṣ) returned from an expedition and the greater and lesser pilgrimages and finished an action, he would say, "Allah is greatest" three times. Whenever he crossed an elevated place, he would say, "There is no deity but Allah, alone, without partner. Sovereignty is His, and praise is His. He has power over everything." Thereafter, send your family news of your arrival through a man. Do not go to them suddenly, lest you see an undesirable thing. Nobody should return from a journey to his family at night, for the Prophet (ṣ) prohibited it. Whenever he returned from a journey, he would first enter the mosque, pray two units, and then enter his house and say, "I have returned home repentant to our Lord. I am repenting such that no sin remains." It is recommended to bring back some delicious eatables for the members of the family. A *ḥadīth* says, "If a person is unable to bring anything back with him, he should bring back at least a piece of stone in his bag." The Prophet (ṣ) laid great emphasis on this, as it cements love and affection.

Secret rules of travelling

Nobody should travel except to increase the progress of religion. If there is chance of loss of any portion of religion, you should return home. Whenever you go out, intend to meet the religious people of that place and try to get benefit from them. Do not stay in one place for more than a week or ten days. If you wish to meet your relatives there, do not stay with them for more than three days, which is the limit for entertaining guests.

Some matters before travelling

What should be known before travelling is of two types: knowledge of dispensations for travellers, and knowledge of the direction of prayer and the fixed times of prayer. Regarding ablution, there are two dispensations: to wipe over socks and to perform dry ablution (*tayammum*). Prayers have also been made easy. They may be shortened, joined, and performed on conveyances or on foot. When travelling, it is also not obligatory to fast.

The following seven dispensations have been made for travelers:

1. To wipe over socks: Ṣafwān ibn 'Assāl said, "While we were on a journey, the Prophet (ṣ) ordered us not to take off socks of leather for three days and three nights." When not travelling, one can wipe over socks for a day and a night. Socks must be put on after a full ablution, must not be torn in any place, and must not to be taken off during the mentioned duration.

2. To perform dry ablution is allowed when travelling provided that water is at a place so far that one would not hear a sound from there, or that there are ferocious beasts near the water: The palms of both hands must be thrust on the earth, and with them the face must be wiped. Then the palms must again be thrust on the earth, and with them the arms up to the elbows must be wiped. With one dry ablution, only one obligatory prayer along with the *sunnah* and optional prayers may be performed.
3. To make obligatory prayers short: The noon, midafternoon and nightfall prayers may be made shortened to two units. It should be performed on time with the intention of shortening it and not under an imam who is performing the full four units. According to Ḥanafī law, one may shorten prayers after crossing a distance of 48 miles from one's residence.
4. To join two obligatory prayers: The noon prayer may be delayed until the time of the midafternoon prayer, or the latter may be prayed with noon prayer during travels. This is the case with the sunset and nightfall prayers, which may be prayed together. The sunset prayer may be performed with the nightfall prayer or vice-versa. It is lawful to perform the Friday prayer when travelling.
5. The direction of prayer: While riding his riding animal, the Prophet (ṣ) prayed *sunnah* prayers facing its direction. Thereon prayers are said by hints of bending and prostration. One need not turn towards the Ka'bah at the start of the prayer.
6. It is allowed to perform *sunnah* prayers while walking by hints and gestures and without sitting for the Testification of Faith (*tashahhud*).
7. It is allowed for a traveller not to fast. He may make up the missed fasts on other days.

Book 8
Music and ecstasy

Introduction

The heart is the seat of secret wealth and is the invaluable mine of jewels. In it lies the most valuable jewel, just as fire lies secretly in stone and iron. It lies hidden in the same way water lies in the depth of the earth. There is no means of waking it up from sleep without pleasant sounds. There is no path of sound entering the heart without the door of the ear. The feelings that lie hidden in the heart are brought out by pleasant, melodious, and rhyming sounds. These do not come out of the heart without movement, just as what is in cauldron does not fall without being heated. Melodious songs take out what is hidden in the heart and creates a wonderful feeling. When songs control the heart, they take out from it its qualities and guilts. So it is necessary to discuss songs in the light of the teaching of Islam.

1

Different opinions about listening to songs

We shall now discuss religious songs and the ecstasy which arises spontaneously. As a result of these songs, the organs of the body tremble. Al-Shāfiʿī, Mālik, Abū Ḥanīfah, Sufyān al-Thawrī and other scholars used words which indicate that listening to religious songs is unlawful.

In his book *Ādāb al-Qaḍā'* (The Decorum of Judgeship), al-Shāfiʿī said that listening to songs is detestable, as it resembles void things, and that he who remains busy listening to songs is a fool, and his deposition is unacceptable. The judge Abū al-Ṭayyib said, "To listen to songs by a marriageable woman is unlawful according to the disciples of al-Shāfiʿī." He also said, "Al-Shāfiʿī said that it is detestable to beat musical instruments with a stick, and that disbelievers (*zanādiqah*) made use of that to divert their attention from hearing the Qur'an.

Mālik prohibited songs, saying, "It is your duty to cancel the sale of a female slave who, after her purchase, is found to be a singer."

Abū Ḥanīfah disliked listening to songs and said that listening to them is a sin. Sufyān al-Thawrī, Ḥammād, Ibrāhīm, al-Shaʿbī and other scholars of Kūfah gave similar opinions.

After quoting the opinion of many scholars, Abū Ṭālib al-Makkī said that listening to songs is lawful, and that ʿAbdullāh ibn al-Zubayr, Muʿāwiyah and other Companions used to hear songs, and that on the most excellent days of the year, the Makkans used to listen to songs as well. The Madīnans also used to listen. ʿAta' had two female slaves who chanted, and his friends would listen to them. Furthermore, al-Junayd, al-Sarī al-Saqaṭī, Dhū al-Nūn al-

Miṣrī, al-Ḥārith al-Muḥāsibī and Abū al-Ḥasan al-ʿAsqalānī used to listen to songs.

Mumshād al-Dīnawarī said, "I asked the Prophet (ṣ) in dream, 'O Messenger of Allah, do you dislike anything of listening to songs?' He said, 'I do not dislike it, but tell them that they should begin it with a verse of the Qur'an and finish it with a verse of it.'" Ṭāhir ibn Bilāl al-Hamadānī al-Warrāq saw in a dream the Prophet (ṣ), who was sitting in a corner of a mosque with Abū Bakr al-Ṣiddīq by his side. The latter was reciting some poetry, and the Prophet (ṣ) was listening. The Prophet (ṣ) then said, 'This is truth in exchange of truth.'"

Al-Junayd said, "Mercy is bestowed on these people on three occasions: eating, as they do not eat unless they are hungry; speaking, as they do not speak except at assemblies of the upright; and listening to songs, as they listen with ecstasy and witness to what is true.

Proof that listening to songs is lawful

Sharīʿah consists of the words and actions of the Prophet (ṣ) and what is inferred therefrom. These things do not prove that religious songs are unlawful.

Inferential proof from the Prophet's words and actions

Generally, singing is a pleasant sound, and pleasant sounds are of two kinds: rhythmic and simple. Rhythmic sounds are also of two kinds: comprehensible, such as poetry, and incomprehensible, such as the sounds of animals. Listening to a pleasant sound should not be unlawful because it is pleasant. Rather, it is lawful according to traditions.

Pleasant sounds without rhythm

The ears have been created to hear the pleasant sounds of songs. Man has five senses and an intellect, and each sense has a perception of what gives pleasure. The pleasure of the eyes is to see. They enjoy seeing beautiful things, such as various kinds of leaves and plants, flowing streams, and beautiful faces. Ugly colours are displeasing to the eye. The nose has been created to smell. It loves to smell pleasant scents and fragrance and dislikes bad smells and the stenches of rotten things. The tongue likes sweet and greasy things and dislikes bitter and distasteful foods. The hands like smooth things more than hard and uneven things. As for the intellect, it feels comfort in knowledge and dislikes illiteracy and ignorance. Such is also the case for the ears. The sounds which they hear is of two kinds: pleasant sounds, such as those of nightingales and pleasant songs, and displeasing sounds, such as those of asses. What is true of other organs is true also of the ears.

Ḥadīth allows the hearing of pleasant sounds. Allah says, "He increases in creation what He pleases" (Qur'an, 35:1). This increase is said to mean pleasantness of voice. The Prophet (ṣ) said, "Allah did not send any prophet who did not have a pleasant voice." He also said, "If a man recites the Qur'an with a pleasant voice, Allah listens to his recitation more intently than does one to the songs of his female singer." A *ḥadīth* praising the prophet Dāwūd says, "Dāwūd used to sing with such a melodious voice that men, jinn, beasts, and birds gathered spell bound to listen to it. Nearly four hundred people died by listening to his songs." The Prophet (ṣ) once praised his Companion Abū Mūsā al-Ash'arī, saying, "He has been given the musical instruments of the songs of the family of Dāwūd."

Allah says, "Surely the most hateful of voices is braying of the asses" (Qur'an, 31:19). This verse also praises pleasant voices. If listening to songs is unlawful, then to listen to the sound of a nightingale is also unlawful. If to hear the sound of a nightingale is lawful, then will it not be lawful to hear pleasant and melodious sounds which have wisdom and good meanings?

Pleasant sounds with rhythm

There is rhythm in pleasant sounds. There are many pleasant sounds without rhythm, and there are many unpleasant sounds with rhythm. With regard to their places of origin, pleasant sounds with rhythm are of three kinds.

The first kind is sounds which issue from inanimate things such as musical instruments and drums, or the sounds of beating instruments with sticks.

The second kind is sounds which issue from the throats of animals, including men, nightingales, and other animals. They are natural sounds which are rhythmic, and therefore listening to them is pleasant. The source of the sounds of animals is the throat. Pleasant sounds were discovered by imitating the pleasant sounds of animals. There is nothing in Allah's creation which men do not imitate. So how could sounds, melodious or not, be unlawful to ears? Nobody says that the pleasant sounds of birds are unlawful. The sounds of animals with life are no different from the sounds of lifeless instruments. So to listen to the sounds of a man, in whatever form it comes out of his throat, is not unlawful. What is unlawful, rather, is to listen to the sounds of the instruments which Sharī'ah expressly prohibits, such as the *kūbah* (drum), pipes, and strings. These are unlawful not because they emit pleasant sounds. If this were the reason, all things man enjoys would have been unlawful. The reason, rather, is that they are connected with wine, which was made unlawful. These instruments incite the drinking of wine, just as living in a room with a strange woman is unlawful because it incites cohabitation. These instruments also remind people of drinking wine. The flutes of shepherds, pilgrims, and drummers, which emit pleasant sounds, are not unlawful, as they have no connection with drunkards. Allah says, "Who has prohibited the embellishment of Allah which He has brought forth for His servants and the good provisions?" (Qur'an, 7:32). So these sounds with rhythm are not unlawful.

The third kind is sounds which are easily understood, namely poems which issue from the throats of men. These are lawful. Easily understood words and pleasant sounds with rhythm, which are individually lawful, cannot be unlawful when they are together. If, however, there are any objectionable words in them, they are unlawful, whether coupled with pleasant sounds or not. Al-Shāfi'ī said, "Poetry is only words. The good of it is good, and the bad of it is bad." If to recite poetry without sound and rhythm is lawful, then to recite it with sound and rhythm is lawful.

When poetry was recited before the Prophet (ṣ), he used to say, "There is surely wisdom in poetry." When constructing the mosque of Madīnah, the Prophet (ṣ) used to hear material with his Companions and recite poetry. He once recited these lines: "O Allah, life is the life of the hereafter, so bestow mercy on the Madīnan Helpers and Emigrants." Further, the Prophet (ṣ) erected a pulpit in the mosque for the poet Ḥassān. He would stand on it and recite poetry deprecating the unbelievers and praising the Prophet (ṣ). The Prophet (ṣ) would then said, "Allah is helping Ḥassān with the Holy Spirit so long as he is defending or boasting of the Prophet (ṣ)." When the poet al-Nābighah recited some of his poems before the Prophet (ṣ), the latter said, "May Allah not break your teeth." 'Ā'ishah said that the Companions used to recite poetry before the Prophet (ṣ), who would only smile. 'Amr ibn al-Sharīd related from his father, "I recited before the Prophet (ṣ) a hundred poems of Umayyah ibn Abī al-Ṣalt. Each time he said, 'Repeat it.'"

Fourth stage

Listening to songs wakes up the heart. What remains strong in the heart is awakened by listening to songs. I say that pleasant songs with rhythm is a secret of Allah for the soul. It creates a wonderful feeling in the heart. Some sounds incite pleasure, some pain, some sleep, some passion. Some sounds move the organs of the body. The heart becomes such if the rings of songs sound in the innermost recess of the heart. Pleasant songs often lull a suckling child into sleep or stop his crying.

Camels are so influenced by songs that even a heavy load seems light to them. A slave was once conducting a camel to a distant place. It was heavily loaded. The slave had a melodious sound. The camel was so impressed by his song that it covered in one day the distance of three days' journey. When the loads were taken from it, it expired. This shows that the effect of songs on the heart is wonderful. For this reason, even birds used to sit on the head of the prophet Dāwūd upon hearing his songs.

Seven types of commendable songs

The first type is the songs of pilgrims. They roam from one country to another with songs and flutes. These songs are lawful, and they recite poetry about the Ka'bah, the Black Stone, the Ḥaṭīm, Zamzam and other signs. These incite people to visit the Ka'bah and other holy places.

The second type is the songs warriors use to urge men to warfare. It is lawful to call to bravery and to lay down one's life for the cause of Allah.

The third type is the songs and poetry of bravery which two warriors recite when they meet on the battlefield. These are lawful because they incite them to fight. It is lawful in lawful fights, but not in unlawful fights.

The fourth type is songs of mourning, which are of two kinds: praiseworthy and blameworthy. It is blameworthy to recite songs which increase sorrow for past mishaps and calamities. The Qur'an says, "So that you may not grieve for what has escaped you" (Qur'an, 57:23). To express sorrow for the dead falls into this class of songs, as it expresses dissatisfaction at the order of Allah. Mourning songs are praiseworthy when men express sorrow for past sins. For his sin, Adam wept for forgiveness and the prophet Dāwūd's songs were for forgiveness. Owing to his melodious songs, many people expired. This action is praiseworthy, and to give encouragement for this is also praiseworthy.

The fifth type is festive songs, which engender joy and happiness during festivals and on other days of expressing happiness. Such songs are sung at the two *'Īds*, marriage festivals, birth ceremonies, the birth of a child, and circumcision. When the Prophet (ṣ) returned to Madīnah after an expedition, women sang from the top of roofs,

"The full moon has risen on us from the mountain passes of al-Wadā'. It is compulsory for us to express gratitude to Allah Almighty." This is commendable.

Furthermore, 'Ā'ishah said, "While I was watching the sports of the Abyssinian boys standing in the mosque on the day of *'Īd*, the Prophet (ṣ) covered me with his mantle." She was then of immature age. One day 'Ā'ishah saw that two girls were beating tambourines at Minā, and the Prophet (ṣ) covered her face with his sheet. When Abū Bakr came, the Prophet (ṣ) removed the sheet from the face of 'Ā'ishah and said, "O Abū Bakr, leave her, as it is a day *'Īd*.

One day, the Prophet (ṣ) asked 'Ā'ishah, "What are these dolls?" She answered, "These are my daughters, and in the midst of them is a horse." He asked, "What are these two over the horse?" She said, "Two wings." The Prophet (ṣ) said, "Two wings for a horse ?" She said, "Have you not heard that Sulaymān, the son of Dāwūd, had a horse with two wings?" With that the Prophet (ṣ) laughed so much that his teeth showed.

'Ā'ishah also said, "The Prophet (ṣ) came to me while two girls who were with me were singing the songs of the Day of Bu'āth. He lay down on his side on the bed and turned his face away. Abū Bakr then came and threatened me, saying, 'The pipe of the Devil before the Prophet (ṣ)?" The Prophet (ṣ) advanced towards Abū Bakr and said, 'Leave them both.'"

These *ḥadīth*s in *Ṣaḥīḥ al-Bukhārī* and *Ṣaḥīḥ Muslim* prove that songs are not unlawful.

The sixth type is the songs of lovers. These increase love for Allah and give satisfaction and pleasure to the mind. These are lawful. But if the union with a strange girl or woman is unlawful, songs for her love are also unlawful.

The seventh type is the songs of one who seeks the love and pleasure of Allah and to meet Him. These are lawful. Listening to songs brings out from the recesses of the heart the ability to see different matters. It also brings out a deep feeling and unspeakable taste which can only be felt and not disclosed. This taste cannot be obtained by any other organs of the body. Sufis refer to intoxication as ecstasy, which appears in the heart as an effect of religious songs which did not exist before. The fire of ecstasy arising in the heart burns the uncleanliness of the mind, just as fire removes the accumulated refuse on invaluable jewels and diamonds. The result is the shining of a heart in which spiritual visions (*mushāhadāt*) and spiritual revelations (*mukāshafāt*) appear. In other words, one's inner eye is opened, an eye by which one sees the secrets of nature. This is the goal of the lovers of Allah and the last stage of their search. He who can reach this stage gains the nearness of Allah. But it is possible only by listening to songs.

He who is stupid expresses wonder at the taste of ecstasy, just as an impotent man express wonder at the pleasure of cohabitation, or a boy at the taste of power and fame. How can he who has no sense of taste, taste? How can he who has no power of reason, have the taste of reason? He who has gained knowledge of Allah loves Him beyond doubt. This love deepens in proportion to his knowledge of Allah. The Prophet's deep love for Allah kept him confined in the cave of Ḥirā' in deep meditation.

Know, dear readers, that every beauty is dear to the sense of that beauty. Allah is ever beautiful and loves beauty. If the beauty is of a material thing, it can be seen by the sense of sight. If the beauty is of glorious attributes and good character, it can be appreciated by the sense of the heart. The word "beauty" has been used metaphorically for these attributes. It is therefore said, "That man has beautiful character and conduct." It does not speak of his figure, but of his qualities. He is loved for these beautiful attributes just as one is loved for his beautiful appearance. If this love is deep, it is called "*'ishq*." Even more wondrous is that a dead man is loved not for this figure but for the innate qualities he had. Every beauty in the world is a spark of the permanent beauty of Allah and a spark of His light. So how can one not love Him who is ever beautiful, the prime source of beauty? He who realises this loves Him most.

Nothing can compare to the beauty of the sun and the moon. Allah is the creator of these beautiful things. So how should He be loved? Love for a created thing has defects. It is a sign of our ignorance. But one who knows Him with the real eye of truth knows of no beauty except the creator of a beauty. He who is cognizant that creation is an attribute of a creator does not go to anybody except him. Everything in the world is the creation of Allah and a sign of His creation. So one realises Him though His creations and realises His attributes and His workmanship, just as one realises the qualities of a writer through his written book. A man of little intellect understands love to be physical union or satisfaction of lust.

The Prophet (ṣ) once told of a young man of the children of Israel who asked his mother from the top of a hillock, "Who has created this sky?" The mother replied, "Allah Almighty." He again asked, "Who has created this earth?" The mother replied, "Allah Almighty." Thus he asked about the mountains and the clouds, and the mother replied as before. He said, "Such is the glory of Allah" and jumped down from the hillock and soon expired. This is nothing but ecstasy from loving Allah who is almighty and great.

Cases in which listening to songs is unlawful

It is unlawful to listen to songs when:

1. they are of a woman whose look excites sexual passion: Beardless boys may also be included in this category if sexual

passion is aroused at their sight. This unlawfulness is not for songs but for women and beardless boys.

2. the instruments used in them are those of drunkards: These remind one of unlawful thing and incite unlawful acts of wine-drinking and consuming intoxicants. They include pipes, strings and the *kūbah,* but not the *daff,* flute or other musical instruments.
3. they have obscene words: Obscene words in poetry, useless talks, and accusations against Allah, His Prophet (ṣ), or his Companions are all unlawful to listen to. Descriptions of a particular woman and not of women in general are unlawful as well.
4. they give rise to evil or immoral desires.
5. it becomes a habit: An excess of anything is bad. If too much food is eaten, it is bad for health. Similarly, just as too much oil rubbed onto the face looks ugly, so also does listening to too many songs become a bad habit.

After strenuous efforts and hard labour, listening to songs and partaking in innocent enjoyments are not bad.

"From your arguments," one might say, "It seems that listening to songs is lawful in some cases and unlawful in others. Why, then, did you say at first that it is lawful?" In answer to this, know that if a person questions the lawfulness or unlawfulness of honey, I must say at first that honey is lawful, but is unlawful for a man of hot temper. If you ask me about wine, I must say at first that it is unlawful, but is lawful for a man in whose throat a morsel of food is stuck. These are the exemptions and not the general rule. So at first I stated the general rule, which is that listening to songs is lawful and that wine is unlawful.

Songs are unlawful not because of their musical sounds but for other reasons. Al-Shāfiʿī does not generally make listening to songs unlawful. He says that he who sings as a profession, his testimony is not acceptable. The reason is that singing is deemed play and sport and it is connected with useless things. Allah will not punish for useless things and play and sport, and they are not unlawful. Allah says, “Allah does not call you to account for what is vain in your oaths” (Qur’an, 2:225). If an oath is taken in the name of Allah without resolve or opposition to Sharī‘ah, it is lawful.

The proofs of those who say that listening to songs is unlawful, and answers to them

They recite the verse of the Qur’an “Of men is he who takes instead frivolous discourse” (Qur’an, 31:6). Ibn Mas‘ūd, al-Ḥasan al-Baṣrī, al-Nakha‘ī and others said that “frivolous discourse” here means songs. The Prophet (ṣ) said, “Allah has made unlawful the singing girl, the selling of her and her price, and teaching her songs.” The word “singing girl” here means a girl who sings before drunkards. We have mentioned before that if there is fear of sin as a result of the singing of women, it is unlawful. This is supported by the songs of slave girls in the house of ‘Ā’ishah in the presence of the Prophet (ṣ). If frivolous discourse is purchased at the price of religion, it leads to misguidance, and so it is unlawful. This is the meaning of ‘frivolous discourse’ in the above verse.

Another proof for the unlawfulness of listening to songs is said to be the verse “Do you then wonder at this announcement? And will you laugh and not weep? While you are indulging in varieties?” (Qur’an, 53:59-61). If this verse makes songs unlawful, then to laugh and to weep, also mentioned in this verse, are unlawful. Also, Allah says, “As to the poets, those who go astray follow them” (Qur’an, 26:224). In this verse, only the infidel poets have been mentioned. It is not understood from this that good poetry has been banned.

Yet another proof is the *ḥadīth* in which the Prophet (ṣ) said, “Satan was the first who sang mourning songs and the first who sang songs.” This does not ban songs, as the prophet Dāwūd used to sing mourning songs for sins. The Prophet (ṣ) heard this song when he returned from an expedition: “The full moon has risen on us from the passes of al-Wadā‘.”

Still another proof is the *ḥadīth* in which the Prophet (ṣ) said, "If a man raises his voice in singing a song, Allah sends to him two devils who climb on his shoulders, place their feet on his chest, and move them until he stops." This *ḥadīth* applies to bad and obscene songs, which we have mentioned above and which give rise to sexual passion.

Further, another *ḥadīth* cited is as follows: "Everything a man plays with is void except his training his horse, his throwing his arrows, and his playing with his wife." The word 'void' does not mean that everything except those three things are unlawful. Rather, it means want of benefit. To hear the pleasant sounds of birds and to partake in innocent sports and enjoyments are not unlawful.

2

Effects and rules of listening to songs

There are three stages in listening to songs: understanding the meaning, ecstasy, and the movement of bodily limbs as a result of ecstasy.

First stage: Understanding the meaning

Understanding varies according to the conditions of listeners. The first condition is the natural state of the mind, to listen to songs and not to have any taste except the taste of listening to songs. This is the lowest stage, as birds and beasts share it with people.

The second condition is to appreciate after understanding the meanings of the songs and to apply the objects of the songs to a particular man. This condition applies to young men, as their sexual passion is aroused by these songs.

The third condition is to apply what one hears to one's intercourse with Allah and to the changing of one's states. At the initial stage, this condition applies to the sojourners to the path of Allah, whose only object is to gain knowledge of Allah. They raise their inner feelings and understand the meanings of songs according to their own conditions.

Let us give some examples here. A Sufi heard a man singing, "The ambassador says, 'See me tomorrow.'" At once his ecstasy rose, and he fell down senseless. When he regained his senses, he was asked why he swooned. He said, "I remembered the words of the Prophet (ṣ) "The inhabitants of paradise will see their Lord once a week."

Al-Raqqī related from Ibn al-Darrāj that he said, "Ibn al-Fawṭī and I passed by a beautiful palace along the Tigris when we found on it a slave girl singing and a beautiful young man looking at her and saying, 'O girl, repeat this song to me.' When she repeated the song, the young man exclaimed, 'It has coincided with my thought!' Suddenly he raised a loud shriek and expired. The owner of the palace freed her from slavery, gifted the palace, gave up everything, and left for an unknown destination. Nothing was heard of him again. His ecstasy was so strong it was as though he was intoxicated by wine.

When asked about songs, al-Khaḍir said, "Surely it is such a slippery stone on which the feet of the learned cannot remain firm." Songs arouse a man's hidden feelings as intoxicants arouse passion. But him whom Allah saves by the light of His guidance is saved.

The poet al-Tha'labī said with regard to the world:

Leave the world and seek her not in marriage.
Her benefits are less than her harms.
Remember always the angel of death, cruel and hard.
Many statements are there about the word's cruel nature,
And with me is a description of her that, by my life, is sound.
She has beautiful face which charms all men,
But her heart is filled with destructive poison.

The second possible meaning of 'listening to songs' is that the listener should apply it to himself with regard to Allah, who cannot be feared as he ought to be. In this case, he fears Allah for show and not out of fear or love for Him. In other words, he is not placed on a high spiritual plane. For this reason, the Prophet (ṣ) said, "O Allah, I am unable to count Your glory. You are as You have praised Yourself." He also said, "I ask Allah's forgiveness seventy times every day and night." This forgiveness is for reaching a higher plane of spirituality from its lower plane.

The third meaning of "listening to songs" is that a man considers his present condition insignificant after seeing the advanced condition of others. This depends on the proportion of the purity of his mind and his intellect. The more his mind is pure, the more his spirituality is developed by listening to songs.

The fourth condition is that of the listener of songs who has reached the highest stage of gnosis after passing beyond different conditions and different stages. He is distant from everything except knowledge of Allah. He even loses his own personality, his own condition, and his own actions and deeds. He is like a man submerged in the ocean. His condition is that of the women who cut their hands unknowingly upon seeing the exquisite beauty of Yūsuf. Thus the Sufi loses himself from all things around him. Those who love Allah deeply cannot look at anything other than Allah. He is like an intoxicated man who loses awareness of all things.

Abū al-Ḥasan al-Nūrī said that he heard a man singing this song: "O darling, I seek from the lasting love. When it comes, intellect leaves me." Once, immersed in ecstasy, he got up, went to an open field, and began to run in it where the sugarcanes were cut, leaving the stems like swords. His feet got wounded, yet he continued running up until the morning. As a result his feet began to bleed, and after some days he died.

This is the degree of those with great faith (*ṣiddīqūn*) and can be attained only by some songs. It is such that a person passes away from his own life and states. He hears songs about Allah, yet hears knowledge about Allah and from Allah. This rank is for he who immerses himself with rays of truth and crosses the boundary of states and works. His passing away is not the passing away of his body but of his heart. By "heart" I mean not the blood and flesh but the secret thing of the spirit which exists by the command of Allah.

This secret thing is like a clean mirror which has no colour of its own, but takes whatever colour is presented to it. Or like a transparent glass which has no colour of its own, but takes the colour of whatever is put in it, and which has no form, but takes the form of whatever thing it is made of. Similarly, whatever is put in the secret thing, the latter takes its form and colour. A poet said:

> Fine is the glass, and fine is the wine, so they mingle and
> the thing becomes hard.
> It seems it is wine, not a cup of wine. It seems it is cup,
> without wine.

This is one of the stages of spiritual learning. From it arises the mistaken idea of those who claim being indwelt (*ḥulūl*) and becoming one (*ittiḥād*). This is close to the claim of the Christians, who claim the uniting of the divine and the human. This resembles the words of those who, seeing the colour red in a mirror, says that the colour of the mirror is red.

Second stage: Ecstasy

After understanding songs comes the stage of ecstasy. Dhū al-Nūn al-Miṣrī said that listening to songs brings truth. Abū al-Ḥusayn al-Darrāj said, "Ecstasy is an expression for what is found when listening to songs." He said also, "Listening to songs takes me to the field of beauty and gives me a sweet drink in the cup of purity, so that I gain thereby the station of contentment."

Al-Shiblī said, "The open form of listening to songs creates disputes, and its internal form gives instructions." A wise man said, "Songs are food to the soul of a spiritual man." 'Amr ibn 'Uthmān al-Makkī said, "No word can explain ecstasy because it is a secret thing of Allah with the believers and men of firm faith." Abū Sa'īd ibn al-'Arabī said that the meaning of ecstasy is lifting a screen, meeting the Lord, seeing unseen things, and the appearance of secret words. He also said, "Ecstasy comes at the time of violent invocation, heart piercing fear, a subtle event, or deriving benefit, a serious slip, seeing unseen things, grief over a lost thing, or repentance for past sins. It is the presentation of an open thing, a secret thing before a secret thing, and an unseen thing before an unseen thing. Then there is walking without feet and invocation without open invocation."

Meaning of ecstasy

Ecstasy arises out of a mental condition which is of two kinds. One kind is spiritual revelations and spiritual visions, which lead to unseen and unthinkable knowledge. Another kind leads to unthinkable change, fear, and repentance. Songs only awaken these states. Muslim al-'Abbādānī said, "Once Ṣāliḥ al-Marrī, 'Utbah al-Ghulām, 'Abd al-Wāḥid ibn Zayd and Muslim al-Aswārī alighted near us on the shore, and I invited them to a feast that night. When they came, I placed before them the feast. Soon after, a singer sang, 'Those who are kept forgetful of next world by delicious food will be thrown into Hell; it will be of no use.' Upon hearing this, 'Utbah al-Ghulām shrieked and fell senseless. They did not eat any food, and I took away the feast before them."

When the heart is pure and clean, it hears the message of heaven and sees also al-Khaḍir, as he appears in various forms to the possessor of hearts. Under these conditions the angels descended on the prophets within their veritable form or in a likeness resembling their form with some resemblance. The Prophet (ṣ) saw Jibrīl twice in his natural form, which occupied the whole space of heaven.

Knowledge which is generated in man in an uncommon condition of the heart is called "insight" (*tafarrus*). The Prophet (ṣ) said, "Fear the insight of a believer, as he sees with the rays of Allah." Hinting to this insight, the Prophet (ṣ) said, "If the Devil did not roam over the hearts of the children of Adam, they would surely see the sovereignty of heaven." The heart is the ground of the Devil and his forces, except those hearts which are pure and clean. Allah says, "Except Your servants from among them, the devoted ones" (Qur'an, 15:40) and "You have no authority over them" (Qur'an, 15:42).

Different kinds of spiritual revelations (*kashf*) and ecstasy

Spiritual revelations are of two kinds: those which can be explained once ecstasy leaves, and those which cannot be explained, as they are unseen things from the unseen world.

Ecstasy is also of two kinds: that which arises spontaneously, and that which comes with difficulty. The Prophet (ṣ) said, "O Allah, grant me Your love, the love of those who love You, and the love of those who bring me near to Your love." The trembling and softness of the heart owing to fear are songs of ecstasy. Allah says, "Those only are believers whose hearts become full of fear when Allah is mentioned" (Qur'an, 8:2) and "Had We sent down this Qur'an on a mountain, you would certainly have seen it falling down, splitting asunder because of the fear of Allah" (Qur'an, 59:21).

So fear of Allah is ecstasy. The Prophet (ṣ) said, "Adorn the recitation of the Qur'an with your pleasant voices." To Abū Mūsā al-Ash'arī he said, "You have been given one of the instruments of the family of Dāwūd." Many a time, the Sufis fell into ecstasy after hearing a melodious recitation of the Qur'an. The Prophet (ṣ) said, "Sūrah Hūd (Qur'an, 11) and similar sūrahs have made me grey-haired." This is nothing but ecstasy. He once fell down senseless after reading the verse "If You should chastise them, then surely they are Your servants" (Qur'an, 5:118) and began to weep. Allah praised such people of ecstasy, saying, "When they hear what has been revealed to the messenger, you will see their eyes overflowing with tears on account of the truth that they recognize" (Qur'an, 5:83). It has been reported that when the Prophet (ṣ) prayed, from his chest could be heard a sound like that of a heated cauldron.

The ecstasy of Companions and their successors

Zurārah ibn Awfā led prayers in the most humble spirit. One day, when he recited, "When the trumpet is sounded" (Qur'an, 74:8), he at once fell down senseless and expired immediately. When 'Umar heard a man reciting the verse "Most surely the punishment of your Lord will come to pass; there will be none to avert it" (Qur'an, 52:7-8), he suddenly shrieked and fell down senseless. He was then brought to his house and suffered for nearly a month. Abū Jarīr once heard a verse recited by Ṣāliḥ al-Marrī, sobbed, then breathed his last. When al-Shāfi'ī heard a judge recite the verses "This is the day on which they will not speak, and permission will not be given to them so that they should offer excuses" (Qur'an, 77:35-36), he immediately fell down unconscious. 'Alī ibn al-Fuḍayl heard a man recite the verse "The day on which men will stand before the Lord of the worlds" (Qur'an, 83:6) and fell down in a swoon.

This was the condition of the Sufis as well. While al-Shiblī was praying behind an imam in Ramaḍān, the imam recited, "If We please, We should certainly take away that which We have revealed to you" (Qur'an, 17:86), and al-Shiblī immediately shrieked and his face changed. Al-Junayd said, "I once saw an unconscious man before al-Sarī al-Saqaṭī, who said to me, 'This man fell senseless upon hearing verses of the Qur'an.' I said, 'Recite to him the verses again.' When they were recited, he regained consciousness. He then said, 'Where have you found this?' I said, 'Ya'qūb lost his sight owing to the loss of his son and regained it because of his son.' They then approved that." Pointing to what al-Junayd said are the words of the poet "I drank it again and found my salvation. I got a taste and drank with satisfaction."

A sage said, "One night I was reading the verse 'Every soul will taste of death' (Qur'an, 3:185). I was reciting it again and again when suddenly an unknown voice said to me, 'How long will you read this verse? You have killed thereby thirty-four jinn who have not risen their heads since they were born.'" Whenever Ibrāhīm ibn Adham heard any man reciting the verse "When the heaven bursts asunder" (Qur'an, 84:1), his limbs would tremble.

If the recitation of the verses of the Qur'an does not affect the mind, he is like a man who hears nothing when called: he is deaf, dumb and ignorant.

It was related that Abū al-Ḥusayn al-Nūrī was once in a company who were quarrelling about a matter, but he was silent. Afterwards he raised his head and recited the following poem:

> At midday, many a cooing pigeon sings heart captivating songs,
> Roaming from branch to branch with a broken heart.
> It brings to mind the love of the days of joy.
> It brings tears as he sheds tears telling woeful tales.
> My weeping sometimes makes his mind soft.
> I complain to him, but he understands it not.
> His complaint also becomes useless: I understand it not.
> I can know him if he understands the pangs of my grieved soul.
> He also cannot forget me, even in times of great sorrow

The narrator said that, after hearing this song, there was none in the company who did not stand up as a result of ecstasy. The dispute among them could not even arouse such ecstasy.

Third stage: The movement of bodily limbs as a result of ecstasy

It is the third stage of the outward expression of the effect of religious songs and involves consists of fall in a swoon, trembling, tearing off clothes, and the like. It has five rules.

1. Consider time, place, and company: Listening to songs has no effect when doing something serious such as eating or praying. When a mind is not engaged, it is fit for hearing religious songs. Regarding place, care should be taken not to listen on public roads, in dark rooms, or in undesirable places where attention cannot remain fixed. Regarding company, it appears that ecstasy seldom arises in the presence of company and is merely a matter of amusement to it. In company, moreover, there is mostly a show of ecstasy and not real ecstasy.
2. A spiritual guide with his disciples should not listen to songs, as it may harm them for three reasons. The first reason in

that some disciples are not so thirsty for spiritual drink that such songs will quench their thirst. They should rather engage themselves in invocation. The second reason is that the hearts of some of them are not so broken as to be able to find taste in it and escape its harm. The third reason is that sometimes songs bring greater harm than benefit to some disciples, who do not consider what is lawful or unlawful. Sahl said, "Ecstasy which does not support the Book of Allah and the Sunnah of the Prophet (ṣ) is void." Al-Junayd said, "I once saw the Devil in a dream and asked him, "Do you exercise any influence on my disciples?" He said, "On two occasions I do: the occasion of listening to songs and of theological speculation. I enter them at these two times."

3. Listen to religious songs attentively, neither paying attention to the audience nor expressing, as far as possible, outward signs of ecstasy, such as shrieking, trembling and dancing: It was related that while Mūsā was telling stories of the children of Israel, a man present tore his clothes to pieces. Then Allah revealed to Mūsā, "Tell the man, 'Break your heart and not your clothes.'"
4. When listening to religious songs, restrain yourself from standing up and from crying: It was related from many Companions that they danced out of joy. After the death of Ḥamzah, a quarrel ensured among 'Alī ibn Abī Ṭālib, Ja'far and Zayd ibn Ḥārithah regarding the maintenance of his children. The Prophet (ṣ) said to 'Alī, "You are from me, and I from you." At this good news, 'Alī began to dance. The Prophet (ṣ) said to Ja'far, "You resemble me in character and conduct." At this Ja'far also began to dance in joy. He then said to Zayd, "You are our brother and chief." He also danced in joy. Then the Prophet (ṣ) put the children in Ja'far's charge, as his wife was their maternal aunt, and a maternal aunt is like a mother. Another traditions states that the Prophet (ṣ) allowed 'Ā'ishah to watch some Abyssinian slaves dance. Ecstasy

sometimes becomes so strong that one cannot restrain oneself and acts contrary to one's habits.

5. If anyone among a group stands up out of ecstasy, the others should stand up as well, as it is one of the good manners of company.
6. Ecstasy should never be feigned.

From what has been stated above, songs sometimes become lawful, unlawful, or blameworthy, depending on the circumstances. It is unlawful for those youths whose sexual passion is strong, as it increases the hidden vices in their hearts. It is lawful for those who enjoy good moral songs. And it is recommended for those religious people who are engrossed in divine love. Allah knows best.

Book 9
Enjoining good and forbidding evil

Introduction

Enjoining good and forbidding evil is the basis of religions and is the mission all the prophets were sent to fulfil. If it were folded up, prophethood would be meaningless, religions would be lost, idleness would reign, ignorance would spread, disturbance would prevail, dangers and calamities would appear, and humankind would be destroyed. It will be discussed in four chapters:

1. Merits of enjoining good and forbidding evil
2. The integrals and conditions of enjoining good and forbidding evil
3. Corrupt practices prevalent in society
4. Enjoining rulers to do good, and forbidding them from evil

1

Merits of enjoining good and forbidding evil

It appears from Qur'anic verses and the words of the Holy Prophet (ṣ), sages and saints that enjoining good and forbidding evil is obligatory.

The Qur'an

Allah says:

> *From among you there should be a party who invite to good and enjoin what is right and forbid the wrong, and these it is that shall be successful.* (Qur'an, 3:104)

This is a communal obligation and not a personal obligation. In other words, if some people do it, other Muslims will be absolved from its sin, but if none does it, all will be sinners.

> *They are not all alike; of the followers of the Book there is an upright party; they recite Allah's communications in the nighttime and they adore (Him).They believe in Allah and the last day, and they enjoin what is right and forbid the wrong and they strive with one another in hastening to good deeds, and those are among the good.* (Qur'an, 3:113-114)

> *And (as for) the believing men and the believing women, they are guardians of each other; they enjoin good and forbid evil and keep up prayer.* (Qur'an, 9:71)

They have been praised by Allah for adopting these measures. Those who do not do these are not believers.

> *Those who disbelieved from among the children of Israel were cursed by the tongue of Dāwūd and 'Īsā, the son of Maryam; this was because they disobeyed and used to exceed the limit. They used not to forbid each other the hateful things (which) they did; certainly evil was that which they did.* (Qur'an, 5:78-79)

In this verse, Allah says that they are fit for being cursed, as they gave up forbidding evil.

> *You are the best of the nations raised up for (the benefit of) men; you enjoin what is right and forbid the wrong.* (Qur'an, 3:110)

In this verse Allah says that Muslims are the best nation only because they enjoin good and forbid evil.

> *So when they neglected what they had been reminded of, We delivered those who forbade evil.* (Qur'an, 7:165)

Allah clearly says in this verse that they got salvation because they used to forbid evil. This verse also proves that forbidding evil is obligatory.

> *Those who, should We establish them in the land, will keep up prayer and pay the poor-rate and enjoin good and forbid evil.* (Qur'an, 22:41)

Allah praised the Companions in the above verse.

> *Help one another in goodness and piety, and do not help one another in sin and aggression.* (Qur'an, 5:2)

This is a clear command from Allah to enjoin good and forbid evil.

> *O you who believe, be maintainers of justice, bearers of witness of Allah's sake, though it may be against your own selves or (your) parents or near relatives.* (Qur'an, 4:135)

This verse speaks of enjoining parents and relatives to do good.

There is no good in most of their secret counsels except (in his) who enjoins charity or goodness or reconciliation between people; and whoever does this seeking Allah's pleasure, We will give him a mighty reward. (Qur'an, 4:114)

If two parties of the believers quarrel, make peace between them. (Qur'an, 49:9)

This peace is to forbid them from rebellion and bring them back to allegiance. If this cannot be done, Allah orders to kill those who do not submit, saying, "Fight that which acts wrongfully until it returns to Allah's command" (Qur'an, 49:9).

Ḥadīth

The Prophet (ṣ) said, "If some people commit sins, and there are other people fit to forbid them but still do not do so, they do not do any religious acts, and a punishment from Allah will soon befall all of them."

When the Companion Abū Tha'labah al-Khushnī asked the Prophet (ṣ) about the meaning of the verse "he who errs cannot hurt you when you are on the right way" (Qur'an, 5:105), the Prophet (ṣ) replied, "O Abū Tha'labah, enjoin good and forbid evil. When you find people following greed and passions, loving the world, and giving opinions according to every wise man, be busy with yourself and give up the affairs of the public, for disasters and calamities will come from behind you like a fully dark night. He who remains as firm as you will get the rewards of fifty of you." The Prophet (ṣ) was then asked, "O Messenger of Allah, will he get the rewards of fifty of them?" He said, "No; the rewards of fifty of you, since you are getting help with good deeds, while they will not get any helper."

When asked about the meaning of the above *ḥadīth*, Ibn Mas'ūd said, "This is not that age. In the present age, enjoining good and forbidding evil are accepted, but soon there will come an age when you will enjoin good, and people will trouble you for it. If you say anything, it will not be accepted from you. When you get guidance, misguided people cannot misguide you."

The Prophet (ṣ) said, "O humankind, Allah said, 'Before you supplicate, enjoin good and forbid evil, or else your supplication will not be answered.'"

He said, "In comparison with jihad in the way of Allah, good deeds are only like a puff of breath in a deep sea. And all good deeds and jihad in the way of Allah are only like a puff of breath in a deep sea in comparison with enjoining good and forbidding evil."

He said, "Allah will ask a servant, 'Who prevented you from forbidding a person from doing evil when you saw it?' If Allah taught him the reply, he would say, 'O Lord, I entertained hope of You and feared men.'"

He said, "Beware of sitting on a pathway." The Companions asked, "We have no choice but to sit on a pathway, and we hold discussions there." He said, "If you are compelled to do so, acknowledge its rights." They asked, "What are the rights of the pathways?" He said, "To shut your eyes, have patience with harms, respond to greetings, and enjoin good and forbid evil."

He said, "Except for enjoining good and forbidding evil and invoking Allah, every word of man does him harm and does not benefit." Then he said, "Surely Allah will not punish the pious for the sins of others so long as they prevent them from wrongdoing."

He said, "When your women become disobedient, your young men commit great sins, and you abandon jihad, what then will be your condition?" The Companions asked, "O Messenger of Allah, will this happen?" He said, "Yes. By Him in whose hand is my life, a more serious thing will happen." They asked, "What?" He said, "When you deem good deeds evil and evil deeds good, what then will be your condition?" The Companion asked, "Will this happen?" He said, "Yes. By Him in whose hand is my life, a more serious thing will happen." The Companions asked, "What?" He said, "When you command to evil and forbade good deeds, what then will be your condition?" They said, "Will this happen?" He said, "Yes. By Him in whose hand is my life, a worse matter than that will happen. Allah will say, "I swear by Myself that I will create for them disasters and calamities which those who are patient with will be puzzled or perplexed."

He said, "Do not wait near a man when he is unjustly killed, as Allah's curse falls also on that man who was there and did not prevent it."

He said, "If a man is present where there is danger, he should only speak truth there, for he will not die before his appointed time, nor will he be deprived of his fixed provision."

From this *ḥadīth* it appears that it is not lawful to enter a place of oppression and sin if one is not able to prevent it. A party of earlier sages used to seek solitude in order not to see evil deeds in markets, festivals, and assemblies, as they understood that they were unable to prevent them.

He said, "When a man was present when a sin was committed and hated it, it was as though he were absent from it. When a man was absent when a sin was committed, but loved it, it was as though he were present."

His presence there is accidental and not out of volition, as it is unlawful.

He said, "Allah Almighty did not send a prophet without disciples. He would live among them until Allah wished in order to instruct them to follow His injunctions and the Book. Afterwards Allah would take his life. After him his disciples would act according to Allah's Book and His command and the ways of the prophet. When they would die, there would come a party of men who would deliver sermons on pulpits, but who themselves did bad deeds. When you see it, it will become the duty of every believer to fight with his hand. If he is unable to do so, then with his tongue. Without this, his Islam will not remain."

Ibn 'Abbās said, "The Prophet (ṣ) was once asked, 'O Messenger of Allah, will any place be destroyed if there are pious men therein?" He said, "Yes." He was asked, "Why?" He said, "They will neglect their duties and remind silent, though they will see them committing sins. For that they will be destroyed."

The Prophet (ṣ) said, "Allah Almighty ordered an angel, 'Throw this place upside down on its inhabitants.' A man said, "O Lord, there is a certain servant of Yours in this place. He has not committed a single sin even for a moment.' Allah said, 'Throw this place on that man and those people, as he did not turn his face to them even for a moment.'"

He said, "Allah sent punishments to a place with eighteen thousand inhabitants whose worship was like that of prophets." The Companions asked, "O Messenger of Allah, why did this occur?" He said, "They did not express anger for the sake of Allah and did not enjoin good and forbid evil."

Mūsā once asked Allah, "O Lord, who is dearest to You?" Allah said, "That servant who humbly comes towards My will just as a vulture rushes towards its object, that servant who remains ready to help My pious servants just as a suckling child keeps attached to its mother's breast, and that servant who gets angry when an unlawful act happens to him, just as an angry leopard does not care whether there are many or few people."

It appears that the merits of enjoining good and forbidding evil are great in the face of such great dangers.

Abū Bakr al-Ṣiddīq asked the Prophet (ṣ), "O Messenger of Allah, is there any jihad besides jihad with the unbelievers?" The Prophet (ṣ) said, "Yes. O Abū Bakr, fighters in the way of Allah are better than martyrs. They are given provision and are alive. They roam about in the world, and Allah praises them before the angels. Paradise has been adorned for them." Abū Bakr asked, "O Messenger of Allah, who are they?" The Prophet (ṣ) said, "They enjoin good and forbid evil, love one another for the sake of Allah, and give up hatred for one another for the sake of Allah." The Prophet (ṣ) then said, "By Him in whose hand is my life, one of them will live in a palace which is placed above all other palaces and above all the palaces of the martyrs. That palace will have three hundred thousand doors. Each door is most valuable and made of emeralds and jewels of green colour, and every door will have light. In that palace, he will have three hundred thousand houris who will look with askance eyes. Whenever any houri looks at a person, he will say, 'Do you remember such and such a day when you enjoined good and forbade evil?'"

Abū 'Ubaydah ibn al-Jarrāḥ said, "I asked, 'O Prophet of Allah, who among martyrs is the most honourable to Allah?" He said, "The martyr who stands before a tyrannical ruler, enjoins him to do good, forbids him from evil, and is killed for it. If the tyrannical ruler does not kill him, the pen will stop writing for him as long he lives."

The Prophet (ṣ) said, "The greatest martyr among my followers will be that person who stand before a tyrannical ruler, enjoins him to do good, and forbids evil, as a result of which the ruler kills him. His place will be between Ḥamzah and Ja'far."

'Umar said, "I heard the Prophet (ṣ) say, "Bad are those of the present age who do not do justice, do not enjoin good, and do not forbid evil."

Words of Companions and early Muslims

Abū al-Dardā' said, "You should enjoin good and forbid evil, or else Allah will place over you a tyrannical ruler who will not honour your elders or be kind to your young. The religious men among you will pray against them, but Allah will not accept their prayer. They will seek help against them, but will not be helped. They will seek forgiveness, but will not be forgiven."

Allah revealed to the prophet Yūsha' ibn Nūn, "I will destroy from your followers forty thousand religious men and sixty thousand sinners." He said, "O Lord, I have understood the reason of the destruction of the sinners, but what is the fault of the religious men?" Allah said, "They were not dissatisfied with them when I was satisfied, and they used to have their meals with sinners."

'Alī ibn Abī Ṭālib said, "The jihad which begins before you are the jihad of your hands, then the jihad of your tongue, then the jihad of your heart. When your heart does not enjoin good and forbid evil, it becomes enveloped with darkness, and its upper portion goes towards its lower portion."

2

The integrals and conditions of enjoining good and forbidding evil

There are four integrals: the person forbidding, the person being forbidden, what is being forbidden, and the forbiddance itself. Each integral has rules and condition.

The person forbidding

The person who forbids evil must have some qualifications. He must be wise and must have strength and ability. An insane man, an unbeliever, and disqualified man are unfit to forbid evil. Ordinary people also are unfit for it, unless rulers order them. Also unfit are slaves, women, and transgressors.

So one must be mature, wise, and a believer. He who disbelieves the bases of religion is unfit. Additionally, one must have moral rectitude. Allah says, "Do you enjoin men to do good and forget your own souls?" (Qur'an, 2:44) and "It is most hateful to Allah that you should say that which you do not do" (Qur'an, 61:3). The Prophet (ṣ) said, "While passing by a party of men in the night of my ascension to heaven, I saw that their lips were cut by scissors of fire. I asked, 'Who are you?' They said, 'We would enjoin good, but we ourselves would not do it. We would forbid evil, but we ourselves would do it.'" Allah revealed to 'Īsā, "Give advice first to yourself. When you follow that advice, give advice to others." It is said that it is lawful for a great sinner to enjoin good and forbid evil.

Levels of enjoining good and forbidding evil

There are five levels of enjoining good and forbidding evil: explaining the wrong nature of the act; admonishing the person politely; reviling him and harsh treatment; forcibly stopping the act, such as by pouring out wine, snatching dresses of silk and stolen articles and returning them to their rightful owners; and intimidation and threatening to strike the person. Except for the fifth degree, one is not required to obtain permission from authorities to enjoin good and forbid evil on any level.

Examples of admonishing rulers

While Marwān ibn al-Ḥakam was once delivering sermon before the *'Īd* prayer, a man said to him, "The sermon is generally given after the prayer." Marwān said to him, "Desist!" Abū Sa'īd said, "The Prophet (ṣ) said, 'If one of you sees a bad thing, let him prevent it with his hand. If he cannot, let him prevent it with this tongue. If cannot, let him hate it in his heart; this is the weakest faith.'" The rulers are also included in this advice.

Al-Mahdī once came to Makkah and stayed there for many days. When he wanted to circumambulate the Ka'bah, it was cleared of the public. 'Abdullāh ibn Marzūq then jumped up and said to him, "Look at what you are doing. Who has given you, with respect to the Ka'bah, a right greater than that of someone who comes from a distant place? Allah says, 'We have made equally for all men, (for) the dweller therein and (for) the visitor' (Qur'an, 22:25). Who has given you power to drive out people?" Al-Mahdī recognized him as one of his officers and brought him to Bagdad after arresting and confining him in a stable. His men tied him with a horse to kill him. But Allah subjugated the horse to him. Baffled at this, they locked him in a room whose key was with the al-Mahdī. Three days later, to the amazement of all, he was found eating vegetables in a garden. He was then taken to al-Mahdī and asked, "Who has taken you out of this room?" Al-Mahdī raised his voice, asking him, "Do you not fear that I can kill you?" The man laughed and said, "I would fear you if you were the owner of life and death." The man remained in jail up to the death of al-Mahdī. When he was released afterwards, he went to Makkah and sacrificed a hundred camels to fulfil the vow of his release.

Ḥibbān ibn 'Abdullāh related that while travelling in a place with Sulaymān ibn Abī Ja'far, the caliph Hārūn al-Rashīd said, "You have a beautiful singing female slave. Tell her to sing before me." When she came, the caliph told him to bring musical instruments. When he was taking it to the caliph, he met a hermit on the way. The hermit took the instrument and broke it into pieces. The man complained about it to the caliph, who called the hermit out of anger. When the hermit entered the caliph's court with a bag of small pebbles, the caliph asked him why he had broken the musical instrument. The hermit said, "I heard your father and his predecessors recite this verse on the pulpit: 'God orders you to do justice, to show kindness, to give charity to the near relatives and forbids you from evil and rebellion.' I saw evil and broke the musical instrument to pieces." The caliph remained silent and allowed the hermit to go. When the hermit left the caliph's court, the latter gave a purse of money to a man and said, "Follow this hermit. If you hear him say, 'I told the caliph such and such,' do not give it to him. If you find him silent, give it to him." When the hermit left, he went to where there were date stones and remained silent. The man gave the purse to the hermit, who in turn said to him, "Tell the Commander of the Faithful to return the money to where took it from." Then he began to pick up date stones and recite the following poems:

> I see the worldly-addicted engrossed in anxieties.
> Along with the increase of their wealth, sorrows increase
> The world gives to the honourable troubles and disgrace.
> It gives him who submits to it an honourable place.
> Give up what is useless to you and unnecessary
> And take to what is for you absolutely necessary.

Sufyān al-Thawrī said, "In 166 A.H., al-Mahdī went on pilgrimage, and I found him throwing stones at Jamrah al-'Aqabah as people were being pushed back on all sides by sticks. I waited there for some time, then said to the caliph, 'O he of handsome face, I heard someone relate this *ḥadīth*: 'On the Day of Sacrifice, I saw the Messenger of Allah throw stones here, and there was no beating, no driving out people, no assault by sticks, and no saying 'Go back all around.' But you are driving the people from the left, right, and front.' The caliph asked, 'Who is this man?' He was told that he was Sufyān al-Thawrī. The caliph then said, 'O Sufyān, had it been the caliph al-Manṣūr, you would not have dared to say this.' He said, 'Had you seen the disasters which befell the caliph al-Manṣūr, the condition you are in now would have been less.'"

A man was once found enjoining good and forbidding evil without the permission of the caliph al-Ma'mūn. When the man was brought before the caliph, he said, "O Commander of the Faithful, we help you in your task. Allah says, 'And (as for) the believing men and the believing women, they are guardians of each other; they enjoin good and forbid evil and keep up prayer' (Qur'an, 9:71)." And the Prophet (ṣ) said, 'A believer in relation to another is like a building, a portion of which strengthens another.' Hearing this, the caliph became pleased with him and said, "You are a fit person to undertake this task.'

Someone who gives advice should have strength and power. He who is unable to undertake this task should hate sinful acts. Inability here means to fear injury and harm from the person to whom advice is given. Allah says, "Cast not yourselves to perdition with your own hands" (Qur'an, 2:195).

There are three kinds of sins. The first is major sins, for which there are prescribed punishments in the Qur'an; it is obligatory to prevent these. The second is sins which are committed continuously, such as drinking wine, wearing silk, and using utensils of gold and silver; it is obligatory to prevent these as well. The third is sins which are expected to be committed in the future.

Four conditions apply to the prevention of these evils. The first is that it must be an evil action according to Sharī'ah, and must be unlawful. The second is that it is to be prevented in the course of its commission. If a man has finished drinking wine, prevention is not applicable, except by way of advice. The third is that the person preventing it must know it is sinful without asking others. If a man commits a sin after closing the door of his house, to enquire about it secretly is unlawful. 'Umar once secretly entered a house and found a man committing a sinful act. Asked about it, the man said, "If I have committed a sin, then you have committed three sins. Asked about them, has said, "Allah says, 'Do not spy' (Qur'an, 49:12), but you have done so. Allah says, 'Go into the houses by their doors' (Qur'an, 2:189), but you have come over the wall. Allah says, 'Do not enter houses other than your own houses until you have asked permission and saluted their inmates' (Qur'an, 24:27), but you have neither asked permission, nor saluted its inmates." After this, 'Umar let him off after imposing on him the condition of repentance.

The fourth condition is that the evil must be known to be evil without effort, otherwise there is no forbidding of evil. These relate to the minor details of different sects. One sect holds that an act like eating a lizard is evil, while according to another sect it is not.

The person being forbidden

The sin which should be prevented must be fit to be prevented according to Sharī'ah. If a man is seen drinking wine, it is compulsory to prevent him from drinking it. Such is also the case of a madman if he is seen committing adultery with a woman. If a man is seen damaging the crops of another, he should also be prevented from doing it to fulfil one's duty towards Allah and towards the one wronged. The rule for a lost thing which one finds is that if it is susceptible to damage, one is not bound to take it.

The forbiddance itself

Know, dear readers, that there are different stages of forbidding sins.

Stage 1: Knowledge of the wrong act

To spy on a sinner is unlawful, so one should not enquire into what is happening at home. But if anyone informs you that a man is drinking wine or doing some unlawful act, it becomes a duty to prevent it. So the first thing is to enquire about the condition of the sinner.

Stage 2: Explaining that something is wrong

Many men do sinful acts out of ignorance. If warning is given, they may themselves desist from the sinful acts. For instance, an illiterate man observes his prayer, but does not bow and prostrate well, or prays with unclean clothes. Had he known this, he would not have prayed in this way. Man is not born learned. Learning has to be acquired.

Stage 3: Forbidding the act verbally

This is done by sermonising, admonition, or showing fear of Allah. If a man commits a sin after knowing that it is a sin, he should be given sermonised and shown fear of Allah's punishment. He should be informed of the traditions of the Prophet (ṣ) which deal with the punishment of the crime. The Muslims are like one soul, and so destructive faults should be removed from the soul. One who gives advice should take precautions so that he himself is free from that vice. He should then remember what Allah said to ʿĪsā, "O son of Maryam, first advise yourself. If you heeded it, then give advice to people or else you will be ashamed before Me." A man once asked Dāwūd al-Ṭāʾī about the condition of a person who enjoins a ruler to good and forbids evil to a ruler or a man in power. Dāwūd said, “I fear being whipped by him.” The man said, “And if the person can bear it?” Dāwūd said, “I fear death.” The man said, “If he can bear it?” Dāwūd said, “I fear for him self-praise begotten by the praise of people.”

Stage 4: Censuring with harsh words

If using gentle words with the wrongdoer could yield good results, harsh words need not be used. When it fails, then use harsh words and abuse him. Such words are like those of the prophet Ibrāhīm: “Fie on you and on what you serve besides Allah; do you not then understand?” (Qur’an, 21:67). One can say, “O fool,” “Do you not fear Allah?” “O sinner,” and “O ignoramus.” The wise man is he who has been described by the Prophet (ṣ) in the following words: “The wise man is he who humbles himself and acts with the afterlife in mind, while the fool is he who follows low desires and hopes for the forgiveness of Allah. There are two rules in this stage: not to abuse except when necessary, and not to use harsh words except when necessary. If this measure does not produce the desired effect, express your anger by ignoring him.

Stage 5: Righting the wrong by hand

This includes pouring out wine, taking off silk clothes from the body, turning someone out of house wrongfully appropriated. This method should be adopted after the failure of the first four stages. Keep the correction within limits, and do not exceed what is necessary.

Stage 6: Intimidation

If all the previous modes of correction fail, this method should be be adopted. For instance, one should say to the drunkard, “Throw away the wine, otherwise I will break your head and strike your neck, or “I will disgrace you.”

Stage 7: Assault

If the previous modes of correction fail, one may assault by hand or stick.

Stage 8: Force of arms

Many a time arms are necessary to ward off evil because a wrongdoer with a party of men are prepared to fight. When the two parties meet, a fight breaks out; it is necessary in order to please Allah and in order to remove the harms of sinful acts. It is allowed for warriors against the unbelievers. Similarly, it is necessary to bring the great transgressors under control.

Qualifications of the person forbidding wrongs

Someone who forbids wrongs and evils should have knowledge that the act is wrong, have piety and have good character.

Regarding knowledge, the place, limit and manner of forbidding wrongful acts should be known and should remain confined within the rules of Sharīʿah. Without such knowledge, one cannot distinguish between right and wrong. Piety is necessary for someone who prevents evil because he should act not in his interest, but for the sake of Allah. Such a man should possess also good character, kindness, and humanity. When anger arises, only good character can control it.

If the person forbidding evil possesses these three qualities, he can be rewarded for forbidding sins. If he does not possess these qualities, he will often exceed the limits of Sharīʿah. The Prophet (ṣ) said, "He who is not patient in enjoining good and for bidding evil and has no knowledge of it should not do it." So it appears that knowledge, patience, and kindness are necessary when giving advice.

Al-Ḥasan al-Baṣrī said, "If you are an adviser for good deeds, first fulfill them yourself or else you will be ruined." Anas related, "We asked the Messenger of Allah, 'O Messenger Allah, should we cease to enjoin others to do good and forbid them evil if we do not act fully according to our sermons and refrain from evil' The Prophet (ṣ) said, 'If you are unable to act fully according to your sermons, still enjoin good. If you are unable to give up fully what you forbid, still forbid it."

A sage advised his sons, "If anyone among you wishes to enjoin good, he should advice himself first with the good qualities of patience and hope for rewards from Allah. He who hopes for the rewards of Allah will not find any difficulty therein." A rule of advice is to be satisfied with patience. For this reason, Allah kept patience attached with advice. The wise Luqmān advised his son: "O dear son, establish prayer, enjoin good and forbid evil. Be patient at the danger that will befall on you for this."

In addition, one who takes up the mission of giving advice should not keep much connection with the world, nor should he have fear. He who depends on men will not be able to prevent sins. A speaker once advised the caliph al-Ma'mūn and spoke harshly to him. The caliph in turn said to him, "O gentleman, be modest, for he who was better than you was sent by Allah to people worse than yourself with the instruction of advising them with gentle words. Allah says, 'Then speak to him a gentle word haply he may mind or fear' (Qur'an, 20:44)."

A slave once came to the Prophet (ṣ) and said, "Give me permission to fornicate." At this the Companions raised a loud cry. The Prophet (ṣ) then said, "Bring him to me." When he sat before the Prophet (ṣ), the latter said to him, "Would you like it if somebody fornicated with your mother?" The slave said, "Never." The Prophet (ṣ) said, "So nobody likes that another should fornicate with his mother." Thus he asked him whether he liked fornication with his daughter, sister, niece, and aunt, and each time he replied in the negative. The Prophet (ṣ) then touched his chest with his hand and supplicated, "O Allah, purify his mind and pardon his sins and private parts. After that, there was no action more heinous in his sight than fornication.

Al-Fatḥ ibn Shakhraf said, "A man with a dagger in hand was once dragging a woman by force. Nobody dared to go near him for fear of being murdered. The woman in his hand was raising loud cries. Suddenly Bishr ibn al-Ḥārith passed by that way. He went to him and touched his shoulder, as a result, the man fell down senseless, and the sage then left the place. The woman also went away. When the man regained his senses, the people asked him, 'What has happened to you?' He said, 'I do not know anything, but I remember that a man came to me and said after touching me, 'Certainly Allah sees you and your actions.' Upon hearing his words, fear entered his heart, and my feet got paralysed. I do not know the man. They said, 'He is Bishr ibn al-Ḥārith. On that very day, he got a fever which ultimately led him to the grave."

3

Corrupt practices prevalent in society

All evil actions are either unlawful or offensive. To prevent what is unlawful is obligatory, and to remain silent at the time of its commission is unlawful. To prevent what is offensive, on the other hand, is recommended, and to remain silent at the time of its commissions is not good, but it is not unlawful.

Evil actions in mosques include not bowing or prostrating well, reciting the Qur'an in a melodious voice, prolonging the call to prayer, the imam's putting on a black robe or a predominately silk robe, telling stories during the Friday sermon, and buying or selling during the Friday prayer.

Evil actions in markets include lying to customers, concealing the defects of commodities, increasing or decreasing weights and measures, selling or buying toys of animals, and selling articles of gold and silver, silk dresses, and the like.

Evil actions in pathways include constructing shops on pathways, encroaching into pathways by extending the veranda of a building, tying animals, obstructing the pathway of people, sacrificing animals on pathways, allowing the water of a building to fall on a pathway, and extending a pipe.

Evil actions in feasts include spreading cushions of silk, serving in cups of gold and silver, beating drums, singing songs, serving unlawful foods and drinks, arousing laughter by telling false stories, spending lavishly on various kinds of food.

Evils actions in buildings include spending unnecessarily on the construction of buildings, as spending money without benefit destroys it. If a man has only a hundred dinars and no other possession, and such money is necessary for the maintenance of his family, his spending it on marriage is considered misuse, and to prevent him from it is obligatory. Allah says, "Do not make your hand to be shackled to your neck nor stretch it forth to the utmost (limit) of its stretching forth, lest you should (afterwards) sit down blamed, stripped off (Qur'an, 17:29); "Give to the near of kin his due and (to) the needy and the wayfarer, and do not squander wastefully. Surely the squanderers are the fellows of the devils" (Qur'an, 17:26-27); "They who when they spend, are neither extravagant nor parsimonious" (Qur'an, 25:67). To prevent miserliness and extravagance is obligatory.

4

Enjoining rulers to do good, and forbidding them from evil

In case of enjoining rulers and kings to do good and forbidding them evil, only the first two modes should be adopted and not the other modes of harsh treatment—abuse, assault fighting. In other words, they should be advised with polite words and with full knowledge of their evil actions. To apply other modes in their case is unlawful, as it creates disturbance and loss of peace and tranquillity. It is not unlawful to take a personal risk provided there is no risk of dangers and difficulties for others, as the Prophet (ṣ) said, "Ḥamzah ibn 'Abd al-Muṭṭalib is the best among martyrs. The next best is he who, standing before a ruler, enjoins him to do good and forbids him evil and is consequently killed by him; his rank is lower than that of Ḥamzah. The Prophet (ṣ) also said, "The best jihad is to speak right words before a tyrannical ruler." He once praised 'Umar ibn al-Khaṭṭāb, saying, "He is an iron man, and the defamation of a backbiter cannot divert him from the matters of Allah."

Those who had firm and sure faith approached rulers with truth, enjoined them to do good, and forbade them evil, risking their lives, possessions, and honour in order to be blessed with martyrdom.

When the leaders of Quraysh wished to take revenge on the Prophet (ṣ), Abū Bakr protested. 'Urwah said, "I asked 'Abdullāh ibn 'Amr, 'What was the greatest trouble Quraysh gave the Prophet (ṣ)?' He said, 'I once went to Quraysh, who were discussing the Prophet's sitting in the Ka'bah, and they said,

'This man has made a fool of us and abused our forefathers and our religion. He has disorganised our unity and abused our idols, and we have shown patience in a great task.' Suddenly the Prophet (ṣ) appeared, kissed the Black Stone, and circumambulated the Ka'bah. Quraysh began to abuse him each time he passed them during the circumambulation. The Prophet (ṣ) then said, 'O Quraysh, do you not hear? Beware! By Him in whose hand is my life, I have not come to you with a sacrificial animal. Quraysh then bowed their heads, and one of them said, 'How excellent is this word!' He then consoled the Prophet (ṣ), saying, 'O Abū al-Qāsim, go away. By Allah, we are not ignorant.' Then the Prophet (ṣ) went away from that place. The next morning, one of Quraysh threw a sheet of cloth round the neck of the Prophet (ṣ) and began to drag him forcefully. Abū Bakr al-Ṣiddīq went to him and said, crying, 'Woe to you! Are you going to kill this man? He only said, 'My lord is Allah." They then let him go.

In another version, it was reported that 'Abdullāh ibn 'Umar said, "When the Prophet (ṣ) was in the precincts of the Ka'bah, 'Uqbah ibn Ubayy caught hold of the Prophet's neck with a sheet of cloth and began to drag him by it with force. Abū Bakr came and drove him out, saying, "Will you kill a man who says, 'Allah is my Lord'? He has come to you with a clear message from your Lord."

It was reported that the caliph Mu'āwiyah kept the allowance of the Muslims in abeyance for some time. While he was delivering a sermon on a pulpit, Abū Muslim al-Khawlānī stood up and said, "O Mu'āwiyah, these allowances are not your paternal properties, nor were they acquired by your father and mother." The caliph grew angry, got down from the pulpit, and said to them, "Sit down in your own places." Then he went to a bathroom, took bath, and came again, saying, "Abū Muslim uttered words which enraged me. I heard the Prophet (ṣ) say, 'Wrath comes from the Devil, who was created of fire and fire can be extinguished by water. So when one of you gets angry, let him take a bath.' Thus, I took bath, and Abū Muslim uttered the truth: These possessions were not acquired by me or my parents' wealth. Take now your allowances."

Ḍabbah ibn Miḥṣan al-'Anazī said, "Abū Mūsā al-Ash'arī was our governor in Baṣrah. When he read a sermon, he used first to praise Allah and invoke blessings on the Prophet (ṣ), then supplicated for 'Umar. I did not like that Abū Bakr should be omitted from the supplication, so I stood up and said to him, 'Why do you not pray for the first caliph Abū Bakr?' He did not pay any heed to my request, but complained about me to 'Umar, who summoned me. I was then sent to 'Umar, who was in Madīnah. He asked me, 'What has occurred between you and my governor Abū Mūsā al-Ash'arī?' I said, 'When he reads the sermon, he supplicates for you only. And I was dissatisfied at this and said to him, 'Why do you not pray also for Abū Bakr, and why do you give 'Umar superiority over him?' Because of this, he complained about me to you.' With that, 'Umar began to weep, saying, 'You are more fit for the post of governor than my governor, and more guided towards truth. Forgive me and Allah will forgive you.' I said, 'O Commander of the Faithful, Allah has forgiven you.' 'Umar again began to weep and said, 'By Allah, shall I tell you about a day and a night of Abū Bakr?' I said, 'Yes. Tell me.'

"'Umar said, 'When the Prophet (ṣ) and Abū Bakr came out one night to migrate to Madīnah, Abū Bakr would sometimes walk in front of him, sometimes behind him, sometimes to his right, and someone to his left. When the Prophet (ṣ) felt pain in his toes because of walking a long way, Abū Bakr lifted him onto his shoulders and carried him until he reached the cave. There, the Prophet (ṣ) said, 'Do not enter this cave until I first enter it. If there is any injurious animal in it, it will first attack me.' When he entered the cave and found nothing, he carried the Prophet (ṣ) into it. There was a small hole in the cave, and Abū Bakr closed it with one of his feet. Shortly after, a snake stung his foot, and he began to shed tears from the pain the snake venom caused. Seeing this, the Prophet (ṣ) said, 'O Abū Bakr, do not weep. Surely Allah is with us.'

"This was a night of Abū Bakr. Regarding a day of his, I can tell you that when the Prophet (ṣ) expired, some desert Arabs rebelled. Some of them said, 'We shall observe prayer, but we will not pay *zakāh*.' When I went to Abū Bakr and advised him to be kind to the rebels, he said to me, 'You were powerful during the days of ignorance, but you have become fearful in Islam. Why should I show kindness to them? When the Prophet (ṣ) expired and revelation stopped, they stopped paying *zakāh*. They used to pay it to the Prophet (ṣ), but before this he fought them over it. So we shall fight against them in this regard. By Allah, it is he who has shown us the true path.' 'This was a day of Abū Bakr.' Then 'Umar sent a letter to his governor rebuking him for not supplicating for Abū Bakr in his sermon.

'Aṭā' ibn Abī Rabāḥ once went to the caliph 'Abd al-Malik ibn Marwān in Makkah. When the caliph saw 'Aṭā', he stood in his honour and asked him, "Do you need anything?" The sage said, "O Commander of the Faithful, fear this sacred place of Allah and His Prophet (ṣ), keep its purity, fear Allah regarding the descendants of the Emigrants and Madīnan Helpers, for by their help you are sitting on this throne. Fear Allah regarding the soldiers guarding the frontiers, for they are the forts of Muslims, and take care of the affairs of Muslims. You will be asked about these matters. And do not be heedless of those who are under your control, nor shut your doors on them." The caliph said, "I will try to follow your advice."

Once, the sage was brought before the caliph al-Walīd ibn 'Abd al-Malik and said to him, "I heard that in hell there is a valley named Habhab, which Allah has reserved for every tyrannical ruler." Upon hearing this, al-Walīd raised a cry and fell senseless.

Ibn Abī Shumaylah, known for his wisdom and good treatment, once went to the caliph 'Abd al-Malik ibn Marwān, who requested that he give him some words of advice. The sage said, "O Commander of the Faithful, on Resurrection Day, humankind will not be saved from its grievous punishment and severe conditions. Only he who pleases Allah by displeasing himself will be safe." The caliph wept at this and said, "I will keep this advice as the object of my life as long as I live."

The tyrannical governor al-Ḥajjāj once called on the scholars of Baṣrah and Kūfah, including al-Ḥasan al-Baṣrī, and began to condemn 'Alī ibn Abī Ṭālib. Ibn 'Ā'ishah said, "We began to support him. But al-Ḥasan cut his thumb and remained silent. Al-Ḥajjāj said to him, 'Why do I find you silent? What is your opinion regarding 'Alī?' Al-Ḥasan replied, 'Allah says regarding 'Alī, 'We did not make that which you would have to be the *qiblah* but that We might distinguish him who follows the Messenger from him who turns back on his heels, and this was surely hard except for those whom Allah has guided aright; and Allah was not going to make your faith to be fruitless; most surely Allah is Affectionate, Merciful to people' (Qur'an, 2:143). 'Alī was one of those believers whom Allah gave guidance. My opinion about him is that he was the cousin and son-in-law of the Prophet (ṣ), and he was dearest to him. Allah adorned him with many virtues. Neither you nor anybody else can have his attributes. My opinion is that Allah is sufficient against any fault that he might have had.' At this the face of al-Ḥajjāj became red, and he stood up in rage. Then he entered his house and we went away.

"One day, al-Ḥajjāj summoned al-Ḥasan and said, 'Do you say that Allah will destroy those who kill the servants of Allah for money?' Al-Ḥasan replied, 'Yes.' Al-Ḥajjāj asked, 'Why do you say this?' Al-Ḥasan said, 'Because Allah made the learned promise that they would make people understand the words of religion and not conceal them.' Al-Ḥajjāj said, 'O al-Ḥasan, bite your tongue! I warn you against making me listen to what I dislike. There is a great deal of difference between your body and mind.'"

Ḥuṭayṭ al-Zayyāt once went to al-Ḥajjāj, who asked him, "Are you Ḥuṭayṭ?" He replied, "Yes. Ask me what you wish. At the Station of Ibrāhīm, I made three promises to Allah: that I will speak the truth whenever anyone asks me anything, that I will have patience when anybody puts me in danger, and that I will express gratefulness when anybody pardons me." Then al-Ḥajjāj said, "What do you say about me?" Ḥuṭayṭ said, "You are the enemy of Allah on earth, and destroy the honour of people and kill them at your whim." Al-Ḥajjāj said, "What do you say about the caliph 'Abd al-Malik ibn Marwān?" Ḥuṭayṭ said, "He is a greater sinner than you. And one of his sins is you." Upon hearing this, al-Ḥajjāj ordered that Ḥuṭayṭ be punished. After he was whipped, the whip of the executioner broke. Then the executioner tied him with ropes and began to cut his flesh with a knife, but he did not utter any expression of pain. When al-Ḥajjāj was informed that the man's end was near, he said, "If he expires, throw his body into the market." Ja'far said, "I and one of his friends went to him and asked him, 'O Ḥuṭayṭ, do you need anything?' He replied, 'A handful water.' When they brought water to him, he drank it, and soon expired. He was only eighteen years old."

'Umar ibn Hubayrah called on the people of Baṣrah, Kūfah, Madīnah and Syria, as well their reciters of the Qur'an. He said to al-Sha'bī, "I wish to cancel the allowances of some people who, rumour has it, say many things against me. My wish is that they should return to my allegiance. What do you say?" Al-Sha'bi said, "A ruler is like a father. Sometimes he is right, and sometimes he makes mistakes, in which case he does not sin." The ruler was pleased to hear his advice. Then he said to al-Ḥasan al-Baṣrī, "What do you say about this?" Al-Ḥasan replied, "I heard the Companion 'Abd al-Raḥmān ibn Samurah al-Qurashī say that the Prophet (ṣ) said, 'Allah will make paradise unlawful to someone who, being appointed to rule over people, does not consider their welfare and provision.'

"Regarding the cancellation of the allowances of the people, I say that to preserve the right of Allah is a more important duty than to preserve your right. Allah has a greater right to be obeyed. There is no permission to show allegiance to the created while being disobedient to Allah. The word of the Commander of the Faithful cannot be placed above the Book of Allah. If his word agrees with it, then accept it. If it disagrees with it, then throw it away. O Ibn Hubayrah, fear Allah. Perchance there may come to you from the Lord of the universe a messenger who will take you to the grave and remove you from the palace." Ibn Hubayrah said, "O sheikh, do not say these words. Allah selected the Commander of the Faithful as a ruler." Al-Ḥasan al-Baṣrī said, "He who gives you better advice regarding religion is better than someone who hopes to please you." Al-Sha'bī then said, "I never saw a man braver and more learned than al-Ḥasan al-Baṣrī."

During the reign of the caliph Abū Ja'far al-Manṣūr, the governor of Madīnah was al-Ḥasan ibn Zayd, about whom some complained to the caliph. The latter asked Ibn Abī Dhu'ayb about the governor, and he said, "Al-Ḥasan conducts his affairs according to his whim, and does not do justice." The caliph then asked him, "What do you say about me?" He said, "I bear witness that you have seized power unjustly and that injustice is prevalent in your rule." The caliph caught hold of his neck and said, "Had I not been here, Persia, Byzantium, al-Daylam and Turkey would have snatched this place from you." After this the caliph released him and said, "By Allah, had I not known that you are a truthful man, I would have killed you."

Al-'Awzā'ī 'Abd al-Raḥmān ibn 'Amr said, "The caliph Abū Ja'far al-Manṣūr once called on me and said, "Advise me." I said, "O Commander of the Faithful, the Prophet (ṣ) said, 'Allah has made paradise unlawful to the ruler who dies displeased with his subjects.' He who dislike truth, hates Allah, as He is the Clear Truth. It is just that you should upkeep the honour of your subjects, establish justice among them, not close your doors on them, be happy in their happiness, and sorry in their sorrows. Under your rule are foreigners, unbelievers, and Muslims, and it is your duty to be just to them.

"O Commander of the Faithful, the Prophet (ṣ) used to have a palm-leaf stock, which he used to clean his teeth and threaten the hypocrites. "The Prophet (ṣ) said, 'Then Jibrīl came down and said, 'O Muḥammad, what is this stick? Thereby you have broken the hearts of your people and created terror in their hearts.'

"Now think of those who shed the blood of their subjects, destroyed their houses, and banished them from their countries. The Prophet (ṣ) once assaulted a desert Arab unwillingly by his own hand. Then Jibrīl came down and said, 'O Muḥammad, Allah has not sent you as an oppressor or a proud man.' Then the Prophet (ṣ) called the desert Arab and said, 'Take revenge on me.' The Arab replied, 'My parents be sacrificed to you. I have forgiven you. I will never do that. If you killed me, I would still pray for your welfare.'

"O Commander of the Faithful, the Prophet (ṣ) said, 'An arrow's space in paradise for one of you is better than the world and its wealth.' Your rule will not last forever, just as it did not last for your predecessors. I have heard 'Umar say, 'If a young goat perishes by the side of the Tigris, I fear I may be asked about it.' How then should it be if a man comes to your court seeking justice and leaves in despair? Do you know the interpretations that have been made concerning this verse about the prophet Dāwūd: 'O Dāwūd, surely We have made you a ruler in the land; so judge between men with justice and do not follow desire, lest it should lead you astray from the path of Allah' (Qur'an, 38:26)?'

"Allah says in the Psalms, 'O Dāwūd, when two parties come to you for justice, do not think that judgement will be givein favour of someone to whom your mind inclines and that he will be victorious over his adversary. In that case, your name will be cut off from the register of Prophethood, and you will not be fit to represent Me. O Dāwūd, I have sent my Prophets to take care of My servants as a shepherd takes care of his flock of sheep. They have been given knowledge of that care and burden of administration, so that they may tie what is broken and enliven the weak by provision.' O Commander of the Faithful, you have been tried by a matter which, if it were presented to the heaven and the earth, they would refuse to bear and would be fearful.

"O Commander of the Faithful, I heard that 'Umar appointed a man to collect *zakāh* from the Madīnan Helpers. After some days, 'Umar heard that he stayed in his house and therefore asked him, 'Why have you not gone out to do your duty? Do you not know that you will get the rewards of a fighter in the way of Allah?' The man said, 'I have heard that the Prophet (ṣ) said, 'If any man is entrusted with public office, he will be raised on Resurrection Day with his hands tied to his neck, and nothing will undo it except justice. Then he will wait on a bridge of fire, which will collapse with him, and all his limbs will break. Then he will be brought and judged. If he is pious, he will get salvation for his good deeds. If he is a sinner, he will be raised with it and will fall to the, abyss of hell.'

"'Umar asked him, 'From whom did you hear this *ḥadīth*?' The man said, 'From Abū Dharr and Salmān al-Fārisī.' When they were brought, they admitted it, and then 'Umar said, 'Woe to me! Who will assume administrative power when there are such evils in it?' Abū Dharr said, 'It will be assumed by him whose nose Allah will cut and whose face He will turn to dust.' Then he began to weep.

"Then I said, 'O Commander of the Faithful, your grandfather al-'Abbās wanted governorship of Makkah, but the Prophet (ṣ) said to him, 'O al-'Abbās, uncle of the Prophet (ṣ), keep yourself away from this trouble. It is better than the burden of administration. You cannot conceive it.'

"The Prophet (ṣ) said this out of kindness to his uncle. He told him that it would not be of any use to Allah, who then revealed to him, 'Warn your near relatives.' The Prophet (ṣ) then said, 'O al-'Abbās, O Ṣafiyyah, O Fāṭimah, daughter of Muḥammad. I am not responsible to Allah for you. My actions will help me, and your actions will help you.'

"'Umar ibn al-Khaṭṭāb said, 'None assumes responsibility for people's affairs except someone who has deep knowledge, who is firm in promise, whose evils cannot openly be spoken of, who does not fear his relatives, and whom the slanders of the slanderers cannot move. There are four kinds of rulers. The first is the powerful ruler who keeps himself and his officers engaged. He is like a warrior in the way of Allah, and the hand of mercy is over him. The second is the weak ruler who does not make efforts in administrative matters. Owing to his weakness, his officers pass time in comforts. He will be ruined and will not get salvation. The third is the ruler who keeps his officers busy in duties, but who himself remains in comforts. This is a calamity about which the Prophet (ṣ) said, 'A bad shepherd is a danger and ruins himself.' The fourth is a ruler who lives in comforts and whose officers live likewise. They are all ruined.'

"O Commander of the Faithful, I heard that Jibrīl once came to the Prophet (ṣ) and said, 'When Allah ordered that the fire of hell be ignited, I came to you. The fire has been placed in hell for Resurrection Day.' The Prophet (ṣ) asked, 'O Jibrīl, describe the fire of hell to me.' Jibrīl answered, 'According to the command of Allah, it burnt for a thousand years, then it assumed a reddish hue, then it burnt for another thousand years, then it assumed a yellowish colour, then it burnt for another thousand years, and finally it assumed a black colour. The fire of hell is at present dense black. Its flames do not rise, nor can they be extinguished. By Him who sent you as a true Prophet, if a piece of cloth of the inmates of hell were exposed to the inhabitants of the world, all would expire owing to its stench. And if an iron chain from it fell into the world, all would expire owing to its stench.' Hearing this, the Prophet (ṣ) wept, and Jibrīl wept, too. Jibrīl then said, 'O Muḥammad, why are you weeping? Your past and future sins have all been forgiven.' The Prophet (ṣ) said, 'Should I not be a grateful servant? O Jibrīl, why are you weeping? You are the trusted spirit and trustworthy regarding the oneness of Allah. Jibrīl replied, 'I fear I may be tried as Hārūt and Mārūt were tried. I cannot trust my rank with Allah.' They both wept until a proclamation came from heaven: 'O Jibrīl, O Muḥammad. Allah has made both of you safe from punishment.

Muḥammad's rank over all other prophets is like that of Jibrīl over the rest of the angels."

"O Commander of the Faithful, I heard that 'Umar said, 'Give me no time, not even a moment, if two people wait long before me seeking justice regarding their property.' The greatest difficulty is to establish the duties to Allah. The greatest honour with Allah is piety. Allah gives honour to whoever seeks it by doing acts of worship. And he disgraces whoever seeks it by committing sins.

'This is my advice to you. Peace be on you." The caliph then gave him a purse as a gift, but he did not accept it, saying, 'I will not trade this advice for a temporary thing of the world.'

The caliph al-Manṣūr sometimes stayed at Dār al-Nadwah in Makkah. In the latter part of the night, he would pray at the Ka'bah and go round it without anyone knowing, and then he would lead the dawn prayer. One night, while going round the Ka'bah, he heard a man saying, "O Allah, I complain to you about the disturbance, rebellion, oppression, and injustice in the country." After hearing this, the caliph sat in a corner, and the man was called to him. When he came, the caliph said, "I heard you saying such and such, and am greatly disturbed to hear it." The man said, "If you grant me security of life, I may tell you." The caliph said, "Have no fear." The man then said, "You are responsible for the disturbance and disorder in the country. Your greed has not entered any other person. Allah placed on you the burden of administrating the Muslims, but you are neglecting to do good to them and are busy in misappropriating their possessions. Between you and the public, there are stumbling block of lime, bricks, iron doors, and guards with arms. You have appointed officers who oppress people and have given them power to wrongfully take people's possessions. You have issued orders forbidding the entry of the public to you except some people. You have made no provision for the oppressed, hungry, naked, weak, and poor. When people see that you have selected some special men for you and do not give permission to anybody except those people, they will say that the caliph has broken the trust of Allah and therefore 'Why should we not break our trust with him?'

"During the reign of Banū Umayyah, whenever the oppressed reached the rulers, they at once meted out justice to them. You amass wealth for one of three reasons. If you say, 'I amass wealth for my children,' Allah says that when a child is born, it does not take wealth or food with it, but it is Allah who gives sustenance out of His kindness and who arranged it beforehand in its mother's breast. If you say, 'I amass wealth to make my reign firm,' Allah says that those who were before you amassed gold and silver and arms and ammunition, but it did not benefit them. When Allah intended to make you caliph, you had no wealth. If you say, 'I amass wealth in order to live more comfortably than I did before,' I say that the rank gained through good deeds is more than what you have now. What will you do with the reign Allah has given you? When the Almighty snatched away your reign and calls you to account, your pomp and grandeur will come of no use to you."

Hearing this, the caliph began to weep bitterly and said, "Would that I had not been created! Would that I were a thing not fit to be mentioned!" Then the sage said, "Keep near you some high-class leaders and guides from the learned." Then the sage went away after saying, "If you recite an invocation morning and evening, your faults will be forgiven, your joy will become lasting, your sins will be forgiven, your supplications will be accepted, your sustenance will increase, your hopes will be realised, and you will die a martyr. The invocation is as follows:

"'O Allah, I bow to Your glory. Just as You are gracious to the kind, so You are above the great with Your greatness. Just as You have knowledge of everything above Your throne, so You have knowledge of everything below the abyss of the earth. To You the machinations of the heart are manifest. Your knowledge of manifest things is secret. Everything before Your glory is humble. Every powerful man is humble to Your power. All affairs in this world and in the next are in Your hands. Give me relief from and a way out of the thoughts I am entering and my faults, and keep my undesirable matter secret. Create in me love for supplicating for things I am not fit for on account of my sins. I ask You for freedom from fear and for Your pleasure. You are doing so much good to me, but I am committing sins. You are giving me love through Your mercy, and I am causing you anger by my sins. Make firm my faith in you, give me courage to invoke You, and shower mercy and blessings on me. You are Forgiving, Compassionate.'"

The above conversation was between al-Manṣūr and al-Khaḍir (peace be on him).

When Hārūn al-Rashīd became caliph, scholars met him, and he fixed their annual allowances. Only his friend Sufyān ibn Sa'īd ibn al-Mundhir did not meet him. So the caliph wrote to him a letter inviting him to come to his palace. When Sufyān received the letter, he wrote this in reply on the back of it:

> From Sufyān to Hārūn al-Rashīd, deluded by wealth and deprived of the taste of faith
>
> I am writing to inform you that I have demolished the path of my love for you and cut off my love for you. I dislike actions for which you cite me as a witness, since you have written that you have opened your treasury to Muslims. You are spending it unjustly and against the provision of Sharī'ah. You are satisfied with what you have done.
>
> O Hārūn, you are spending the wealth of the state extravagantly without the consent of the people. Are the widows, orphans, and learned satisfied with your actions? Know that you will have to face the Almighty very soon. Dressed in silk robes, you have taken your seat on the throne. You have hung a long screen over your doors and kept your tyrannical soldiers as guards. They drink wine, but beat drunkards. They commit fornication, but mete out prescribed punishments for fornicators. They steal, but they cut off the hands of thieves. Why do you not punish them before they punish others?

He handed over the letter to the messenger of the caliph without enclosing it in an envelope and without any seal. The messenger handed over the letter to the caliph, who accepted it cordially. He then used to keep it by his side and read it at the end of each prayer until his death.

The caliph al-Rashīd stayed for some days at Kūfah after pilgrimage, and people came to him. Bahlūl the Crazy was one of them. When Hārūn came to him, Bahlūl proclaimed loudly, "O Commander of the Faithful!" Hārūn uncovered his face and said, "At your service, O Bahlūl." Bahlūl said, "You should be modest and humble in your journey."

With that, the caliph began to weep and said, "Give me more advice." Bahlūl said, "O Commander of the Faithful, if any man spends something out of the wealth Allah gave him and gives charity, he is written as a pious man." Then the caliph presented him with something which he refused to accept, saying, "I do not need it."

These are some examples of how past sages and learned men enjoined good and forbade evil. They cared very little for the powers of the rulers and trusted entirely in Allah. They were satisfied with the belief that Allah would grant them the reward of martyrdom.

Book 10
The character and conduct of the Prophet (ṣ)

Introduction

All praise is due to Allah, who created the universe and taught His greatest prophet, Muḥammad, the best of manners, purified his character and conduct, and chose him to be His friend. All praise is due to Allah, who gives to whoever makes his character and conduct beautiful the blessing of following the Prophet's attributes, and who deprives whomever he wishes to destroy of assuming the character of the Prophet (ṣ).

Good outward conduct is the fountain of good inward conduct. The movements of the bodily limbs are the result of the thoughts of the heart, and external actions are the result of character and conduct. Striving to know Allah and to acquire wonderful, secret powers are the fountains of actions. And the light of this secret power is expressed outwardly, making the body beautiful and giving rise to good attributes after removing evils.

A person who does not have fear in his heart has no fear expressed in his bodily limbs. The beauty of the conduct of prophethood is not expressed in a person whose heart is not illumined with the light of Allah. What I included in first and second books of this volume, I do not wish to repeat them here.

1

The Prophet's learning through the Qur'an

The Prophet (ṣ) would supplicate Almighty Allah, asking Him to for good manners, for the good treatment of others, and to be adorned with good character and conduct. He would say in his supplication, "O Allah, make my constitution and conduct good" and "O Allah, save me from bad character and conduct." Acceptance of his prayer is seen in the following verse: "Call upon me, I will answer you" (Qur'an, 40:60).

Allah revealed the Qur'an to the Prophet (ṣ) and through it He taught him good manners. His character is the Qur'an. Sa'd ibn Hishām said, "Once, I went to 'Ā'ishah and her father and asked them about the character and conduct of the Prophet (ṣ). 'Ā'ishah replied, 'Do you not read the Qur'an?' I said, 'Yes.' She said, 'The character of the Messenger of Allah is the Qur'an.'"

His conduct is expressed in the following verses:

> *Take to forgiveness and enjoin good and turn aside from the ignorant.* (Qur'an, 7:199)

> *Surely Allah enjoins the doing of justice and the doing of good (to others) and the giving to the kindred, and He forbids indecency and evil and rebellion.* (Qur'an, 16:90)

> *Bear patiently that which befalls you; surely these acts require courage.* (Qur'an, 31:17)

> *Whoever is patient and forgiving, these most surely are actions due to courage.* (Qur'an, 42:43)

So pardon them and turn away; surely Allah loves those who do good (to others). (Qur'an, 5:13)

They should pardon and turn away. Do you not love that Allah should forgive you? (Qur'an, 24:22)

Repel (evil) with what is best, when lo! he between whom and you was enmity would be as if he were a warm friend. (Qur'an, 41:34)

Those who restrain (their) anger and pardon men; and Allah loves the doers of good (to others). (Qur'an, 3:134)

Avoid most of suspicion, for surely suspicion in some cases is a sin, and do not spy nor let some of you backbite others. (Qur'an, 49:12)

In the battle of Uḥud, when the head cover of the Prophet fell, and he was separated from his Companions, blood was oozing from his face. Wiping the blood, he said, "How will people who dyed the face of the Prophet with blood while he called them to their Lord attain salvation? Then Allah revealed the verse "You have no concern in the affair." (Qur'an, 3:128)

This was only to teach him good manners.

The Qur'anic verses concerning the teaching the Prophet (ṣ) good manners are many. It was the first object of Allah to teach the Prophet (ṣ) good manners, character, and conduct. In this regard, the Prophet (ṣ) said, "I have been sent to perfect good conduct." Allah praised the character of the Prophet (ṣ) by saying, "Most surely you conform (yourself) to sublime morality" (Qur'an, 68:4). Thereafter, the Prophet (ṣ) explained to the people that Allah loves good character and hates bad character.

'Alī said, "How strange that a Muslim does not benefit his Muslim brother who comes to him in need. If he hopes for rewards and fears punishment, he should hasten to good conduct, as it shows the path of salvation." A man then asked 'Alī, "Did you hear this from the Prophet (ṣ)?" He said, "Yes. And I have heard from him advice better than this. When the prisoners of the tribe of Tayyi' were brought to him, one of their girls came to the Prophet (ṣ) and said, 'O Muḥammad, if you wish, release me, but do not dishonour me before the tribe of the Arabs. I am the daughter of the leader of my people, and my father was the caretaker of my people. He would set captives free, feed the hungry, spread peace, and never refuse a beggar in need. I am the daughter of Ḥātim al-Ṭā'ī.' The Prophet (ṣ) said, 'O girl, his qualities you mentioned are those of a believer.' The Prophet (ṣ) said to his Companions, "Free her, as her father loved good character and conduct." Thereupon, Abū Burdah ibn Nayyār stood up and said, 'O Messenger of Allah, does Allah love good conduct?' The Prophet (ṣ) replied, 'By Him in whose hand is my life, none will enter paradise unless he has good conduct.'"

The Prophet (ṣ) said, 'Allah adorned Islam with good character and beautiful actions.' Among such qualities are being good company; having good manners; being modest; doing good to others; feeding others; spreading peace; visiting the ill, be they pious or impious; following the bier of a Muslim; treating neighbours well, be they believers or non-believer; honouring Muslims; accepting invitations; forgiving others; settling disputes among others; giving charity; being the first to greet; pardoning the faults of others; giving up music, musical instruments, and jests Islam prohibits; not backbiting; speaking the truth; giving up miserliness, greed, deceit, and treating enemies badly; not cutting off blood tie; and giving up bad conduct, pride, glory, haughtiness, indecencies, hatred, rebellion, enmity, oppression and the like, as all these are attributes of a believer.

Anas ibn Mālik said that the Prophet (ṣ) did not give up good advice, enjoined us to stick to it, and would warn us against backbiting and prohibited it. The following verse suffices for all these maxims: "Surely Allah enjoins the doing of justice and the doing of good (to others)" (Qur'an, 16:90).

Mu'ādh ibn Jabal said, "The Prophet (ṣ) advised me thus: 'O Mu'ādh, I advise you to fear Allah, to speak the truth, to fulfil promises, to pay trusts, not to breach trusts, to save your neighbour, to show kindness to orphans, to be modest in speech, to spread peace, to do good deeds, to hope less, to cleave to faith, to study the Qur'an, to love the next world, to fear reckoning, and to act humbly. O Mu'ādh, I forbid you to call a truthful man a liar. Do not follow any sin, disobey the learned, be a leader, disobey a just man, or create disorder in a land. I instruct you to fear Allah while passing by each stone, each tree, and heaps of earth. Repent anew after committing any sin. Repent secretly for secret sins and openly for open sins.'"

2

The Prophet's character and conduct

The Holy Prophet (ṣ) was the most patient, bravest, just, and chaste of men. His hand never touched a strange woman. He was the most charitable man. He did not pass a single night hoarding a dirham or dinar. Whenever excess money came to him, and if there was no one to whom he could give it, he did not return home until he gave it to the poor and needy. He would not keep for more than a year the provision of his family members Allah was pleased to give him. He would take one fifth of the dates and wheat which easily came to him. What remained in excess he would give in charity. He would give charity to any beggar, even out of his own provision which he had saved.

He would repair his shoes, join his wives in their work, and cut meat with them. He was the most bashful among men and could not stare at anyone for long. He accepted the invitation of slaves and free men and the offering of even a cup of milk. He did not use what was given as *zakāh*, and would accept the invitation of widows and the poor. He exacted the truth even when it brought harm to him and his Companions.

He would say, "I do not accept the invitation of any infidel." He would bind stones against his stomach to appease his hunger, and ate whatever he had. He did not return any present, nor did he take precautions with lawful food. If he got dried grapes in lieu of bread, he ate them. If he got baked meat, he ate it. He would eat any bread, wheat, sweets, or honey he received. He considered milk sufficient if he did not get any other food.

He would eat neither leaning against a pillow nor at a high table. The soles of his two feet served as his towel. He never ate bread for three consecutive days until he met Allah; this was a voluntary act on his part.

He would accept wedding invitations, visit the sick, and attend funerals. He was the most modest, and his tongue was the most eloquent, never prolonging his speech.

His constitution was the most beautiful. No worldly duties could keep him busy. He would put on whatever he got. His ring was made of silver, and he would wear it on the little finger of his right or left hand.

He would mount his servant behind him on any conveyance—horse, camel or ass. Sometimes he walked barefoot, and sometimes he wore neither turban nor cap. He would go to a distant place to see a sick man.

He loved perfumes and hated foul smells.

He would sit with the poor and eat with them. He would honour the noble, advising them to do good deeds, and show kindness to relatives. He did not treat anybody harshly. He would accept any excuse offered to him.

He would at times joke without lying, never bursting into laughter. He considered innocent sports and games lawful and played with his wives, sometimes holding races with them. He would drink the milk of camels and goats with his family members, and would give them equal shares of food and clothes.

He would never waste time; rather, he spent it for the sake of Allah. He would walk in the gardens of his Companions for recreation.

He neither hated the poor for their poverty nor fear kings for their mighty power. He would urge everyone, regardless of social status, to Allah.

Allah adorned him with all virtuous qualities as well as perfect rule, although he was illiterate. His childhood was spent with shepherds and he used to graze sheep and goats. He was an orphan, his parents having died in his infancy.

3

The Prophet's good manners

If the Holy Prophet (ṣ) abused anybody, he would compensate him and show him kindness. He did never cursed any woman or slave. Once, while on the battle field, he was asked, "O Messenger of Allah, it would have been better if you had cursed them." He said, "Allah sent me as a mercy and not as a curser." When he was asked to curse a particular person or an unbeliever, he did not curse him, but rather prayed for his welfare. He never beat anybody with his own hand except for the sake of Allah. Similarly, he took revenge never for personal wrongs, but for the preservation of Allah's honour.

He would select the easier of two things as long as it did not involve sin or the severing of ties. In addition, He would fulfil the needs of anyone, whether a slave or freeman, who required his help.

Anas ibn Mālik said, "By Him who sent him as a Prophet, he never said to me, 'Why have you done this' or 'Why have you not done this?' His wives did not rebuke me, either."

The Prophet (ṣ) would sleep on whatever bed he had, otherwise he would sleep on the ground.

Allah described the Prophet (ṣ) in the Torah: "Muḥammad is the Prophet of Allah and His chosen servant. He is neither harsh, coarse, nor clamorous in marketplaces. He is not vengeful, but rather prone to pardon. His birthplace was Makkah, his emigration was to Madīnah, and his reign is in Syria. He and his Companions wear waistband wrappers and urge to the Qur'an and wisdom. He washes his bodily limbs." He is thus described in the New Testament as well.

It was his nature to be the first to greet whomever he met. He would wait where he was to meet a man. When he shook hands with someone, he would never be the first to release it. And when he met with any of his Companions, he would shake their hands, clasping it, and strengthening his grasp over the person's hand.

He neither stood up nor sat without mentioning Allah. When anybody sat by him at the time of his prayer, he used to make it short, then ask him, "Do you need anything?" When he fulfilled the person's need, he would return to his prayer.

His sitting place was no different from that of his Companions, as he sat where he went. He was not found sitting among his Companions with his legs outstretched. He would sit mostly facing the Ka'bah, and honour whoever came to him. He would even spread his own sheet of cloth for non-relatives, and offer guests his own pillow. Everyone thought that the Prophet (ṣ) honoured him more. Whoever came to him could see his face.

He would call his Companions by their surnames out of respect, and surnamed whoever had none. He would call women by the names of their issues, and call others by their surnames. He would call the boys by their surnames, thereby softening their hearts.

He was the least angry of all, and was very affectionate and kind.

Nobody could speak loudly in his assembly. When he rose therefrom, he would recite, "O Allah, You are pure. All praise is Yours. I bear witness that there is no deity but You. I seek Your forgiveness and turn to you."

4

The Prophet's words and laughter

Of the Arabs, the Prophet (ṣ) had the most eloquent and pleasant speech. He said, "I am the greatest orator among the Arabs." He seldom spoke. And when he did, he did not speak much.

His words fell gradually from his lips like pearls. 'Ā'ishah said, "The Messenger of Allah did not speak like you." They said the Messenger of Allah spoke very little, and concisely. It was neither too long nor too short. The words came one after another like pearls. Whoever heard them remembered them.

He was the most pleasant in speech among his Companions. He kept silent for long, and did not speak without necessity. He would speak not evil words, but only the truth. Nor did he use ornamental words.

His Companions never disputed before him. He would say, "Do not refute the Qur'an by comparing one part with another, as it has been revealed for many purposes."

He would smile much before his Companions, exposing his teeth. It was related, "A Bedouin once came to the Prophet (ṣ), whose face became changed on seeing him. Seeing anger in his face, the Arab said, 'By Him who sent him as a true prophet, I will not ask him until he smiles.' Then he said, 'O Messenger of Allah, we heard that the Antichrist will bring soup for people, who will then remain hungry. My parents be sacrificed for you, do you forbid me to eat it until I perish? Or do you order me to eat it with satisfaction? Would I become an infidel after faith in Allah?'

The Prophet (ṣ) laughed at this, so much so that his teeth showed. Then he said, 'No. Rather, Allah will make you free from the food, just as he will make the believers free.'" He would smile most when the Qur'an was being revealed to him.

When something happened, he would entrust it to Allah and renounce his own strength and power, supplicating, "O Allah, show me truth as truth and enable me to follow it. And show me falsehood as falsehood and enable me to shun it. Save me from doubt, so that I do not follow my passion without Your guidance. Make my desire to obey You. Be pleased with my soundness. Show me the different shades of truth. You guide to the straight path whomsoever You will."

5

The Prophet's eating

The Holy Prophet (ṣ) ate whatever he received. To him the best food was what everyone partook of. When the dining cloth was spread, he would say, "In the name of Allah. O Allah, render the food favourable and praiseworthy and cause it to have the favour of paradise."

Whenever the Prophet (ṣ) sat to eat, he sat as a praying man sits, not placing one leg over the other, and said, "I am a mere servant and eat as a servant eats."

He would not have any hot food, saying, "There is no grace in it. Allah will not feed us with fire, so make this food cold."

He would eat whatever was presented him with three fingers, sometimes with the help of the fourth.

Once, a dish made of clarified butter, honey, and wheat was presented him. When he ate it, he said, "How good it is." He used to eat bread, curry, dates, and salt. Of all fresh fruits, the dearest to him was grapes, cucumber, and watermelon. He used to eat gourd with bread and sugar and sometimes with dates. His ordinary meal consisted of dates and water. Sometimes he mixed milk with dates.

Meat was his most favourite curry. He said, "Meat increases the power of hearing and is the king of foods in this world and the next. If I asked my Lord to feed me meat every day, He would do so." He would eat cooked meat with gourd. He liked gourd and said, "It is the fruit of a plant of my brother Jonah." 'Ā'ishah said, "The Prophet (ṣ) said to me, 'O 'Ā'ishah, when you cook meat, mix it with much water, as it makes the broken-hearted strong.'" He would eat the meat of hunted birds, but did not himself hunt.

He used to eat bread with butter and liked goat neck and thigh. Of curries, he liked gourd; of condiments, vinegar; of dates, dried dates. He prayed for these three things, saying, "These have come from paradise. They are medicines for poison and insomnia."

Of vegetables, he liked endives, mountain balms, and garden purslanes.

He disliked kidneys because of their proximity to urine. He also disliked several parts of a goat: the genitals, ovaries, blood, goitre, gall bladder and the like. He did not eat onions and garlic, but did not condemn them.

He would eat what he liked and did not eat what he did not like. He disliked eating the meat of *ḍabb* (a spiny-tailed lizard) and spleen, but he did not prohibit them to be eaten.

He would clean his dish with his hand, saying, "Most blessings are in the remnants of the food." Likewise, he would not clean his hands with a towel until he licked his fingers well, such that they assumed a reddish hue, and said, "Nobody knows in which part of the food is the blessing." When he finished his meal, he would say, "O Allah, all praise is Yours. You have given me food and drink and satisfaction. So praise to You, who cannot be denied, who is eternally present, and who is indispensable." He was accustomed to wiping his hands well, then washing his hands and mouth with excess water, each time mentioning the name of Allah.

He would drink water slowly and not hastily in one breath. He would not blow in the cup of water when drinking, and supply food to the person by his side. He was once given milk and honey mixed together, but he refused to drink it, saying, "Two drinks at the same time, and two curries at the same time!" I do not make them unlawful, but I consider them bad for the reckoning of resurrection day, as they are additional things in this world. I like modesty and Allah raises him who humbles himself for Allah.

In his home he was more modest than an unmarried girl. He would not order the preparation of any food, but rather eat whatever was given him and remain silent if not given.

6
The Prophet's clothing

The Prophet (ṣ) would wear a sheet, gown, shirt, or whatever he received. Green would please him, but most of his clothes were white. He said, "Dress your living in white garments, and shroud your dead therein."

He would wear a gown in jihad. His shirt reached his thighs. He had only one shirt dyed with saffron, and in it he led prayers. He would sometimes wear only a padded garment and say, "I am but a slave, and dress as a slave dresses."

He had two special garments for the Friday prayer which he did not put on at other times. Sometimes he had only one garment, with which he cohabited with his wives. He also had a black garment which he gave away. Thereupon, Umm Salamah said, "What happened to that black garment?" He replied, "I clothed someone with it." She said, "You look more beautiful when the black garment mixes with your beautiful constitution."

He would sometimes go out with a seal tied with a thread in hand. He used to impress his letters with the seal, saying, "It is better to put a seal on a letter than to back-bite."

He would wear a cap under his turban. If he had no turban, he would put the cap on instead. Sometimes he took off his cap and fixed it in front of him as a prayer stake. When he had no turban or cap, he covered his head with a sheet of cloth. And he had a turban named al-Sahab, which he presented to 'Alī.

Whenever he put on a garment, he began from the right side and said, "All praise is due to Allah, who has given this garment to cover my private parts and to adorn myself among others." When he wished to take off a garment, he began from the left side. When he put on a new garment, he donated his old garment to a poor man and said, "If a Muslim gives his wearing garment to another Muslim, nobody except Allah will dress him, and he remains in the custody of Allah as long as that cloth remains with him, be he alive or dead."

He had a bed of skins stuffed with palm fibres. It was two cubits long and a cubit and a span wide.

He had the habit of naming animals, arms, and possessions. The name of his flag was al-ʻIqāb. The names of his swords were Dhū al-Faqār, al-Mikhdham, al-Rasūb and al-Qaḍīb. The middle portion of his swords were moulded with silver, and he would wear a belt of leather which had three rings of silver. The name of his bow was al-Katūm; his quiver, al-Kāfūr; his camel, al-Qaṣwā'; his she-mule, al-Duldul; his ass, Yaʻfūr; and his goat whose milk he drank, ʻAynah.

He also had an earthen pot he used as an ablution pot and a drinking vessel.

7

The Prophet's pardoning

The Holy Prophet (ṣ) was the most patient among men and the most forgiving in spite his having power to retaliate. If someone presented to him a necklace of gold or silver, he would give it to some of his Companions. One day, a desert Arab stood up and said, "O Muḥammad, if Allah ordered you to do justice, I do not see you doing it." The Prophet (ṣ) replied, "Woe to you! Who act justly to you after me?" When the Arab was about to leave, the Prophet (ṣ) said, "Bring him back to me gently."

On the day of Khaybar, the Prophet (ṣ) was taking silver coins for the people in the cloth of Bilāl when a man said to him, "O Messenger of Allah, do justice." The Prophet (ṣ) said to him, "Woe to you, if I do not do justice, who will do justice after me? If I do not do justice, I shall be ruined and suffer loss." 'Umar then said, "Should I not kill him? For he is a hypocrite!" The Prophet (ṣ) replied, "God forbid that people should say I kill my Companions."

The Prophet (ṣ) was once in jihad when the unbelievers found the Muslims heedless. So one of them raised a sword over the head of the Prophet (ṣ) and asked him, "Who will prevent me from killing you?" He at once replied, "Allah." Suddenly the sword fell from his hand, and the Prophet (ṣ) picked it up and said, "Who will prevent me from killing you?" The man said, "Hold it firmly." The Prophet (ṣ) said, "Say, 'I bear witness that there is no deity but Allah, and that I am His Messenger.'" The man said, "I have no enmity towards you. I shall not kill you. I shall not go with you, but I shall not join those who fight against you." Then the Prophet (ṣ) set him free. The man went to his tribe and said, "I have come to you today from the best man."

Anas ibn Mālik related that a Jewess poisoned the food of the Prophet (ṣ) at Khaybar. When he began to eat it, he smelled the poison and stopped eating. The woman was brought to the Prophet (ṣ), who asked her about the poisoned food. The woman said, "I intended to kill you." The Prophet (ṣ) said, "Allah will not give you that power." The Companions exclaimed, "Should we not kill her?" To which the Prophet (ṣ) replied, "Do not kill her."

On another occasion, a Jew enchanted the Prophet (ṣ), and Jibrīl informed him of this. He then took out the enchantment and came round, but took no revenge against the Jew.

'Alī said, "The Prophet (ṣ) sent me, al-Zubayr, and Miqdād, to a certain place and said, 'Continue until you reach Rawḍah Khākh, where you will find a woman with a letter which you must take from her.' We then reached the place and told the woman to give the letter to us. The woman denied knowledge of any letter. She was then compelled to hand it over. We then brought it to the Prophet (ṣ). On it was written, 'From Ḥāṭib ibn Abī Balta'ah to the polytheists of Makkah …' This letter was written to inform them secretly of the affairs of the Prophet (ṣ). The Prophet (ṣ) said, 'O Ḥāṭib, what is the matter?' He said, 'O Messenger of Allah, do not hasten to punish me. I have mixed with my people. The Emigrants who are with you have in Makkah their relatives who look after their families there. I had hopes that, though I have got no relationship with Quraysh, I would find a man among them who would take care of my relatives there if I show kindness to them. I have not done this out of infidelity, or preferring infidelity after Islam, or out of apostasy.' The Prophet (ṣ) said, 'This man has spoken the truth.' But 'Umar ibn al-Khaṭṭāb said, 'Allow us to kill this hypocrite,' to which the Prophet (ṣ) replied, 'He joined the battle of Badr with us. And how do you know? Perhaps Allah examined the people of Badr,' and said, 'Do whatever you like. Allah has forgiven you.'"

The Prophet (ṣ) was once distributing the booties when a Madīnan Helper stood up and said, "Allah is not pleased with this distribution." When this was mentioned to the Prophet (ṣ), his face turned red, and he said, "May Allah show you mercy. My brother Mūsā was given similar troubles, but remained patient."

The Prophet (ṣ) said, "Let nobody communicate anything about my Companions, as I wish to have a sound mind when I come to you."

8
The Prophet's dislikes

The skin of the Prophet (ṣ) was thin, and his interior and exterior were clean. His pleasure and wrath were visible in his face. When he got very angry, he would touch his head repeatedly. He would not disclose to anybody what appeared bad to him.

A man wearing a yellow dye once came to the Prophet (ṣ), who disliked it, yet said nothing until he left. When he departed, he said to the people, "If this man were asked to forego the yellow dye, it would be better."

A desert Arab once urinated in the mosque in the presence of the Prophet (ṣ). The Companions were about to assault him when the Prophet (ṣ) said to him, "These mosques are not for urinating and uncleanliness."

A desert Arab once came to the Prophet (ṣ) and begged him for something. He gave that thing to him and said, "I have treated you well." The desert Arab said, "Never! You have not treated me well." At this the Companions got angry, but the Prophet (ṣ) prohibited them from doing any harm to the man. Then the Prophet (ṣ) went into his room and brought something for him to eat, saying, "I have done you good." Then the man said, "May Allah bless your family and relatives." The Prophet (ṣ) said to him, "What you said first seemed unpleasant to my Companions. If you like, say to them what you have said to me just now. What is in their mind will then vanish." The man said, "I shall say it to them."

When the desert Arab came around again, the Prophet (ṣ) said, "I added what the desert Arab told me. It seemed to me that he was pleased with it. I asked him, 'Are you satisfied?' and he replied, "Yes. May Allah bless your family and relatives." The Prophet (ṣ) added, "The smile of the desert Arab in relation to me is like that of a man who had a camel which left. It then sped up lest people follow it. The driver of the camel said, 'You all go away and leave the camel and myself alone. I know it better and shall show kindness to it.' The driver of the camel gave it some food and called it to him. When it came, he loaded it and rode it. The desert Arab would have entered hell for using harsh words had I not prohibited you from retaliating against him and assaulting him."

9

The Prophet's generosity

The Holy Prophet (ṣ) was the most charitable man, and he was the most charitable during Ramaḍān, withholding nothing.

Describing the Prophet (ṣ), 'Alī said, "His hand of charity spread to its utmost, and his tongue was the most truthful. His conduct was the most modest, and he was the most honourable in lineage. Fear struck whoever saw him first. Whoever mingled with him loved him.

Someone said in praise of him, "I did not see anyone like him before or after him."

A man once begged the Prophet (ṣ) in the name of Islam, and he gave him. He then begged him further and he gave him a flock of sheep which was grazing between two hillocks. The beggar then went to his people, saying, "Accept Islam because Muḥammad gives so much that he does not fear poverty." He never refused anyone who begged him for something.

Ninety thousand dirhams were once brought to the Prophet (ṣ), and he distributed it among his Companions. After that a man came to him and begged him for something. The Prophet (ṣ) said to him, "I have nothing now, go and buy something, and when we have some (money) we will pay for it." 'Umar ibn al-Khaṭṭāb said, "O Messenger of Allah, Allah has not imposed on you a burden you cannot control." His words did not appear pleasing to the Prophet (ṣ). That man said, "Spend and do not fear poverty from Allah." The Prophet (ṣ) then smiled, his pleasure visible in his face.

When the Prophet (ṣ) returned from the battlefield of Ḥunayn, the desert Arabs came to him and begged him, so much that he was compelled to take shelter in a corner of a tree. They caught his sheet, and he said, "Give me back my sheet. If I had sheep equal in number to these thorny plants, I would distribute them all to you, and you would not find me a miser or a coward."

10

The Prophet's bravery and heroism

The Holy Prophet (ṣ) was the greatest hero and bravest man. 'Alī said, "In the battle of Badr, we all took refuge with the Prophet (ṣ), who braved the enemies. We found him the bravest on that day." 'Alī also said, "When the fight began and friends and foes met with one another, we feared for the Prophet (ṣ), as he was closest to the enemies. Nobody was nearer to the enemies than him."

When he ordered people to fight, he became pleased and prepared himself. At that time, he was considered the most superior in strength. 'Imrān ibn Ḥuṣayn said, "The Prophet (ṣ) attacked the enemy who came to him first." The Companions said that the Prophet (ṣ) had a firm hold on the enemy. In the battle of Ḥunayn, when the Prophet (ṣ) was surrounded by the enemies, he alighted from his mule and said, "I am surely the Messenger of Allah. There is no untruth in it. I am the descendant of 'Abd al-Muṭṭalib." On that day, he was the bravest of all.

11

The Prophet's modesty

In spite of the lofty position of the Prophet (ṣ), he was the most humble and modest. Ibn 'Āmir said, "I saw the Prophet (ṣ) throwing stones (at Jamrah) on a camel. There was no assault in it, no driving out, and no saying, 'Go aside! Go aside!'" He sat on a sheet of cloth on the back of a mule and took someone behind him.

He would visit the sick, follow funeral biers, accept invitations from servants and slaves, repair shoes, and sew garments. He would help his family members in their household duties.

His companions would not stand up in his honour, as they knew he disliked it. He would salute children when passing by them. One day, a man was brought to the Prophet (ṣ) and was afraid to see him. The Prophet (ṣ) said, "Be quiet. I am not a king. I am the son of a humble Qurayshite woman who used to eat gourd."

He would sit with his Companions like an ordinary man. So whenever a stranger came to see him, the stranger could not recognise him until he was introduced to him.

'Ā'ishah said, "Eat reclining—may Allah make me your ransom—as it easier for you." The Prophet (ṣ) leaned towards the ground so much that it seemed his head would touch it. He would say, "I shall eat like a slave and sit like a slave." He never in his lifetime ate using a plate.

12

The Prophet's figure and constitution

The Prophet (ṣ) was neither tall nor short. When he walked alone, he appeared like a man of medium height. If a tall man walked with him, he looked taller. When two tall men walked on either side of him, he appeared the tallest, but when they became parted, people called them tall.

He was handsome, neither too white nor too brown. He was of pure reddish hue. Praising him, someone said that his limbs which were exposed to sunlight, such as the face and neck, appeared more white than red.

The sweat of his face was like pearls, and was more fragrant than musk.

His hair was very pleasant, neither straight nor curly. When he combed it, it appeared like lines in sand. It is said that his hair touched his shoulders. Sometime he parted his hair into four plaits, each ear exposed between two plaits. Sometimes he kept his hair above his ears, at which time his neck appeared shiny as pearls. Grey hairs could be seen in his head and beard. Their number was no more than seventeen.

The Prophet (ṣ) had a most pleasant constitution. Some likened him to a full moon. His forehead was wide, and the place between his eyebrows was bright as pure silver. His eyes were black tinged with a reddish hue. His eye lashes were profuse. His nose was thin, and his teeth were neither widely spaced nor too close together. When they were exposed while he smiled or laughed, they shone like lighting.

His lips were most beautiful, and the ends of his face were the softest. His face was smooth. His beard was thick, and he did not trim it. He would, however, clip his moustache.

He had the most beautiful neck, neither long nor short. If the rays of the sun fell on his neck, it appeared like a cup of silver mixed with gold. His chest was broad, even like a mirror, white like moonlight. There was a thin line of hair extending from his chest up to his navel. There was no hair on his stomach, but thereon were three lines, one of which was covered by a waist band.

His shoulders were wide and had hair. The place between his shoulders was also wide, and therein there was an impression or "seal of prophethood," which was closer to the right shoulder. In it was a spot mixed with black and yellow. There were hairs around it which appeared like the hairs of a horse.

He had hands full of flesh, and his fingers were like silver sticks. His palms were softer than wool and were so fragrant that it seemed that perfume was applied to them. When someone shook his hand, that person's hand would smell fragrant. If his pure hand touched the head of a boy, the boy was distinguishable from other boys on account of the pleasant scent of his hand.

His thighs were bulky, and his constitution was proportionate and beautiful. In his latter days, he became rather fleshy, but he was not fat like his first stage of life.

The Prophet (ṣ) walked firmly and steadily. He said concerning his constitution, "I am similar to Adam, but in character and conduct I am similar to Ibrāhīm." He also said, "I have ten names with my Lord: Muḥammad; Aḥmad; Abolisher, through whom Allah abolishes disbelief; Last, there being no one after; Assembler, after whose step Allah assembles them; Messenger of Mercy; Messenger of Repentance; Messenger of War; Follower, who follows all prophets; and al-Qutham." Abū al-Bakhtarī said that "al-Qutham" is defined as a complete, perfect person.

13

The Prophet's miracles

The character and conduct of the Holy Prophet (ṣ); his actions; his habits; his management of affairs; his treatment of the different classes of people; his showing them the straight path; his wonderful answers to various, difficult and subtle questions; his untiring efforts for the good of people; his good guidance regarding the open laws of Sharī'ah—all these matters lead one to the conclusion that these were beyond the power of a man without help from an unseen hand. They are impossible on the part of a hypocrite or a liar. On seeing his constitution and qualifications, people testified that he was a great, truthful man sent by Allah.

Allah gave him these qualities, though he was illiterate, had no education, and always lived with illiterate Arabs. Being illiterate, an orphan, and weak, how could he acquire such good character and conduct, such knowledge about Allah without worldly knowledge? His true and correct knowledge about earlier prophets show that he is a true messenger of Allah, because he knew these truths by revelations. How could he know what was is beyond man unless he received revelation? His miracles prove that he is a true prophet of Allah. I shall relate some of his miracles without going into details.

- When Quraysh told the Prophet (ṣ) to divide the moon into two parts, the Prophet (ṣ) supplicated Allah, who split the moon into two portions clearly visible to those present.

- During the siege of Madīnah by the allied armies which lasted more than a month, the Prophet (ṣ) supplied provisions to all.
- He fed eighty people with only four *mudds* of maize and a little goat.
- The daughter of Bashīr had a few dried grapes with which the Prophet (ṣ) fed all his soldiers to satisfaction, and there still remained excess.
- Water gushed forth from the fingers of the Prophet (ṣ), so much so that his soldiers drank to their hearts content and also performed ablution therewith.
- There was no water in a well at Tabūk, and it dried up. The Prophet (ṣ) threw a little water of his ablution into the well, which immediately gushed forth so much water that thousands of soldiers drank to their satisfaction.
- There was no water in a well at al-Ḥudaybiyah. The Prophet (ṣ) threw the remaining ablution water into it, which immediately gushed forth abundant water. Fifteen hundred men drank to their satisfaction.
- The Prophet (ṣ) threw a handful of dust in the faces of his enemies, as a result of which they instantly became blind. Soon after, this verse was revealed: "You did not smite when you smote (the enemy), but it was Allah Who smote" (Qur'an, 8:17).
- The Prophet (ṣ) would deliver sermons standing on the trunk of a palm tree in the mosque. When it was replaced by another, the trunk began to emit a mild sound which was heard by all his Companions. When he touched it with his hand, it became calm.
- The Prophet (ṣ) urged the Jews to wish for death while at the same time informing them that they had no desire for it. An obstacle came between them and their speech, and they were unable to express their wish to die. This is mentioned in the Qur'an.

- The Prophet (ṣ) warned 'Uthmān of a great danger as a result of which he would enter paradise. History bears testimony that he was murdered in his very house while reading the Qur'an.
- A man joined jihad, but the Prophet (ṣ) said he would enter hell. This became evident when the man committed suicide.
- While the Prophet (ṣ) was emigrating to Madīnah, Surāqah ibn Mālik pursued him in order to capture him and get a reward. But the feet of his horse sank, and dust followed him in his steps. When he sought the Prophet's help in escaping the danger, he prayed for him. This continued three times, the Prophet (ṣ) praying for him each time. After he was released for the third time, the Prophet (ṣ) prophesised that Surāqah would soon wear the bangles of the Persian king Khosroes. After the conquest of Persia by Muslims, these bangles were procured from the king and were given to him to wear.
- Al-Aswad al-'Ansī was a liar and claimed prophethood during the lifetime of the Prophet (ṣ). He was a resident of Sana'a, Yemen. One night, he was found assassinated in that town. In that very night, the Prophet (ṣ) gave the people news of his death and named his murderer.
- During the night of the emigration to Madīnah, a hundred Qurayshites surrounded the house of the Prophet (ṣ) to kill him. But he escaped from their clutches by throwing dust on their heads, which made them unable to see him leave.
- The Prophet (ṣ) said to some of his Companions, "The last man among you will die of arson." This prophecy came true.
- The Prophet (ṣ) told two trees to cover him while he urinated. The two trees shifted from their sites, covered him from public view, and then went away to their old sites after he was done.
- The Prophet (ṣ) was of medium stature, but when he walked with two tall men on either side of him, he was seen the tallest of them.

- The Prophet (ṣ) said he would kill Ubayy ibn Khalaf al-Jumaḥī in the battle of Uḥud. During this battle, the Prophet (ṣ) inflicted a minor injury on him, which led to his death.
- The Prophet (ṣ) was given food mixed with poison to eat. The person who ate it first expired, but the Prophet (ṣ) lived for four years, even after eating that food. That food told the Prophet (ṣ) that it was poisoned.
- In the battle of Badr, the Prophet (ṣ) predicted the fate of the leaders of the Quraysh. This happened exactly as he predicted.
- The Prophet (ṣ) said to his daughter Fāṭimah that she would meet him first after he died. She died six months after the Prophet (ṣ).
- The Prophet (ṣ) said to his wives, "She who has a longer hand will meet me first after my death." Zaynab bint Jaḥsh, the most charitable among his wives, was the first to die after the Prophet (ṣ).
- A camel had no milk in its udder. As soon as the Prophet (ṣ) touched it, it began to give milk. Ibn Masʿūd embraced Islam on seeing this miracle of the Prophet (ṣ).
- When an eye of a Companion came out of its socket, the Prophet (ṣ) restored it, and the Companion's eye sight improved.
- The greatest living miracle of the Holy Prophet (ṣ) is the Qur'an, which exists even today. He challenged people to produce a chapter like it. The Qur'an says, "Say, 'If men and jinn should combine together to bring the like of this Qur'an, they could not bring the like of it, though some of them were aiders of others'" (Qur'an, 17:88). But nobody has succeeded in producing a book or even a sentence like it up until the present. This alone is a sufficient and living testimony that the Holy Prophet Muḥammad (ṣ) is a true messenger of Allah.

Index of Qur'anic verses

(2:44), 258
(2:57), 18
(2:143), 274
(2:168), 84
(2:172), 7, 79
(2:173), 196
(2:188), 4, 84
(2:189), 164, 262
(2:195), 261
(2:198), 58
(2:223), 47
(2:225), 234
(2:232), 25
(2:251), 169
(2:275), 84
(2:278-279), 84

(3:92), 179
(3:103), 123
(3:104), 250
(3:105), 188
(3:110), 251
(3:113-114), 250
(3:128), 289
(3:134), 150, 289
(3:169), 203
(3:185), 242

(4:19), 40
(4:21), 40
(4:25), 37
(4:28), 31
(4:34), 51
(4:86), 165
(4:114), 252
(4:129), 45
(4:135), 251

(5:2), 251
(5:13), 289
(5:78-79), 251
(5:83), 241
(5:105), 192, 252
(5:118), 241

(6:36), 143
(6:91), 93
(6:108), 164

(7:10), 58
(7:32), 227
(7:56), 72
(7:89), 32
(7:165), 251
(7:199), 157, 288

(8:2), 241
(8:17), 314
(8:63), 123

(9:71), 250, 261
(9:109), 86

(11:69), 17
(12:25), 42

(12:100), 152
(12:105), 207

(13:38), 25

(15:40), 240
(15:42), 240
(15:88), 196

(16:28), 115
(16:90), 72, 288, 291

(17:24), 44
(17:26-27), 269
(17:29), 269
(17:53), 152
(17:86), 242
(17:88), 316

(18:28), 136

(20:16), 136
(20:44), 266

(21:67), 264

(22:25), 67, 259
(22:41), 251

(23:12-14), 49
(23:51), 3
(23:96), 169

(24:22), 132, 163, 289
(24:27), 164, 262
(24:32), 25
(24:36), 77
(24:47), 77
(24:61), 10, 142

(25:63), 138
(25:67), 269
(25:74), 25

(26:100-101), 126
(26:216), 149
(26:224), 234

(28:54), 169
(28:77), 72, 76

(31:6), 234
(31:15), 136
(31:17), 288
(31:19), 226

(33:53), 10

(35:1), 226

(36:12), 68
(37:137-138), 207

(38:26), 277

(39:7), 29
(39:18), 194

(40:1-3), 148
(40:60), 288

(41:34), 289
(41:53), 207

(42:26), 135
(42:38), 140
(42:43), 288

(48:29), 143, 156

(49:9), 252
(49:12), 101, 147, 164, 262, 289

(50:18), 69

(51:20-21), 207
(51:24), 17

(52:7-8), 242
(52:21), 29

(53:29), 136
(53:59-61), 234

(55:8-9), 71

(56:20), 17
(56:21), 17
(56:60), 29

(57:23), 229

(58.22), 133

(59:9), 152
(59:21), 241

(61:3), 258

(62:10), 58

(66:4), 43
(66:6), 45

(67:2), 29

(68:4), 122, 289

(73:20), 58

(74:6), 39
(74:8), 241

(75:13), 68

(77:35-36), 242

(78:11), 58

(81:9), 49

(83:1), 71
(83:1-3), 71, 145
(83:6), 242
(83:13-14), 114
(83:14), 87

(84:1), 242

(106), 7

(112), 7, 46, 216

(113:3), 31

Index

al-'Abbās, 146, 278
'Abd al-Malik ibn Marwān, 112, 113, 273, 275
'Abd al-Muṭṭalib, 270, 309
'Abd al-Raḥmān ibn 'Awf, 40, 72, 141, 162
'Abd al-Raḥmān ibn Samurah al-Qurashī, 275
'Abd al-Wāḥid ibn Zayd, 240
abdāl, 33, 171
'Abdullāh al-Marwazī, 215
'Abdullāh ibn al-Zubayr, 224
'Abdullāh ibn 'Amr, 270
'Abdullāh ibn Marzūq, 259
'Abdullāh ibn Mas'ūd, 18, 102, 103, 115, 163, 199, 234, 252, 316
'Abdullāh ibn 'Umar, 126, 271
'Abdullāh ibn Unys al-Anṣārī, 209
'Abdullāh ibn Zubayr, 51
Abū al-Bakhtarī, 312
Abū al-Dardā', 91, 148, 149, 160, 172, 193, 196, 256
Abū al-Ḍayfān, 13
Abū al-Ḥasan al-'Asqalānī, 225
Abū al-Ḥasan al-Nūrī, 140, 238
Abū al-Haytham, 10
Abū al-Ḥusayn al-Darrāj, 239
Abū al-Ḥusayn al-Nūrī, 243
Abū al-Qāsim, 271. *See also* Muḥammad (prophet)
Abū al-Rabī' al-Zāhid, 187
Abū al-Ṭayyib, 224
Abū 'Alī al-Ribāṭī, 215
Abū Ayyūb al-Anṣārī, 10, 106
Abū Bakr al-Ṣiddīq, 10, 41-43, 61, 86, 94, 101, 103, 106, 109, 114, 131, 132, 162, 163, 192, 225, 230, 255, 270-273
Abū Burdah ibn Nayyār, 290
Abū Dharr, 106, 111, 138, 148, 167, 176, 178, 278
Abū Ḥanīfah, 197, 224
Abū Ḥāzim, 113, 114, 140
Abū Hurayrah, 102, 106, 122, 140, 157, 158, 176, 199, 215
Abū Isḥāq, 61. *See also* Ibrāhīm ibn Adham
Abū Ja'far al-Manṣūr (caliph), 113, 276
Abū Jarīr, 242
Abū Mas'ūd al-Anṣārī, 184
Abū Mūsā al-Ash'arī, 107, 226, 241, 272
Abū Muslim al-Khawlānī, 271
Abū Nu'aym, 212
Abū Qatādah, 18
Abū Sa'īd al-Khudrī, 106
Abū Sa'īd ibn al-'Arabī, 239
Abū Sulaymān al-Dārānī, 28
Abū Ṭalḥah, 178
Abū Ṭālib al-Makkī, 224
Abū Tha'labah al-Khushnī, 252
Abū 'Ubaydah ibn al-Jarrāḥ, 116, 256

Abū Umāmah al-Bāhilī, 146
Ādāb al-Qaḍā', 224
Adam, 5, 9, 33, 126, 229, 240, 312
adhān, 50
'Adī ibn Ḥātim, 96
'Adn, 12
ahl al-dhimmah, 166
Aḥmad ibn Ḥanbal, 92, 93, 104, 187
'Ā'ishah, 17, 35, 37, 41, 42, 44, 45, 87, 100, 107, 109, 132, 152, 158, 160, 161, 166, 169, 176, 212, 218, 228, 230, 234, 244, 274, 288, 296, 298, 310
'Alī ibn Abī Ṭālib, 11, 19, 32, 38, 43, 49, 67, 102, 106, 107, 113, 126, 135, 138, 141, 162, 195, 199, 244, 257, 274, 289, 300, 303, 307, 309
'Alī ibn al-Fuḍayl, 242
'Alī ibn al-Ḥusayn, 141
'Alī ibn Ma'bad, 92
'Alqamah al-'Uṭāridī, 137
al-A'mash, 38, 197
Āminah, 172
'Amr ibn al-Sharīd, 228
'Amr ibn 'Uthmān al-Makkī, 239
Anas ibn Mālik, 11, 14, 40, 106, 144, 160, 162, 165-167, 188, 265, 290, 294, 303
Anṣār, 10, 38, 109. *See also* Madīnan Helpers
al-'Aqīq, 188, 195
'aqīqah, 51, 181
al-Aqra' ibn Ḥābis, 181
Arab, 19, 48, 114, 159, 167, 273, 277, 290, 296, 302, 305, 306, 308, 313
'arīsh, 93
Āsiyah, 41
Asmā', 51, 53
al-Aswad al-'Ansī, 315
Aṭā' ibn Abī Rabāḥ, 143, 273
'Awn ibn 'Abdullāh, 197
al-'Awzā'ī 'Abd al-Raḥmān ibn 'Amr, 19, 61, 276
'Aynah, 301
Ayyūb (prophet), 41
al-Azd, 116
Azdī, 37

badal, 88
Badr, 303, 309, 316
Bahlūl, 283
Bahrain, 92
Balance, the, 34
Banī 'Āmir, 130
Banū Mudlij, 178
Banū Umayyah, 281
Baqiyyah ibn al-Walīd, 130
al-Barā' ibn 'Āzib, 167
Barīrah, 10
Bashīr, 314
Baṣrah, 67, 272, 274, 275
Bilāl, 225, 302
Bishr al-Ḥāfī. *See* Bishr ibn al-Ḥārith
Bishr ibn 'Abdullāh, 188
Bishr ibn al-Ḥārith, 94, 137, 187, 267
Black Stone, the, 229, 271
Bu'āth, Day of, 230
Burayrah, 101
Byzantium, 116, 276

Christian(s), 126, 166, 176, 239
Companion(s), 9, 18, 19, 26, 27, 32, 38, 43, 59-61, 74, 86, 97, 99, 102, 106, 107, 109, 111, 126, 134, 142, 146, 153, 157, 159, 161, 163-165, 167, 181, 183, 187, 189, 199, 213, 214, 224, 226, 228, 233, 241, 244, 251-253, 255, 256, 266, 275, 289, 290, 292-296, 302-305, 307, 309, 310, 314-316

Ḍabbah ibn Miḥṣan al-'Anazī, 272
daff, 233
Dār al-Nadwah, 280

Dāwūd (prophet), 99, 126, 226, 229, 234, 241, 251, 277
Dāwūd al-Ṭā'ī, 187, 263
al-Daylam, 276
Devil, the, 6, 17, 19, 21, 30, 31, 33, 46, 60, 134, 148, 150, 163, 165, 169, 194, 230, 240, 244, 271. *See also* Satan
dhimmī, 133
Dhū al-Faqār, 301
Dhū al-Nūn al-Miṣrī, 21, 94, 147, 192, 224, 239
Dhū al-Qarnayn, 208
al-Duldul, 301

Egypt, 209

Fatḥ al-Mawṣilī, 140
al-Fatḥ ibn Shakhraf, 267
Fāṭimah (daughter of the Prophet), 32, 44, 51, 278, 316
Fayyāḍ ibn Najīḥ, 31
Firdaws, 12
al-Fuḍayl ibn 'Iyāḍ, 87, 111, 127, 144, 170, 187, 188

Galen, 197
Guarded Tablet, the, 147

Ḥā Mīm, 148
Habhab, 273
ḥadīth(s), 9, 11, 25, 29, 30, 32-34, 37, 38, 41, 43, 46, 49, 52, 58, 61, 70, 73, 77, 78, 84, 88, 91, 98, 99, 110, 123, 135, 143, 144, 147, 148, 151, 156, 179, 189, 195, 208, 209, 211, 213, 219, 226, 230, 234, 235, 252, 254, 261, 278
al-Ḥajjāj, 20, 106, 107, 111, 274, 275
Ḥammād, 78, 112, 224
Ḥamzah ibn 'Abd al-Muṭṭalib, 244, 256, 270
Ḥanafī, 220
harīsah, 32
al-Ḥārith al-Muḥāsibī, 104, 152, 225
Hārūn al-Rashīd, 106, 107, 260, 282, 283
Hārūt, 279
al-Ḥasan al-Baṣrī, 9, 10, 28, 73, 126, 139, 141, 143, 234, 265, 274-276
al-Ḥasan al-Masūḥī, 152
al-Ḥasan ibn 'Alī, 15, 32, 50, 92, 106, 109, 127, 181, 199
al-Ḥasan ibn Zayd, 276
Ḥassān ibn Thabit, 228
Ḥāṭib ibn Abī Balta'ah, 303
Ḥaṭīm, the, 229
Ḥātim al-Aṣamm, 17, 112, 188
Ḥātim al-Ṭā'ī, 290
Ḥibbān ibn 'Abdullāh, 260
Ḥirā', 191, 231
Hishām ibn 'Abd al-Malik (caliph), 112, 193
Hishām ibn 'Urwah, 187
Holy Prophet, ix, 3, 35, 142, 195, 250, 292, 294, 298, 302, 307, 309, 313, 316
al-Ḥudaybiyah, 314
Ḥudhayfah al-Mar'ashī, 148, 187
Ḥudhayfah ibn al-Yamān, 111, 142, 199
ḥulūl, 239
Ḥunayn, 161, 308, 309
al-Ḥusayn ibn 'Alī, 32, 51, 181, 195
Ḥuṭayṭ al-Zayyāt, 274, 275

Ibn 'Abbās, 15, 26, 31, 87, 143, 146, 156, 169, 177, 188, 199, 254
Ibn Abī Dhu'ayb, 276
Ibn Abī Laylā, 187
Ibn Abī Shumaylah, 113, 273
Ibn al-Darrāj, 237
Ibn al-Fawṭī, 237
Ibn al-Karībī, 152

Ibn al-Mubārak, 87, 144, 187
Ibn 'Āmir, 310
Ibn Hubayrah, 276
Ibn Shabramah, 187
Ibn Sīrīn, 44
Ibn 'Umar, 9, 51, 107, 131, 141, 143, 167, 195, 211, 214
Ibn 'Uyaynah, 187
Ibrāhīm (prophet), 13, 17, 18, 264, 274, 312
Ibrāhīm al-Nakha'ī, 148, 188, 198
Ibrāhīm ibn Adham, 18, 27, 34, 60, 61, 78, 141, 187, 242
'Īd(s), 44, 199, 230, 259
'iddah, 37
iḥrām, 37
'Ikrimah, 31
Ilyās (prophet), 37
Imam Aḥmad, 38
Imam al-Shāfi'ī, 21, 22, 42, 63, 106, 107, 144, 150
'Imrān ibn Ḥuṣayn, 309
al-'Iqāb, 301
iqāmah, 50
Iraq, 195
Iraqi, 195
'Īsā (prophet), 25, 35, 60, 125, 129, 145, 170, 193, 251, 258, 263
'ishq, 232
Israel, 99, 115, 149, 232, 244, 251
Israeli, 199
istikhārah, 216
ittiḥād, 239

Jābir, 31, 39, 41, 49, 60, 159, 176
Jābir ibn 'Abdullāh, 209
Ja'far al-Ṣādiq, 9, 137, 149
Ja'far ibn Abī Ṭālib, 20, 244, 256
Jamrah al-'Aqabah, 261
Jarīr ibn 'Abdullāh, 106, 161
Jerusalem, 85, 141, 208, 211
Jews, 126, 166, 169, 314
Jibrīl, 32, 131, 174, 195, 240, 276, 277, 279, 280, 303
jihad, 27, 33, 44, 47, 60, 65, 78, 179, 181, 189, 210, 213, 253, 255, 257, 270, 300, 302, 315
Judgement Day, 73
Juhaynah, 159
al-Junayd al-Baghdādī, 31, 137, 152, 192, 224, 225, 242, 244
Juwayriyah, 109

Ka'bah, 112, 210, 211, 220, 229, 259, 270, 271, 280, 295
al-Kāfūr, 301
kashf, 241
al-Katūm, 301
Khadījah, 151
al-Khaḍir, 237, 240, 282
al-Khawwāṣ, 212
Khaybar, 302, 303
Khaythamah, 141
Khosroes, 315
al-Khuld, 12
kūbah, 227, 233
Kūfah, 72, 224, 274, 275, 283
Kurā' al-Ghamīm, 15

Laylā, 130
Luqmān, 41, 42, 60, 138, 266

Madīnah, 15, 43, 59, 97, 113, 162, 188, 199, 208, 209, 211, 228, 230, 272, 275, 276, 294, 314, 315
Madīnan Helpers, 10, 38, 109, 113, 224, 228, 273, 278. *See also Anṣār*
al-Mahdī (caliph), 259
Makkah, 112, 178, 208, 259, 260, 273, 278, 280, 294, 303
Makkans, 224
Mālik ibn Anas, 188, 224
Mālik ibn Dīnār, 38, 129, 142
al-Ma'mūn (caliph), 137, 261, 280, 266
Ma'rūf al-Karkhī, 171

Mārūt, 279
Marwān ibn al-Ḥakam (caliph), 106, 259
Maryam, 251, 263
Masrūq, 141
Maymūn ibn Mahrān, 140
Messenger of Allah, 16, 19, 27, 30, 36, 37, 44, 50, 52, 84, 122-124, 133, 142, 157, 159, 166, 167, 170, 176, 180, 183, 184, 199, 225, 252-255, 261, 265, 288, 290, 294, 296, 302, 303, 307, 309. *See also* Muḥammad (prophet)
miḥrāb, 12
al-Mikhdham, 301
Minā, 230
Miqdād, 303
Misṭaḥ ibn Uthāthah, 132
Mu'ādh ibn Anas, 162
Mu'ādh ibn Jabal, 76, 159, 291
Mu'āwiyah (caliph), 106, 109, 114, 224, 271
mudds, 314
mufti, 61, 98
Muhājirūn, 109
Muḥammad (prophet), 142, 160, 171, 277-279, 287, 290, 294, 302, 307, 312. *See also* Messenger of Allah
Muḥammad ibn Sulaymān, 112
Muḥammad ibn Wāsi', 127, 142
Mujāhid, 31, 127, 147
mukāshafāt, 231
Mumshād al-Dīnawarī, 225
Mūsā (prophet), 93, 126, 127, 131, 153, 160, 169, 170, 180, 200, 210, 244, 255, 304
Mūsā ibn Wardān, 215
mushāhadāt, 231
Mus'ir, 147
Muslim al-'Abbādānī, 240
Muslim al-Aswārī, 240

Nabataean, 42
al-Nābighah, 228
al-Nakha'ī, 148, 188, 198, 234
Negus, 18

Persia, 276, 315
Persian, 100, 315
Pharaoh, 41

al-Qaḍīb, 301
al-Qaṣwā', 301
qiblah, 274
qīrāṭ, 172
Qubā', 51
Qur'an, 12, 17, 20, 21, 25, 49, 58, 65, 67, 84, 88, 98, 104, 108, 115, 123, 156, 187, 191, 225, 226, 229, 234, 241, 242, 250, 268, 288, 294, 296, 297, 316
Quraysh, 7, 270, 271, 303, 313, 316
Qurayshite, 310
al-Qutham, 312

al-Rabī' ibn Khuthaym, 188
Rabī'ah ibn Umayyah, 162
Rāfi', 50
Raḥīm, 178
Raḥmān, 40, 50, 72, 141, 162, 178
Rajab, 13
rak'ah, 27
Ramaḍān, 15, 52, 242, 307
al-Raqqī, 237
al-Rasūb, 301
Rawḍah Khākh, 303
Resurrection Day, 26, 29, 34, 45, 50, 58, 69, 74, 79, 92, 113, 117, 124, 143, 151, 158, 162, 164, 168-171, 174, 188, 273, 278, 279
al-Ribāṭī, 215

Sa'd ibn Abī Waqqāṣ, 188
Sa'd ibn al-Rabī', 141

Sa'd ibn 'Ubādah, 43
Ṣafiyyah (wife of the Prophet), 40
Ṣafwān ibn 'Assāl, 219
al-Sahab, 300
Ṣaḥīḥ al-Bukhārī, 49, 230
Ṣaḥīḥ Muslim, 49, 230
Sahl al-Tustarī, 87, 188, 244
Sa'īd ibn al-'Āṣ, 143
Sa'īd ibn al-Musayyib, 112, 187, 208
Sa'īd ibn Zayd, 188
al-salām, 160
Ṣāliḥ al-Marrī, 240, 242
Salmah, 111
Salmān al-Fārisī, 11, 278
al-Sammāk, 196
Samnūn, 131
Sana'a, 315
al-Sarī al-Saqaṭī, 93, 152, 224, 242
Satan, 94, 152, 234. *See also* Devil, the
al-Sha'bī, 146, 187, 208, 224, 275, 276
al-Shāfi'ī, 187, 196, 200, 224, 242
Sharī'ah, 3, 17, 57, 62, 63, 67, 89, 96, 98, 101, 108, 110, 112, 132, 147, 225, 227, 234, 262, 265, 282, 313
Sharīk ibn 'Abdullāh, 187
Shawwāl, 37
al-Shiblī, 239, 242
Shurayḥ, 187
siddīq, 87
ṣiddīqūn, 91, 238
son of 'Imrān, 126
Station of Ibrāhīm, the, 274
Sufi, 12, 236, 238
Sufyān al-Thawrī, 12, 14, 18, 87, 111, 113, 187, 188, 196, 212, 224, 261
Sufyān ibn Sa'īd ibn al-Mundhir, 282
Sufyān ibn 'Uyaynah, 196
Sulaymān (prophet), 71, 210, 230
Sulaymān al-Dārānī, 28, 32
Sulaymān al-Khawwāṣ, 187
Sulaymān ibn 'Abd al-Malik, 112-114
Sulaymān ibn Abī Ja'far, 260
sunnah, 17, 87, 220
Surāqah ibn Mālik, 315
Syria, 148, 208, 275, 294

tābi'ūn, 187
Tabūk, 217, 314
tafarrus, 240
Ṭāhir ibn Bilāl al-Hamadānī al-Warrāq, 225
tashahhud, 220
Ṭāwūs al-Yamānī, 112, 113, 193, 195
tayammum, 219
Thābit al-Bunānī, 196
al-Tha'labī, 237
tharīd, 17, 19
al-Thawrī, 135
Throne, the, 73, 123, 128, 143, 151, 178
Tigris, the, 237, 277
Torah, the, 15, 88, 187, 211, 294
Turkey, 276

'Ubādah ibn al-Ṣāmit, 111
Ubayy ibn Khalaf al-Jumaḥī, 316
Uḥud, 172, 289, 316
Umāmah al-Bāhilī, 146
'Umar ibn 'Abd al-'Azīz, 92, 111, 114, 116
'Umar ibn al-Khaṭṭāb, 10, 26, 27, 33, 41-44, 51, 60, 62, 74, 75, 78, 87, 91, 92, 101, 102, 107-109, 116, 127, 136, 146, 148-150, 162-164, 166, 179, 187, 195, 209, 216, 241, 256, 262, 270, 272, 277, 278, 302, 303, 307
'Umar ibn Hubayrah, 275
Umayyah ibn Abī al-Ṣalt, 228

umm ghīlān, 138
Umm S'ad, 218
Umm Salamah, 300
'Uqbah ibn Ubayy, 271
'Utbah al-Ghulām, 140, 240
'Uthmān al-Makkī, 239
'Uthmān in 'Affān, 109, 161, 315
Uways al-Qarnī, 193
'Uzayr, 200

al-Wadā', 230, 234
al-Walīd ibn 'Abd al-Malik (caliph), 112, 273
Wuhayb ibn al-Ward, 188

Ya'fūr, 301
Yaḥyā ibn Kathīr, 93
Yaḥyā ibn Mu'ādh, 87
Ya'qūb (prophet), 180, 242
Yazīd ibn 'Abd al-Malik (caliph), 106
Yazīd ibn Mu'āwiyah (caliph), 97
Yemen, 181, 209, 315
Yūnus (prophet), 11
Yūnus ibn 'Ubayd, 72
Yūsha' ibn Nūn, 256
Yūsuf (prophet), 152, 180, 238
Yūsuf ibn Asbāṭ, 100, 148, 187
Yūsuf ibn Muslim, 188

zakāh, 87, 89, 90, 92, 96, 101, 108, 116, 127, 161, 179, 273, 278, 292
Zamzam, 229
zanādiqah, 224
Zayd ibn Ḥārithah, 244
Zayd ibn Thābit, 106
Zaynab, 109
Zaynab bint Jaḥsh, 31, 316
Zoroastrians, 102
al-Zubayr, 303
Zurārah ibn Awfā, 241